Reference Guides to Rhetoric and Composition

Series Editor, Charles Bazerman

Reference Guides to Rhetoric and Composition
Series Editor, Charles Bazerman

The Series provides compact, comprehensive and convenient surveys of what has been learned through research and practice as composition has emerged as an academic discipline over the last half century. Each volume is devoted to a single topic that has been of interest in rhetoric and composition in recent years, to synthesize and make available the sum and parts of what has been learned on that topic. These reference guides are designed to help deepen classroom practice by making available the collective wisdom of the field and will provide the basis for new research. The Series is intended to be of use to teachers at all levels of education, researchers and scholars of writing, graduate students learning about the field, and all who have interest in or responsibility for writing programs and the teaching of writing.

Parlor Press and The WAC Clearinghouse are collaborating so that these books will be widely available through low-cost print editions and free digital distribution. The publishers and the Series editor are teachers and researchers of writing, committed to the principle that knowledge should freely circulate. We see the opportunities that new technologies have for further democratizing knowledge. And we see that to share the power of writing is to share the means for all to articulate their needs, interest, and learning into the great experiment of literacy.

Existing Books in the Series

Invention in Rhetoric and Composition (2004, Lauer)
Reference Guide to Writing across the Curriculum (2005, Bazerman, Little, Bethel, Chavkin, Fouquette, and Garufis)
Revision: History, Theory, and Practice (2006, Horning and Becker)
Writing Program Administration (2007, McLeod)
Community Literacy and the Rhetoric of Local Publics (2008, Long)
Argument in Composition (2009, Ramage, Callaway, Clary-Lemon, and Waggoner)

Argument in Composition

John Ramage, Micheal Callaway,
Jennifer Clary-Lemon, and Zachary Waggoner

Parlor Press
West Lafayette, Indiana
www.parlorpress.com

The WAC Clearinghouse
http://wac.colostate.edu/

Parlor Press LLC, West Lafayette, Indiana 47906

Printed in the United States of America

S A N: 2 5 4 - 8 8 7 9

Library of Congress Cataloging-in-Publication Data

Argument in composition / John Ramage ... [et al.].
p. cm. -- (Reference guides to rhetoric and composition)
Includes bibliographical references and index.
ISBN 978-1-60235-109-7 (pbk. : alk. paper) -- ISBN 978-1-60235-110-3 (hardcover : alk. paper) -- ISBN 978-1-60235-111-0 (adobe ebook)
1. English language--Rhetoric--Study and teaching (Higher) 2. Persuasion (Rhetoric)--Study and teaching (Higher) 3. Report writing--Study and teaching (Higher) I. Ramage, John D.
PE1431.A77 2009
808'.0420711--dc22

2009032671

Series logo designed by Karl Stolley. Copyediting by Ethan Sproat.
This book is printed on acid-free paper.

Parlor Press, LLC is an independent publisher of scholarly and trade titles in print and multimedia formats. This book is available in paperback, cloth, and Adobe eBook formats from Parlor Press on the World Wide Web at http://www.parlorpress.com. For submission information or to find out about Parlor Press publications, write to Parlor Press, 816 Robinson St., West Lafayette, Indiana, 47906, or e-mail editor@parlorpress.com.

The WAC Clearinghouse supports teachers of writing across the disciplines. Hosted by Colorado State University's Composition Program, it brings together four journals, three book series, and resources for teachers who use writing in their courses. This book will also be available free on the Internet at The WAC Clearinghouse (http://wac.colostate.edu/).

Contents

Series Editor's Preface

Charles Bazerman

In the large and growing house of rhetoric and writing, argument and its sister persuasion share an extensive and venerable room, being built since the founding of rhetoric in ancient Greece. The core concerns of classical rhetoric are all carried out through argument: deliberation on governance and citizenry, determination of guilt and innocence, asserting rights and obligations, forging alliances and agreements, rallying action against enemies, increasing communal commitment. Core institutions of society have been formed to create structural conditions (such as procedures, criteria, and exigencies) to bring arguments to successful resolutions for communal action: courts, legislatures, religions, electoral democracy.

The great chamber of argument and persuasion has large doorways to many neighboring rooms that see themselves in different terms. Philosophy, the long-standing dialectical opponent of argument, itself structures its discussion through argument. Academic disciplines are argumentative fields, though organized as cooperative endeavors. Team deliberations on planning and choices—whether architectural, medical, or military—depend on the expression of varied views, though often elliptically framed within specialized knowledges, goals, and roles.

Argument can serve private purposes. Through argument with others an individual can work through personal beliefs, values, commitments, and life choices. Social occasions of argument provide opportunities for the individual to investigate and think through individually shaped questions in the context of contending views. Modern concepts of individual development, consciousness, conscience, and responsibility depend on an individual having access to and participating in argument to come to personal persuasions.

While some see engaged argument as an oral phenomenon, confronting the embodiment of alternative views in one's interlocutors, writing has transformed the range and depth of arguments, the evidence available, and the structured situations within which arguments occur. Even courtroom argument has been transformed by written laws, libraries of case precedents, prepared briefs, written depositions, written rules of evidence, and other documents that have made law a bookish profession. Many spheres of literate interaction that facilitate modern society at a distance rely on argument, whether for the value of a financial investment, the most effective plan for preserving the ecology of a watershed, or the significance of volunteering in a non-profit project. Within the specific academic world of composition, arguing facilitates learning to think in an educated, intelligent, informed, disciplinary, articulate manner.

This *Reference Guide to Argument in Composition* provides access to a wide range of resources that bear on the teaching of writing. The ideas of major theorists of classical and contemporary rhetoric from Aristotle to Burke, Toulmin, and Perelman and their relevance to instruction are succinctly presented. The authors clearly sort through and state their position to related pedagogies of teaching informal fallacies and propaganda, and present the reasons for preferring an argument approach over other available approaches for the teaching of composition. The authors also identify the role of argument in pedagogies that are not overtly called argument, including pedagogies that foreground feminism, liberation, critical cultural studies, Writing Across the Curriculum, genre, service learning, technology, and visual rhetoric. The lists of further reading and the annotated bibliography provide opportunities for learning more about the approaches presented in this guide.

Much of the book self-exemplifies the value of an argumentative approach by overtly arguing for the value of taking an argumentative approach, for the value of adopting the perspectives and concepts of particular theorists over others, and for the superiority of argumentative approaches for the teaching of writing over others. In making these arguments the book challenges the readers for themselves to sort through their thoughts about the value of argument and how to best incorporate it in their pedagogy. I particularly recommend readers take seriously the arguments against ossification of argumentative systems and for always considering the specific situations within which each argument takes place.

Preface

Argument in Composition is addressed to all teachers, including some who may not in fact be teachers of composition, who might wish to incorporate the teaching of argument into their courses. In designing the book, we have aimed at a level of generality somewhere between that of a textbook on argument and a theory of argument. Or, in the language of Kenneth Burke, our approach is pitched to the level of "talk about" argument as opposed to "talking" argument or "talking about the talk about" argument. Those of our readers who wish straight argument talk should consult any of the numerous fine textbooks devoted to the subject. Those who wish a narrower but deeper understanding of argument should consult the many primary sources we refer to throughout this book. Our emphasis on this mid-level of generality derives from our purpose: to help teachers translate theory into pedagogy and to make informed choices about which argument textbooks (if any) make best sense for their courses. We hope the first three chapters of *Argument in Composition* equip our readers to formulate their own classroom approach to argument and to read more critically the materials catalogued in the rest of the book.

As the above allusion to Kenneth Burke might suggest, *Argument in Composition* is heavily influenced by Burke's approach to rhetoric. While Burke's theory receives little if any explicit attention in most argument textbooks (beyond the often oversimplified treatment of his pentad), we believe it to be the most cogent and comprehensive framework available for unifying the sundry approaches to argument—Toulmin's schema, stasis theory, informal fallacies, the rhetorical situation, and so forth—that form the backbone of most contemporary argument textbooks. Because Burke serves as the primary lens or "terministic screen" through which we view argument, some commonly used terms are not featured in the main body of our text. In some cases such terms, through no fault of their own, are incongruent with or peripheral to our approach. We do not, for example, give extensive attention to the enthymeme. We do cite it in our glossary of argument terms and more importantly, we cite John Gage's thoughtful analysis of the term. Certainly we recognize the important place of the enthymeme within the history of argument instruction and its potential usefulness for some contemporary classroom teachers. We just have trouble making it fit our own approach. Other terms are not discussed primarily because we feel that they are already included under different names within our own rubric. In the case of the rhetorical situation, for example, we discuss Lloyd Bitzer's notion of exigence because we believe it uniquely describes a concept critical to students of argument. We do not, however, mention another element of the Bitzer's rhetorical situation, "constraints," in the belief some of the other argument tools that we discuss, notably stasis theory, more clearly and usefully fulfill the role filled by constraints in Bitzer's theory.

Argument in Composition is, inevitably, itself an argument as much as it is a compendium of approaches to argument. We have tried to present our argument without being too argumentative. At the same time, we would be the first to acknowledge that our field, "rhetoric and composition," is a far from settled one. There are indeed arguments to be made for and against the inclusion of expressive writing in an argument class (we try to make an argument for inclusion). There are also arguments for and against the inclusion of visual argument in such a class. In the case of visual argument, our position is more complex. We applaud the goal and recognize the importance of visual argument. We cite work being done in the area. But we decry the lack of useable tools—or a common vocabulary for that matter—that might make such work accessible for undergraduates. For now, we would probably advise teachers either to wait until better tools are available or to get to work developing their own tools. In the meantime, we view visual argument to be something like those intriguing websites one eagerly hunts down only to be greeted by a screen announcing that they remain "Under Construction."

Argument in Composition

1 Introduction: Why Argument Matters

Anyone who remains skeptical about the important role argument plays in college writing curricula across the country today need only look to the sheer abundance of textbooks devoted to the subject. Every major textbook publisher features at least three or four competing argument texts. Moreover the quality of the current generation of argument texts certainly exceeds the standard—though it was not, truth be told, a particularly high standard—set by generations of argument texts prior to the mid-1980s. While a number of thoughtful critical thinking textbooks written by philosophers were successfully adapted to writing courses in argument during the seventies, the standard argument texts comprised a pretty rum lot.

In fact argument was seldom taught as a stand-alone subject in writing curricula prior to the 1980s. Typically, argument was taught as part of some taxonomic scheme such as the so-called "current-traditional" curriculum. The current-traditional, or "modes-based" writing courses that dominated college curricula for decades were organized around supposedly functional categories of writing such as narration, description, process and so forth, each of which came complete with a prescribed format. The most striking feature of these modes in retrospect was how arhetorical they were. Students were given little sense of why an audience might wish a description of a family pet or favorite teacher or an excruciatingly detailed account of how to make a peanut butter sandwich; and the main thing they were told about audiences generally was to assume they were a bit thick and needed things spelled out for them in, well, excruciating detail. Students progressed over the course of the semester from simple to complex tasks in a manner prescribed by a loosely behaviorist learning theory. Because it was considered the most complex of the modes, argument was typically accorded pride of place at the end of the syllabus. But being placed in the final position also ensured that it frequently got short shrift, even total neglect, at the end of the term.

Many teachers were in fact relieved not to teach argument given the difficulties their students had with it in the context of current-traditional instruction. In retrospect, those difficulties were hardly surprising. While the relationship between arrangement and aim remains pretty much self explanatory when one's task is to describe the process of making a sandwich, that same relationship is complicated by several orders of magnitude when one sets out to persuade an audience that a constitutional ban on same sex marriage may or may not be a grand idea. Whatever transference might have occurred among earlier assignments, it appeared to stop abruptly when it came to argument. As we've since learned, when the cognitive demands of an assignment fall outside our students' "zone of proximal development," all sorts of other problems—with spelling, with grammar, with syntax, with style—erupt like a pox. Argument, many writing teachers reluctantly concluded based on their sad experience in such courses, should either be taught later in the curriculum or elsewhere in the university.

Clearly, thus, many of the problems students had learning how to construct arguments in a current-traditional writing course could be laid at the feet of the approach. It was as if we tried to prepare students for calculus by assigning them a series of arithmetic problems, pretending that solving addition, subtraction, multiplication and division problems prepared one to solve quadratic equations. Not every composition course was of course organized around current-traditional principles. But few of the texts apparently intended for use in stand-alone argument courses were any more promising. They mostly consisted of anthologies of canonical arguments interlarded with unhelpful advice and potted assignments. The usually brief—and one rarely wished them longer—prefaces and introductions rehearsed some classical terms, informal fallacies and model syllogisms and invited students to apply the material, some way some how, to the essays that followed. Needless to say the complexities of the essays handily eluded the dubious pieties of the opening chapter, leaving students and teachers alike to wonder if perhaps, indeed, argument was not beyond the ken of mere mortals.

What caused all this to change over the past twenty years or so? Here we run up against a confusion of the chicken and egg variety—Did our approaches to argument gain in sophistication and usefulness because of a growing recognition of how much argument mattered in the world, or did the growing sophistication and usefulness of our approaches make us progressively more aware of the capacity for argument to matter in the world? In all likelihood, the two phenomena occurred more or less simultaneously and mutually reinforced each other. Or more accurately, our belated awareness of the many fine tools available to students of argument, tools that were in many cases adapted from tools a couple of thousand years old, rendered the study of argument more fruitful and the transmission of argument skills more reliable. For whatever reasons, thus, we find ourselves today in the midst of a sort of golden age in the history of argument instruction. Later on we will look further back into the past to see just how this came about and where the present era might fit in the history of argument instruction. For now we want to concentrate on our current understanding of argument and our motivation for teaching it.

Coming to an Understanding of Argument

In our classes, we like to make an initial approach to argument directly and inductively by examining two or more arguments on an issue, working out with our students which features of our examples are most likely to be shared with other arguments. This approach is illustrative of a more general approach to teaching that we favor: bottom-up, problem-based learning, grounded in application and ascending toward principles as opposed to the more traditional top-down, "presentational" mode of knowledge transmission (i.e., lecturing). There are to be sure costs as well as benefits to our inductive approach to learning. In exchange for actively learning important elements of argument we have foregone thoroughgoing, albeit passive, "coverage" of our topic. The best we can hope for from our initial examination of argument is a better understanding of some of its more prominent features and a better sense of how to think critically about the subject. That is one of the points of the exercise and of our course—the meaning of complex terms like "argument" is always contested because they are in effect inexhaustible.

Whatever the danger that students might mistake our selected parts for the whole, the benefits of our approach in our view significantly outweigh the potential costs. While we could transmit a good deal more declarative knowledge about argument through lecture, there is no guarantee that the knowledge we transmit would arrive at its intended destination, or that if it did arrive it would be sufficiently free of noise not to garble our signal or that students would have a clear notion of what to "do" with whatever knowledge survived the transmission. Our experience of lecturing on the definition of argument suggests that the most common question we manage to provoke about the material we present is the following: "Which of this will be on the test?" We do not take that to be a positive sign. Defining matters on which there is general agreement is, among other things, boring. Defining matters that are uncertain and contested is considerably more engaging. In our initial discussions on argument, we want our students to get a sense that the definition of any complex notion like argument is contestable, that the values and beliefs we bring to the exercise of defining the term influence our choice of its meaning, and that in turn how we define it determines how we practice it.

Every semester, at the end of our inductive exercise in definition, we are left not with the same tidy set of conclusions about the meaning of argument that we have rehearsed in our lectures, but with different, oftentimes unexpected, conclusions that arose out of freewheeling conversations. To be sure, we steer that conversation enough to ensure that at least a handful of points about argument are made, and not every point offered up in our classes survives the interrogation to which we submit it. (Like the ancient master of dialectic, Socrates, we are not above putting in the fix occasionally.) But each semester produces new insights into the meaning of argument. The important point to remember is that there will be plenty of time later to address the most crucial issues of definition left unanswered at the outset. In the meantime, students are more likely to be engaged by and ready to apply ideas that they have hand in producing.

The arguments that follow are not ones that we would use in a typical undergraduate class. The issues they raise are appropriate to a more theoretical discussion of argument than the one we seek to promote at the outset of an undergraduate class. Certainly we make no claims for them as argument exemplars. But neither are they randomly selected. They are "meta-arguments" of a sort that raise questions about the nature of argument central to our approach and preview issues that recur in the pages that follow. The two arguments and the ensuing discussion obviously cannot replicate an open-ended classroom encounter with the material. In order for you to at least get a feel for that experience, we invite you to read them the way we ask our students to read them. Before looking at our discussion, ask yourself how the two essays are different and how they are similar in both the way they argue and the conclusions they reach. The conclusions you reach can then be used to interrogate our own conclusions about the two arguments.

John Leo, "Cultural Relativism Leaves Some Blind to Evil" (2001, Universal Press Syndicate), 10/15/01

The House of Bishops of the Episcopal Church put out a disgraceful statement on the terrorist attacks. After urging believers to "wage reconciliation" (i.e., not war), the bishops said: "The affluence of nations such as our own stands in stark contrast to other parts of the world wracked by crushing poverty which causes the death of 6,000 children in the course of a morning." The number 6,000 and the reference to a single morning, of course, are meant to evoke Sept. 11 in a spirit of moral equivalence.

In plain English, the bishops seem to think that Americans are in no position to complain about the Manhattan massacre since 6,000 children around the world can die in a single day. The good bishops are apparently willing to tolerate 6,000 murders in New York* because the West has failed to eliminate world poverty, and perhaps should be blamed for causing it. But the terrorist attack has nothing to do with world hunger or disease. And the bishops' statement is a moral mess. How many murders can Episcopalians now overlook because of the existence of crushing poverty? If 6,000, why not 60,000?

This is a minor example of what could be a major problem over the long haul. A large number of our cultural and moral leaders are unable to say plainly that evil exists in the world and that it must be confronted. Instead they are content to babble about "cycles of violence" and how "an eye for an eye makes the world blind," as if the cop who stops the violent criminal is somehow guilty of the crime, too.

Part of this philosophy arises from the therapeutic culture. Accusing someone of being evil is bad thinking. There is no evil, no right and wrong, only misunderstandings that can fade if we withhold judgment and reach out emotionally to others. Everything can be mediated and talked out.

---

* The number of casualties of the 9/11 attacks had not yet been fixed, at slightly fewer than 3,000, at the time of Leo's writing.

More of it comes from the moral relativism at the heart of the multicultural philosophy that has dominated our schools for a generation. Multiculturalism goes way beyond tolerance and appreciation of other cultures and nations. It teaches that all cultures and all cultural expressions are equally valid. This sweeps away moral standards. Every culture (except America, of course) is correct by its own standards and unjudgeable by others.

Teachers at all levels have been warning us for years about where this is headed. We are seeing large numbers of the young unable or unwilling to make the simplest distinctions between right and wrong. Even horrorific acts—mass human sacrifice by the Aztecs and genocide by the Nazis—are declared undjudgeable. "Of course I dislike the Nazis," one upstate New York student told his professor. "But who is to say they are morally wrong?" The same argument, or non-argument, can apply to the terrorists of September as well.

Only a minority of students think this way, but multiculturalism, with its radical cultural relativism, is becoming a serious problem. It leaves a great many students dubious about traditional American values and cynical about any sense of common purpose or solidarity. This is particularly so when the mantra of the cultural left that America is "racist-sexist-homophobic" is added to the mix.

This hybrid philosophy—no judgment of other cultures, but severe judgment of our own—is already beginning to color many responses to the terrorist attacks. It peeks out from behind the "root causes" argument and the need to "understand" the terrorists and to see their acts "in context." Often what is meant by the root-cause people is that reckless and imperial America brought the attacks on itself.

The philosophy also shines through many statements of concern about bias against Muslim Americans. Of course Muslims must not be singled out for attack or scorn. But a good many official statements about Sept. 11 made only brief reference to the horror of the attacks before launching long and lopsided attention to the possibility of anti-Muslim bias.

Terrorism is the worst threat the nation has ever faced, and at the moment Americans are solidly united to confront it. The multicultural-therapeutic left is small but concentrated in businesses that do most of the preaching to America—the universities, the press, the mainline churches and the entertainment industry. They will have to be pushed to move away from sloppy multiculturalism and all-purpose relativism. Let the pushing begin.

Stanley Fish, "Condemnation without Absolutes"

During the interval between the terrorist attacks and the United States response, a reporter called to ask me if the events of Sept. 11 meant the end of postmodernist relativism. It seemed bizarre that events so serious would be linked causally with a rarefied form of academic talk. But in the days that followed, a growing number of commentators played serious variations on the same theme: that the ideas foisted upon us by postmodern intellectuals have weakened the country's resolve. The problem, according to the critics, is that since postmodernists deny the possibility of describing matters of fact objectively, they leave us with no firm basis for either condemning the terrorist attacks or fighting back.

Not so. Postmodernism maintains only that there can be no independent standard for determining which of many rival interpretations of an event is the true one. The only thing postmodern thought argues against is the hope of justifying our response to the attacks in universal terms that would be persuasive to everyone, including our enemies. Invoking the abstract notions of justice and truth to support our cause wouldn't be effective anyway because our adversaries lay claim to the same language. (No one declares himself to be an apostle of injustice.)

Instead, we can and should invoke the particular lived values that unite us and inform the institutions we cherish and wish to defend.

At times like these, the nation rightly falls back on the record of aspiration and accomplishment that makes up our collective understanding of what we live for. That understanding is sufficient, and far from undermining its sufficiency, postmodern thought tells us that we have grounds enough for action and justified condemnation in the democratic ideals we embrace, without grasping for the empty rhetoric of universal absolutes to which all subscribe but which all define differently.

But of course it's not really postmodernism that people are bothered by. It's the idea that our adversaries have emerged not from some primordial darkness, but from a history that has equipped them with reasons and motives and even with a perverted version of some virtues. Bill Maher, Dinesh D'Souza and Susan Sontag have gotten into trouble by pointing out that 'cowardly' is not the word to describe men who sacrifice themselves for a cause they believe in. Ms Sontag grants them courage, which she is careful to say is a 'morally neutral' term, a quality someone can display in the performance of a bad act. (Milton's Satan is the best literary example.) You don't condone that act because you describe it accurately. In fact, you put yourself in a better position to respond to it by taking its true measure. Making the enemy smaller than he is blinds us to the danger he presents and gives him the advantage that comes along with having been underestimated.

That is why what Edward Said has called 'false universals' should be rejected: they stand in the way of useful thinking. How many times have we heard these new mantras: "We have seen the face of evil"; "these are irrational madmen"; "we are at war against international terrorism." Each is at once inaccurate and unhelpful. We have not seen the face of evil; we have seen the face of an enemy who comes at us with a full roster of grievances, goals and strategies. If we reduce that enemy to "evil," we conjure up a shape-shifting demon, a wild-card moral anarchist beyond our comprehension and therefore beyond the reach of any counterstrategies.

The same reduction occurs when we imagine the enemy as "irrational." Irrational actors are by definition without rhyme or reason, and there's no point in reasoning about them on the way to fighting them. The better course is to think of these men as bearers of a rationality we reject because its goal is our destruction. If we take the trouble to understand that rationality, we might have a better chance of figuring out what its adherents will do next and preventing it.

And "international terrorism" does not adequately describe what we are up against. Terrorism is the name of a style of warfare in service of a cause. It is the cause, and the passions informing it, that confront us. Focusing on something called international terrorism—detached from any specific purposeful agenda—only confuses matters. This should have been evident when President Vladimir Putin of Russia insisted that any war against international terrorism must have as one of its objectives victory against the rebels in Chechnya.

When Reuters decided to be careful about using the word "terrorism" because, according to its news director, one man's terrorist is another man's freedom fighter, Martin Kaplan, associate dean of the Annenberg School for Communication at the University of Southern

California, castigated what he saw as one more instance of cultural relativism. But Reuters is simply recognizing how unhelpful the word is, because it prevents us from making distinctions that would allow us to get a better picture of where we are and what we might do. If you think of yourself as the target of terrorism with a capital *T*, your opponent is everywhere and nowhere. But if you think of yourself as the target of a terrorist who comes from somewhere, even if he operates internationally, you can at least try to anticipate his future assaults.

Is this the end of relativism? If by relativism one means a cast of mind that renders you unable to prefer your own convictions to those of your adversary, then relativism could hardly end because it never began. Our convictions are by definition preferred; that's what makes them *our* convictions. Relativizing them is neither an option nor a danger.

But if by relativism one means the practice of putting yourself in your adversary's shoes, not in order to wear them as your own but in order to have some understanding (far short of approval) of why someone else might want to wear them, then relativism will not and should not end, because it is simply another name for serious thought.

Discussion of Leo and Fish Part I: Some Theoretical Background

We begin with the most controversial element of our discussion: our belief that Fish's argument is the stronger one and that our grounds for preferring it are not just ideological but professional and technical as well. The first part of this confession is probably less surprising to most than the second part of it. Many readers of this book will find Leo's argument less persuasive, just as many readers of, say, the conservative newspaper *The Washington Times* would probably find Fish's argument less persuasive. The basis for this division is congruent with the different assumptions about argument held by our two authors. Leo would surely claim that our readers have misread his essay and been hoodwinked by Fish because they—that is to say "you"—are in thrall to "moral relativism.'" By the same token, Leo would doubtless find the readers of *The Washington Times* a more perspicacious lot largely because they have somehow managed to elude indoctrination by a "therapeutic culture" overseen by the intellectual elite—that is, once again, "you." That is to say, for Leo, the differences between our two hypothetical readings are not so much differences in *interpretation* as they are differences in *meaning*. Competent, uncorrupted readers will find the correct meaning in each of the texts, incompetent, corrupt readers will not. There is no room in Leo's world for Fish's "rival interpretations" of texts or events because in the end there is only one correct reading.

Fish, meanwhile, would find the differences in the two readings unremarkable, and certainly no matter for scandal. While he would be prepared to argue against a reading of the two essays that deems his argument inferior to Leo's—indeed one imagines he would be greatly exercised by such a judgment—he would not interpret an unwillingness to acknowledge the superiority of his position as a sign of moral corruption. The *Washington Times* readers simply constitute a community of readers who share different beliefs and assign different meanings to terms like truth and justice than would an audience of Fish-sympathizers. He would be prepared to present arguments showing why they are wrong and he is right—in effect he does so in his essay—but he would accept at the outset that in his arguments he could not appeal to any set of universal standards adhered to by both his supporters and Leo's supporters that would underwrite his conclusions and put paid to Leo's in the eyes of all parties to the dispute. (Because Fish sees the boundaries between communities as far less permeable than we do, he is less optimistic about the prospects for inter-community dialogue than we are.) Leo, meanwhile, assumes that such universals, known to all and perversely ignored by some, do exist, though he is careful not to name them or elaborate on their entailments. Leo's absolutes to-be-named-later, like religious deities whose names are never to be spoken, are more impressive in absentia than in the flesh.

Our own view inclines us less toward Leo and more toward Fish for several reasons. For one thing, Leo's assumptions about the nature of truth and meaning are incompatible with a number of assumptions shared by most members our own community. The most important of those assumptions is the belief that argument has heuristic power, that through the dialogues we carry on with ourselves or with other people, doing what Aristotle called "proving opposites," we do not just defend truth and vanquish error, we actually modify accepted truths and discover new ones. Implicit in this view is the belief that truth cannot be, as Leo appears to assume it is, independent of human judgment or the language we use in forming those judgments. If truth truly is absolute, independent of us and incorrigible by us, and if language is merely a transparent medium of expression not what Burke calls a "terministic screen" that shapes what it reveals, rhetoric is a trivial business deserving of the sort of scorn that the early absolutist Plato heaped on the first of our breed, the Sophists.

While our position here, a position consistent with if not identical to that held by most members of our community, may look suspiciously like the position Leo characterizes as "moral relativism," we do not believe it is. Describing us or Fish as moral relativists is more a caricature of our position than a representation of same. Just because we accept the inevitability of multiple positions on any given issue of significance is not to say we accept—like Leo's hapless student who "dislikes" Nazis but cannot bring himself to denounce them—the moral or cognitive equivalence of all positions on an issue. As rhetoricians we cannot claim membership in the "I'm Ok, You're OK," school of human relations; indeed if such a view prevailed, rhetoricians would be out of work. Rhetoric and argument have no place in either of the two worlds that for Leo represent the sum of all possibilities: his world of One Truth, or the world he imagines us inhabiting where there are countless equivalent truths. In the world of One Truth, rhetoric and argument might serve either to propagandize for the one true faith or to seduce people away from that faith, but it could have no legitimate effect on the truths that form the faith's foundation. In a world of multiple equivalent truths, not only would we be powerless to alter each other's position, there would be no reason to try absent good reasons to prefer one position over another.

Our position, thus, is neither absolutist nor relativist; we prefer to think of it as "realist" in the sense that Kenneth Burke uses that term. In a realist world, rhetoric and argument are essential activities precisely because it is a world that recognizes the significant, though not limitless, role that human agency plays in resolving the world's problems and the important part that language plays in enabling human agency to realize its ends. In particular, language has the realistic capacity to "induce cooperation" among human beings even while it lacks the magical power to "induce motion in things" (*Grammar* 42). While Burke recognizes the enormous power of language to effect change, his realism also requires belief in a world independent of language's shaping power. Our knowledge of this extra-verbal realm comes to us negatively, through the power of things, events and bodies to resist our assertions and claims and thwart our designs. This power of "recalcitrance" in the world encourages an attitude of humility like that which Burke finds in the pragmatist William James, whom he refers to admiringly as "an expert in the *comparative degree* of adjectives of value." James rejected "absolutism (which is really the *superlative,* identifying the One as the Best)" and preferred to think "in terms of *more* rather *all.* . . . To optimism or pessimism, he preferred 'meliorism'" (*Attitudes* 12). While absolutists like Leo sometimes allow the perfect to become the enemy of the good, deeming anything less than *all* insufficient and corrupt, realists look to make things better by degree by inducing cooperation among people and working *toward* collectively defined ends that are themselves constantly being redefined. In such a world, rhetoric and the arts of persuasion are not trifling tools for distracting the masses, they are "equipment for living."

In the world we describe, justice and truth are important, albeit lower case, terms in our vocabulary. What the words mean to a given group of people at one moment in time may not be precisely the same as the meaning they possess at a different time under different circumstances, or to a different group of people in the same time and place. But every group in every circumstance imagines itself pursuing justice and truth. Or as Fish puts it more strikingly: "No one declares himself to be an apostle of injustice," even those whose methods may strike us as heinous. Different groups may use different means to arrive at different meanings for important terms like truth and justice, but these differences are not "subjective" any more than Leo's meanings are "objective." Only Leo's failure to articulate a specific meaning for his notion of truth can preserve its aura of universality. Leo's community, like Fish's, has worked out a definition of the term that is consistent with the principles of that community. But unlike Fish, Leo and the members of his community appear to disown the process that produced their version of truth in the first place. Upon arrival in the realm of Absolutes, they pull up their ladders after them and denounce ladder-users. Like the Platonic world of Pure Forms, Leo's Truth appears to exist apart from the world, unaffected by the interactions of mortals. Exceptional souls may occasionally glimpse an essence amid the accidents of life, and after experiencing such epiphanies may attempt to share them with others, but beyond this, humans have no role in constructing truth. The difference between the two positions has been neatly captured by philosopher Richard Rorty:

> If we see knowing not as having an essence, to be described by scientists or philosophers, but rather as a right, by our current standards, to believe, then we are well on the way to seeing *conversation* as the ultimate context within which knowledge is to be understood. Our focus shifts from the relation between human beings and the objects of their inquiry to the relation between alternative standards of justification, and from there to the actual changes in those standards which make up intellectual history. (*Philosophy* 389-90)

In Rorty's terms, the debate between Leo and Fish may be framed as a debate between those who represent knowledge as an accurate description of essences versus those who understand it as "a right by our current standards to believe." Those who subscribe to the first position relegate rhetoric and persuasion to a decidedly secondary status. The discovery of knowledge is to be left to scientists and philosophers expert in "the relation between human beings and the objects of their inquiry." Those who subscribe to the second position place rhetoric and persuasion at the center of knowledge-making. Through "conversation" they work out "the relation between alternative standards of justification." Which is, more or less, what rhetoricians have been doing for more than two millennia.

Discussion of Leo and Fish Part II: Getting from Duality to Commitment

In this second part of our discussion of the Fish and Leo essays, we want to return our focus to the classroom and how as teachers we might use these essays to work out a tentative definition of argument for ourselves and apply the lessons of the debate to our teaching. From a teaching perspective, what is especially interesting about Leo's argument is how neatly his position and the position he assigns his opposition mimic the mindsets of two problematic groups of students we encounter frequently our classes. Borrowing from William Perry's schema of cognitive and moral development, we term these two positions "duality and multiplicity." They represent two of the earliest stages in Perry's developmental schema and pose markedly different challenges in the classroom. A student in duality assumes there are clear cut right and wrong answers to every question and that the job of the teacher is to present those answers clearly and then test students on their recall of the correct answer. Problems arise when: a) we challenge them to come up with their own answers and/or, b) they believe we are offering them answers that conflict with answers they have previously assimilated from other authorities. If we are doing our jobs, we will do both of these things, which in turn will cause them either to retreat into their old truisms or to risk placing their faith—religious, political, or ideological—into doubt. Students in duality may well see us as threats to their very identity, as shadowy an unknowable as Leo's terrorists in our attempts to unsettle their world view. It is important, thus, to keep in mind how high the stakes and great the risks may be for such students when we ask them to "prove opposites" and truly listen to opposing arguments.

Those in multiplicity, meanwhile, adopt a *laissez faire,* live-and-let-live approach to intellectual differences very much like the one Leo attributes to "multiculturalists." Like those in duality, they too subvert the dialectic process, but by different means. Those in duality subvert the dialectic process by pronouncing One True Thesis and dismissing all alternatives as pretenders. Those in multiplicity, meanwhile, pronounce all alternative theses equally valid and imagine them leading parallel existences that never intersect. In neither case can a thesis engage an antithesis to produce any sort of synthesis. Those in multiplicity are open to new ideas, but they are incapable of critically engaging those ideas, of choosing from among those ideas the ones that make best sense in a given set of circumstances, or of combining elements of various ideas to construct a better one. Insofar as college is a place where students forsake duality for multiplicity—though few students appear to enter college deep in the throes of duality—Leo is half right in claiming that colleges encourage students to adopt something like "fuzzy ethics" as a world view. Probably at one time or another, most college students—including some of us—have embraced the sort of flaccid tolerance of alien ideas that Leo sneeringly refers to as "moral relativism," as an alternative to the more toxic forms of intellectual intolerance bred by dualism. But contrary to Leo, most of us see our task as moving students beyond both stages toward a stage of higher order moral reasoning that embraces complexity and contrariety without lapsing into indifference.

Perry calls this ultimate stage of development "commitment in relativism." It is a position not unlike the one that Stanley Fish represents in "Condemnation without Absolutes." While it remains an ideal more than a realistic possibility for most people, it is a worthwhile aspiration for teachers of argument to hold out for their students. Those who achieve commitment in relativism acknowledge the impossibility of perfect certitude balanced by their need to act on imperfect knowledge. They are at once strongly committed to their principles and aware that no set of principles is infallible or incorrigible. Knowledge, they have come to understand, is a never-ending process not an ultimate possession, and the price one pays for that knowledge is doubt and self-questioning. Having weaned themselves from absolutes, having accepted the necessity of choosing the best from among imperfect alternatives and having taken responsibility for those choices by advancing them in the world, those committed in relativism are perfectly capable of not only condemning positions hostile to their own, but of putting themselves in the shoes of their adversaries and achieving some level of identification with them.

Of course there is no readily apparent way of getting students who are mired in relativism (where most entry-level college students find themselves according to Perry) all the way to commitments in relativism in a single class. Few students will get close to this last stage by the conclusion of their college careers. But so long as the goal is clear, and our methods of teaching and our manner of interacting with our students are congruent with that goal, we have a better chance of nudging students along toward something more satisfying to them and to us than if we operate in a vacuum.[1] If we prefer Fish's argument to Leo's, so long as our preferences our grounded in the imperatives of our discipline and of our pedagogical model, we should feel free to share that preference with our students along with the reasons for our preference.

Leo and Fish Part III: The Elements of Argument

One of the first challenges we face when introducing our notion of argument to students is dispelling the faulty assumptions about argument they bring with them into our classrooms. They have, after all, acquired their own notions of argument long before they began formal study of the matter. They have seen arguments conducted in their homes and schools, read about them in books and newspapers, viewed them on television, listened to them on radio and watched them in movies countless times by the time they walk into classrooms where we presume to teach them how to write arguments. Given the random way in which students acquire early knowledge of argument, it is not surprising that they may need to be "untaught" some assumptions before the teaching can begin. In the case of the Leo-Fish essays, the first thing that may strike students as odd is the fact that the two essays do not speak directly to each other in a clash of ideas. While the Leo and Fish essays appeared on the same day, October 15, 2001, dealt with the same phenomenon, and arrive at strikingly different conclusions via strikingly different routes, they appear to have been written in ignorance of each other. Neither offers a point-by-point refutation of the other, and when they contradict each other, it is more a case of a random intersection of contrary ideas than an intentional posing of opposites.

When we claim that most important arguments of the day are carried on in a similarly indirect fashion, many students are, not surprisingly, puzzled. Their personal experience with argument is likely to incline them toward a "debaters' model" of argument, as a direct contest of opposing ideas carried out between two (or a few) people bent on winning. One attends to such arguments for their entertainment value—the possibility that they might end violently gives them an edge—or to figure out on which side one might throw in one's lot. One would neither engage in nor attend to such arguments—or the faux versions of same featured on TV news shows and talk radio—in order to evaluate the arguments carefully, winnow out the least persuasive ones, and fashion new arguments from opposing arguments. The dominant model of argument is not, in brief, a dialectical model so much as it is a zero-sum game model, veering toward a contact sport, that does not invite active participation of those who attend to it or a search for higher truths of those who engage in it.[2]

Our preferred model of argument elevates the search for better ideas over what Burke calls "advantage-seeking." But like Burke, we acknowledge that at least some element of advantage-seeking is to be found in every argument, no matter how civil the arguers' tone, no matter how accommodating they may be of opposing views. No one argues *purely* to discover better ideas, and it is important early in the semester when weaning students from their overly agonistic models of argument, not to overstate the high-mindedness of our own enterprise and thereby to set them up for further disillusionment. Argument, after all, typically involves some investment of one's ego and one's heart as well as one's mind and one's judgment. Most of us undertake the risks of argument—the risk of alienating people, of arousing opposition, of missing the point and having that fact pointed out, not always kindly, in a public setting—only if our fondest beliefs or self-interests are at stake. Even the most selfless of arguers wishes, if not to win an argument, to at least "get it right." To lose an argument, or even to have one's argument called into question, may well require one to go back and reexamine beliefs that anchor one's identity. So argument is risky, in part because we are seeking advantage for our interests and beliefs or are striving to prevent others from winning an advantage for their interests and beliefs. But that said, most of us—even, or perhaps especially, terrorists—truly believe that in serving our interests larger interests are served and that in forwarding our beliefs we are working toward truth and justice for others. To be sure, all of us find ourselves sometimes serving as apostles of, if not injustice, ideas that are, at best, the least unjust of a bad lot. But there is a certain nobility in even this pursuit and students should be reminded of this fact early in the semester.

What provokes the arguments of Fish and Leo is an event, 9/11, that caused many Americans to alter their perceptions of and assumptions about the world. Until September 11, 2001, no foreign power had managed to invade the country or kill significant numbers of American citizens on American soil in centuries. After 9/11, our sense of invulnerability and of our role in the world required reexamination while our beliefs about the rest of the world's attitude toward us had to be radically revised. In sum, the events of 9/11 represent a classic instance of what in rhetoric is referred to as an "exigence." According to Lloyd Bitzer, who coined the term forty years ago as part of his revisionist look at the rhetorical situation, "Any exigence is an imperfection marked by urgency; it is a defect, an obstacle, something waiting to be done, a thing which is other than it should be" (304). An exigence cannot be, in the language of debate, an "inherent" problem, some unchangeable aspect of the human condition, say, that defies solution; and it cannot be a problem that can be solved directly by extra-verbal means. "An exigence is rhetorical when it is capable of positive modification and when positive modification requires discourse or can be assisted by discourse" (304). The terrorist of attack of 9/11 demanded "discourse" of every one of us, whether we mulled over our responses in silent soliloquies or submitted them aloud or in print for public scrutiny. What did we make of the attack? How should we respond, as a nation and as individuals? Most Americans tried to articulate their feelings about the attack and to find some way of forming an ethical judgment of it. We often looked to trusted pundits like Leo, and academics like Fish who shared their thoughts in the media, to help us find expression for thoughts that eluded us and ideals that might guide us.

Both Fish and Leo share the requisite sense of urgency about what needs to be done in response to the exigence. For Leo, the lesson of 9/11 is that time has come to begin pushing the "multicultural-therapeutic left" away from its sloppy relativism and to offer a united, presumably "monocultural," front in opposition to the terrorist threat. It is a line of thinking that appears to anticipate some lines of thought pursued subsequently by our political leadership: the world changed on 9/11 calling for an overhaul of our political priorities and our value system (or a return to our core values), including the sacrifice of some liberties in exchange for better security; our enemy is "terrorism" or some variation thereof ("Islamic fascism," "international terrorist movement" "Muslim extremists") that is monolithic, shadowy, and nihilistic in nature; in opposing this enemy we must be uncompromising and go it alone if other members of the international community do not share our vision. By the same token, Fish's essay appears to anticipate many of the arguments put forth by eventual critics of the Iraq war, after Iraq became in effect a testing ground for ideas very much like those supported by Leo. What resulted is a textbook example of what has happened throughout history when absolutist ideas are tested on reality. The monolithic model of evil ran afoul of the heterogeneous nature of a deeply divided society. While terrorist groups did enter the fray after the American occupation, most of the violence after 2003 was sectarian violence, inflicted by specific groups, each "with a full roster of grievances, goals and strategies" seeking advantage for their interests.

One of the interesting questions raised by the notion of exigence is the degree to which the "defect" or "obstacle" it names is in the world versus in the eye of the beholder. Our own "realist" reading of the two essays would place exigence in both places. That is, Fish and Leo's essays are at once responses to an event in the world independent of the power of language to change or reverse it, and continuations of the two writers' lifelong working out of their belief systems. While Leo may imply that 9/11 changed the world, the world he describes in the wake of 9/11 is a world that has much in common with the dystopia he has been decrying for many years, and his prescription for dealing with the post-9/11 world is consistent with proposals for reform he has been making since the 1960s.

Likewise Fish's liberal response (though Fish typically eludes labels like liberal/conservative, his position on this particular issue lines up with the position that many liberals ultimately took on the issue) to the exigence of 9/11 echoes ideas that he has been articulating for over thirty years in the realms of literary and legal theory. His insistence that we attend to the particulars of our enemies' complaints in order to understand their motivations and what we are up against is of a piece with his insistence that we attend to the details of texts and work out their meaning in the context of their authors' intentions. His contention that in justifying our responses to 9/11 we can only appeal to those contingent truths that we hold to in common with other members of a community who shares our beliefs—"the record of aspiration and accomplishment that makes up our collective understanding of what we live for"—is of a piece with his belief in communities of readers who work out standards for meaning and interpretation among themselves.

Our interest in connecting Leo and Fish's arguments about 9/11 to their larger world view goes beyond any interest we might have in correctly labeling their political positions. Understanding the source of their claims is, we would argue, key to understanding the tone the two writers take in expressing those claims. Establishing a reasonably clear way of talking about matters of tone early on in an argument course is critical. It is critical because of the difficulties so many students face in finding an appropriate voice in their arguments. Part of this difficulty can be traced back to the different stages of development students occupy when they arrive in our classes. Students leaning toward dualism, for example, may adopt an overly aggressive tone in their arguments. (While few full-fledged dualists show up on day one in our classes, it is a position to which some, particularly first year college students, retreat when they feel threatened intellectually.) Remember, much is at stake for a dualist placed in the position of justifying ideas that they assume should require no justification. One symptom of this anxiety will be a tone of aggressive, if unearned, certitude. Claims, no matter how shaky, will be delivered with little support, no qualification and absolute conviction. Controversial categorical judgments, particularly moral judgments, will be handed down as if by fiat. Opposing arguments will be dismissed out of hand no matter how strong they may appear to a third party. Any reader not in complete agreement with the author of such an argument may well feel more bullied than persuaded.

Their counterparts in multiplicity, meanwhile, tend also to see their claims and judgments as self-evident, not because they are the One True Thing but because, hey, everyone gets to believe whatever they want. The tone favored by those in multiplicity will be considerably less belligerent than the tone adopted by their peers in dualism. They are not threatened by disagreement—after all, people inevitably see things differently; an argument for them is just a way to let people know "where they are coming from." In truth, their claims are often difficult to disagree with. The more abstract the position they take, after all, the more difficult it is to dispute their basic premise that there is no real need to discriminate among positions. If the dualist tends toward an excessively belligerent tone, the multiplist tends toward an excessively bland one.

By way of helping students recognize the intellectual origins of tone and the limitations they face if they are unable to moderate their tone, it is helpful to analyze matters of tone in essays like those of Fish and Leo. Because these writers are considerably more sophisticated than most student writers, their tonal differences, though significant, are less stark than those we see in our classes. Underlying differences in tone between Fish and Leo's essays are differences in outlook that we've already touched on. In particular, Fish's tone can be traced back to his belief that truth must be rediscovered and renegotiated as contexts change, and that truth consists not of a correspondence between one's vocabulary and a state of affairs in the world, but of the most persuasive justification among competing versions of the truth. Leo's tone, meanwhile derives from his belief that there is one universal truth that is not altered by circumstances. Those who think straight, like Leo, possess absolute truth and good. Those, like the bishops, who think sloppily obscure our vision of truth and good and allow error and evil into the world. At the risk of overstating those differences, we would describe Fish's tone as being closer to that of a mentor or guide, someone concerned simultaneously to clear up confusions and to complicate his readers' understanding of things. It is an asymmetrical relationship to be sure, Fish is the teacher and we are his pupils, but insofar as he seems to believe we are capable of following a complex line of reasoning, it is not condescending. Leo's tone, meanwhile seems closer to that of a gadfly or scold, brisk and judgmental. His concern is to clarify matters by simplifying them in order to facilitate sound moral judgment.

Leo's tone is established in early his first sentence when, before telling us what the bishops' statement actually says, he pronounces it "disgraceful;" and then, after offering two snippets from the statement, he proceeds to tell his readers what the bishops *really* mean, "[i]n plain English," before concluding that it is "a moral mess." Moral and linguistic clarity are of a piece for Leo. He gives short shrift, thus, to those who natter on about "root causes" and understanding acts "in context." To set the record straight, he offers a "plain English" translation of this morally and linguistically sloppy talk, avowing that what the bishops really mean to say is that "reckless and imperial America brought the attacks on itself." Throughout his critique, Leo offers scant evidence in support of his generalizations and few details that might help his audience identify the multiculturalists, moral relativists, and denizens of therapeutic culture in their midst. A single quote from "one upstate New York student" supports a broad generalization about lamentable educational practices common throughout American higher education, while the bishops' statement is presented as "a minor example of what could be a major problem"—the inability of moral leaders "to say plainly that evil exists."

If Leo's characterization of the bishops' statement is in fact accurate and fair-minded, the tonal aspects of his essay might be attributed more to legitimate moral outrage than to habits of mind congruent with his belief system. But even one sympathetic to Leo's view would have problems squaring his summary of the bishops' statement with the full text of that statement. It begins in fact by announcing "a new solidarity with those in other parts of the world for whom the evil forces of terrorism are a continuing fear and reality" (Bishops). To be sure Leo and the bishops do not appear to define evil in the same way, nor do the bishops seem content to let the epithet "evil" serve as their full explanation of the motivation for the terrorists' act. But they do "say plainly that evil exists" and that terrorist acts like 9/11 qualify as evil acts.

Our concern here is not to debunk Leo's critique of the bishops. Our concern is to emphasize the extent to which the tone of Leo's essay derives not from an "objective" awareness of a world independent of his perceptions of it, so much as it derives from the belief system through which he perceives that world. While Leo would doubtless find such a contention scandalous, a relativist canard, Fish would not. The differences in tone between the two writers, we would argue, is not a function of one being less objective than the other, but of one being more aware than the other that total objectivity is a will-o-the-wisp. In lieu of absolute truth and objectivity, Fish embraces something on the order of intersubjectivity. We are, in his view, united by "particular lived values" and share "the record of aspiration and accomplishment that makes up our collective understanding of what we live for." Fish's pragmatic view of truth as fallible and particular is reflected in his tone, a tone that rivals Leo's in its briskness but is less judgmental, more cautious about the naming of things. At the heart of his essay, in fact, lies his rejection of reductive labeling, his concern to complicate soundbite versions of postmodernism, of relativism, and of terrorism. While Fish says he finds the reporter's question about "the end of postmodern relativism" that begins his essay "bizarre," he goes on to offer a thoughtful response to it, attributing the reporter's misunderstanding of the term not to some moral lapse, but to the fact that it is part of "a rarefied form of academic talk" to which the reporter is not normally privy.

In announcing our own preference for Fish's style, we are of course mostly reaffirming our general sympathy with his world view. But that preference in turn, is not merely "subjective" in the way that someone like Leo would use that term. Our sympathies with Fish's point of view and his manner of expression are professional as well as personal. The ideas that he expresses and the way he expresses them are in greater harmony with our disciplinary imperatives than are Leo's ideas and the manner of expression that his ideas give rise to. Fish's thoughts and tone are, in our view, more likely to result in better thinking about the issue at hand than are Leo's thoughts and tone. Whether one argument fares better than the other in the marketplace of ideas is another matter altogether. Such judgments are harder to make and more audience-specific than the judgment about the effects of the arguments on understanding of the issues. In order to better understand this complex, often misunderstood relationship between arguments that win the day with audiences and arguments that lead audiences to reexamine issues we turn now to a continuum of argument practices and the metric used to arrange arguments along that continuum.

Argument and "the purification of war"

The subheading for this section is taken from the Latin epigraph to Burke's *A Grammar of Motives—"Ad bellum purificandum."* It is at once a most modest sentiment—one would, after all, sooner see war ended altogether—and a most ambitious one—as war grows exponentially more savage in the new century, we long for anything that might mitigate its gruesome effects. It's also an epigraph that could serve to introduce Burke's entire oeuvre, as it captures neatly the primary goal of rhetoric as he imagines it—the transformation of destructive urges into creative and cooperative acts, enmity into identification, war into argument. As we noted earlier, Burke is enough of a realist to hold that this transformation can never be complete—in every argument there will remain a residual element of aggression and advantage-seeking no matter how noble the cause in whose name the argument is made. But Burke is also enough of an idealist to believe that interests other than those of the arguer are always served by argument. The only case in which the needs and beliefs of an audience may be ignored is when the arguer is confident that their cooperation will be secured by force if their argument fails and they deign to argue for pretty much the same reasons that dictators hold elections. Joseph Heller neatly captures the spirit of "might makes right" disguised as argument, a hegemonic practice all too familiar to twenty-first century audiences, in an exchange from the novel *Catch-22*. The exchange features the novel's protagonist, Yossarian, confronting his nemesis, Milo Minderbinder, after Milo has pretended to offer an Italian thief some dates for a bedsheet and then refused to hand over the dates after the thief has given him his bedsheet.

> "Why didn't you just hit him over the head and take the bedsheet away from him?" Yossarian asked.
>
> Pressing his lips together with dignity, Milo shook his head. "that would have been most unjust," he scolded firmly. "Force is wrong and two wrongs never make a right. It was much better my way. When

> I held the dates out to him and reached for the bedsheet, he probably thought I was offering a trade."
>
> "What were you doing?"
>
> "Actually, I was offering to trade, but since he doesn't understand English, I can always deny it."
>
> "Suppose he gets angry and wants the dates?"
>
> "Why, We'll just hit him over the head and take them away from him," Milo answered without hesitation. (68)

This then is what argument looks like at the far left end of the continuum where force looms menacingly behind every persuasive gambit. What sorts of argument practices does one find at this end of the continuum? Propaganda and advertising come immediately to mind. Parental arguments that end with that time-honored phrase that simultaneously announces victory and admits defeat—"Because I said so!"—surely falls somewhere toward the left end of things. Then as one moves to the right toward more "purified" forms of combat, one encounters the practice of law, labor negotiation and education. Finally, at the furthest remove from might makes right, we have those purest of persuasive practices that seem not to be persuasive at all; the example Burke uses is that of writing a book. We will take a closer look at the characteristics of these different practices shortly, but before we do, we need to articulate the principle used to distinguish among these various forms of persuasion, a principle that Burke refers to variously as "standoffishness" or "self interference."

To understand this principle it is helpful to keep in mind one of Burke's favorite metaphors for responsible persuasion, the practice of courtship, which is itself a "purified" version of considerably less seemly practices. If courtship reigns at the far right end of the continuum, one would expect to find the persuasive equivalent to something like sexual harassment at the left end of the continuum. Sexual harassment is a predatory relationship based on asymmetry whereby one party uses their power over the other to coerce affection. In the middle, the arts of seduction come into play, as the seducer pretends to be whatever their prey wishes them to be and tells their prey whatever they wish to hear in order to achieve their own gratification. At the right end of the continuum, meanwhile, a couple engages in courtship, a respectful relationship based on mutuality whose ends inevitably include sex along with a great many other aspirations. To be sure, each of the people in a courtship relationship will do what they can to make themselves desirable to the other person, to persuade them of their viability as a partner. Certainly sexual attraction will play a role in the relationship. But each is willing for the time being to delay gratification in the name of increasing their sense of identification with the other person, overcoming the estrangements of class, gender, nationality, religion or whatever categories of difference we might use to sort out the human race. Whereas in the earlier cases relationships were little more than a means to the end of sexual gratification by one of the two parties (in Martin Buber's formulation, a classic "I-it" relationship), the courtship relationship is an end in itself ("I-Thou") for both partners. If one were to extend the courtship metaphor beyond the left end of the continuum, one would find oneself in the murky realm of rape and sexual assault, while off the right end of the continuum, one would find oneself in the luminous realm of celibacy, as when a nun declares herself a bride of Christ. All practices that fall along the continuum, meanwhile, are some combination of self-interest and physical desire, and a willingness to interfere with one's natural urges in the name of other ends.

To return now to actual persuasive practices as they fall along the self-interference continuum, we begin with propaganda and advertising. These practices are, Burke maintains, very much "addressed" insofar as they are obsessively focused on audience. It is an asymmetric relationship with the advertiser or propagandist having at least some control, in the case of some propagandists, a virtual monopoly, over their audience's access to information and understanding. While both propagandists and advertisers are quick in their public pronouncements to lavish praise on their audiences, particularly their intelligence, their own advice to each other about how to win over audiences manifests scant regard for the people they are pitching, particularly for their intelligence. Both groups spend a lot of time and extraordinary amounts of money exploring the psyches and emotional soft spots of their audiences. No other group among those who practice the arts of persuasion comes close to spending as much time as advertisers and propagandists figuring out ways to exploit their audience's vulnerabilities. Hitler's *Mein Kampf,* for example, is both a classic of propaganda theory and a thoroughgoing analysis of audience psychology. Noting Hitler's skill at manipulation of his audience, Burke calls attention to the very calculated way "he gauges resistances and opportunities with the 'rationality' of a skilled advertising man planning a new sales campaign. Politics, he says, must be sold like soap—and soap is not sold in a trance" (*Philosophy of Literary Form* 216). Contemporary advertisers, meanwhile, are relentless in the pursuit of connections between demographic and psychographic information—there are sixty-four distinct groups of consumers arranged in a psychographic grid used by advertisers—and consumer buying habits. While old style behaviorist theories are out of favor with most academic psychologists these days, advertisers and propagandists are still in the business of manipulating stimuli to get the desired response. Like engineers who still rely on the old Newtonian paradigm to build bridges and skyscrapers, the propagandists and behaviorists seem to find that their outmoded mechanistic paradigm works just fine when it comes to selling soap and politics.

While all propaganda is by definition predatory in ways suggested above—we will consider recent uses of propaganda more extensively later in the book—advertising embraces a wider range of practices, some of which are fairly benign. Advertising is, for example, used to promote charitable contributions as well as soap. Indeed, within every category of persuasive practices one will find a range of practices that are to varying degrees advantage-seeking on the one hand or "standoffish" on the other. Some advertisements may do little more than feature positive references to their product by disinterested third parties. At times, even propaganda may serve an altruistic public policy goal; and instead of telling "the Big Lie" as Goebbels famously recommends, it may simply withhold information that would complicate its argument. But taken as a whole, these practices do not promote self interference in any serious way. Only to the extent that one alters one's script in recognition that a different script is more likely to find favor with one's audience does one interfere with one's impulses. But this is more a matter of subordinating one form of gratification to another; in the end, one's audience is always a means to one's ends.

As one moves toward the center of the continuum, legal persuasive practices serve as our model. While there are many who would place lawyers' arts farther to the left on our continuum, legal argument is considerably more constrained in its ability to seduce or dupe its audience than are propaganda and advertising. There is, moreover, considerably more parity between arguer and audience in the legal arena than there is in the political and consumer arenas. Withholding information, for example, which might be applauded as part of a virtuoso campaign to spin things in the realms of politics and advertising, can be a punishable offense in the realm of the law. Because of the adversarial nature of the legal system, the various lapses in one's arguments are vulnerable to disclosure and exploitation. (Our political system is also nominally adversarial, but there are few rules or judges to control political discourse, and the public tolerance for fallacious reasoning and even outright mendacity does little to encourage self interference among politicians.) The law offers all sorts of formal constraints on the desire of lawyers to manipulate their audience. The closest lawyers can come to the use of demographic and psychographic information to gain some advantage for their point of view is restricted to the use of jury consultants who use elaborate schemes to select sympathetic juries. For all its flaws, legal reasoning imposes various forms of interference on participants in the legal system all the way to the top of the system where Supreme Court Justices hope to write opinions for posterity.

Burke uses the curious metaphor of writing a book to explain his "purest" form of persuasion, the equivalent of a great courtship. Here, the principle of self-interference is neither imposed by concerns about audience nor by rules, conventions and fears of punishment or disclosure. The restraint required of pure persuasion is entirely self-imposed. An author's self-interference is in response to the demands of book he is creating, "demands conditioned by the parts already written, so that the book becomes to an extent something not foreseen by its author, and requires him to interfere with his original intentions" (*Rhetoric* 269). This interference is not so much ethical as aesthetic, and the purity of pure persuasion is the formal purity of "art for art's sake" more than it is the moral purity of saintliness. That said, Burke attributes to pure persuasion "a high ethical value" (271) insofar as it imposes a different order of obligations on those who experience it, something like "truth for truth's sake." The purest forms of argument are dialectic in nature, a working out of ideas that have a momentum and integrity of their own, heedless of the needs and desires of an audience. Just as an art for art's sake movement often produces art that strikes its audience as indifferent or hostile to its expectations, argument at the far right end of the continuum may enjoy scant success in the marketplace. But like the best works that emerge from an art for art's sake movement, purely persuasive arguments may eventually enjoy a belated acceptance by audiences, in part because they have changed the way people think about the issue at hand.

In the end, of course, pure persuasion of this sort is not a goal for students of argument so much as it is a tendency within argument, a counter-balance to opposing tendencies toward an exclusive—and all too often predatory—focus on audience. In introducing students to the concept of pure persuasion, we like to remind them of an alternate meaning of the term argument—the "gist" or "essence" of an extended piece of discourse. Looking for the argument, the central point, of any piece of discourse is a habit of mind common to all critical readers. The more complex the piece of discourse we are reading, the more likely it is that the argument we tease out of the prose will be the product of opposing ideas, not an unambiguous thesis or major claim always appearing—where so many of our students have been taught to look—in the last sentence of the first paragraph. A gist is a synthesis of disparate ideas and a joint product of the reader/viewer/listener's interpretive powers and the properties of the discourse they are interpreting. It is not what remains after one idea trumps another, a trophy or laurel leaf that goes to the victor, it is a creative act, a rhetorical version of the ontologist's essence. In the end, it is why we teach argument: To complicate our students' thinking about the world, to help them learn how to withhold judgment (to cultivate the art of "standoffishness") of their own ideas as well as others,' long enough to test them against opposing ideas and to respect what emerges from that combination.

Why students Need Argument

Up to this point, we have offered a definition of argument congruent with our disciplinary imperatives and personal beliefs. In this next section we shift our focus to what students might hope to get out of a writing course concentrating on argument. What unique role does the study of argument serve in the curriculum and in their lives? As we design our courses and our assignments we need to keep that role in mind and to shape our pedagogy around it. In what follows, we will focus on three particularly crucial functions of argument: as a vehicle for teaching the most readily transferable set of skills one might learn in a writing course; as a vehicle for constructing and defending identity; and as a vehicle for ethical reasoning.

Argument and Critical Literacy

While there is no single name for the highly mobile cluster of skills students might learn in a writing course focused on argument, we will refer to them here as "critical literacy." Critical literacy remains a somewhat amorphous concept, and for reasons we will soon cite, a somewhat controversial one. We will try to stipulate a definition of the term that clarifies our usage of it and minimizes some of its more controversial aspects. In setting out to define critical literacy it seems fair to say that we know more about what it is not than we do about what it is. What it most assuredly is not is whatever was being done in the name of the current-traditional writing curriculum with its emphasis on pre-fabricated forms and dumb readers. The current-traditional curriculum not only did not encourage students to think *outside* the box, it actively encouraged them to think of everything *as* a box, even the inherently chaotic, idiosyncratic business of writing. Its apparent goal was literacy in its older sense of minimal competency, albeit ratcheted up to the college level. It did not encourage personal engagement or reflection. It certainly did not offer students much in the way of skills and understandings that might travel with them elsewhere in the curriculum. Few philosophy courses in the university required "process" papers and fewer sociology courses stressed the "description" paper. (Some in our profession in fact favor the abolition of first year writing requirements precisely because they believe that the current-traditional model or some variant thereof remains the dominant model of writing in the profession. If one agrees that they are right about the currency of that model, they have a point.)

Perhaps the key distinguishing characteristic of critical literacy as we understand that term and the one that most clearly distinguishes it from its older, minimalist version, is its emphasis on reflective knowledge, the capacity Coleridge referred to as "knowing your knowledge" versus merely possessing it. In contrast to the demands placed on students writing a sound process paper, consider the challenges facing students setting out to construct a sound argument. They must be able to imagine counter-arguments, anticipate audience response, particularly skepticism and ignorance, and move deftly between claims of truth, reasons that warrant those claims, and evidence that supports the reasons. They must assess the adequacy of the support for their claim and qualify it accordingly. They must learn how to evaluate evidence and how to fairly summarize and question authorities with differing points of view. Perhaps most importantly, students must be prepared to risk their beliefs and assumptions about the world. It is not possible in the arena of argument simply to "plug [in a formula] and chug [out an answer]." Students have to understand issues in the context of an ongoing conversation about those issues, accepting at the outset that, as Stanley Fish suggests above, not all parties to that conversation will accept their beliefs and assumptions at face value.

In the interest of further clarifying critical literacy it might be helpful to contrast it to yet another approach to the teaching of composition that succeeds the current-traditional model. The critical thinking movement in composition was led by people like psychologist Dick Hayes and composition theorist Linda Flower who teamed up to show how problem solving methods could be imported into the writing classroom. They were among the first in the field of composition who, in Janet Emig's famous phrase, treated writing in a fully developed way as a "mode of thinking" and helped people see how the acquisition of writing ability entails higher order reasoning. But while the critical thinking movement was useful in helping the discipline move past current-traditional approaches, it did not cultivate reflective understanding in the same way that critical literacy sets out to do. Moreover, the problem-solving skills it focused attention on were taught as if they were value free, a set of skills not unlike those required to solve puzzles. Their value-free assumptions limited their applicability to argument, a genre that often takes us far afield into issues that are value laden and emotionally charged.

One of the easiest ways to distinguish a critical thinking approach to teaching writing from a critical literacy approach is to focus on the notion of problem-solving. Simply put, critical thinking proponents focus on how to solve problems, while critical literacy proponents focus on how to discover problems. One of the most important figures in the critical literacy movement in the 1980s, Brazilian philosopher Paolo Freire, coined the term "problematize" to describe what he set out to do with his educational program in South America. Friere's work with peasant populations proved to be so controversial that the government felt compelled to shut it down eventually. In the process of teaching basic literacy, Freire was teaching revolutionary politics by causing pre-literate "mythic" thinking to give way to critical literacy. The power of naming situations, as Freire's peasants soon discovered, contains the seeds for challenging and redefining those situations. At one level, Freire's pedagogical experiments confirmed one of Kenneth Burke's most important insights: that proverbs, which comprise a sort of linguistic shorthand for naming recurrent situations, constitute "*strategies* for dealing with *situations*" (*Philosophy* 296). For Burke as for Freire, names are never neutral. Before we can name anything, we must first size it up, "discern 'the general behind the particular' (301), and the name that we choose in turn implies an attitude toward it. Insofar as an attitude is an incipient act, language and politics are inextricably linked.

Educators have been reluctant to embrace the political dimension of critical literacy for obvious reasons. As witnessed by John Leo's antipathy toward the "therapeutic," "multiculturalist" political sympathies of college faculty, there is already a great deal of fear about the possibility that schools are indoctrinating instead of educating students. The fact that critical literacy belongs to an ancient tradition of education stressing that "the unexamined life is not worth living," and that it encourages such non-partisan virtues as self-reflection and self-questioning has not dissuaded some conservative critics from denouncing it as little more than a propaganda tool. While some of the more ardent proponents of critical literacy, like the truest believers in any cause, appear sometimes to believe that theirs is the one true faith and that non-believers are in league with the John Leo's of the world, many of our most thoughtful practitioners and innovative teachers profess allegiance to critical literacy on largely pedagogical grounds.

Moreover, those who may be tempted to believe that by teaching students to challenge the status quo, question tradition and authority and think dialectically about the world they ensure a generation of students committed to progressive politics flatter themselves. Critical literacy is simply too complex an instrument to serve as a reliable tool of indoctrination. Its emphasis on *how* to think, on foregrounding processes and tacit understanding, combined with its skeptical attitude toward content and coverage, leaves entirely open the question of what students might *do* with their education. The very qualities of critical literacy that allow it to transfer so readily to other courses, that make it so adaptable to history, economics and sociology courses, are the very qualities that render it a flawed vessel of indoctrination. As Michael Berube reminds us, citing what he calls the principle of "reversibility," there is no way to ensure that training students in advanced literacy can be "a unidirectional vehicle for political change" (145 *Employment*). Our most reflective thinkers may turn out to be hedge fund wizards as surely as they turn out to be political revolutionaries.

But beyond the fear of appearing partisan in our approach to teaching writing, there is a deeper animus toward the teaching of reflection that is not on the surface political. Philosopher Hans Blumenberg, for example, takes note of the increasing pressure on educators to set aside the goal of the examined life and to "abandon the idea . . . that is governed by the norm that man must know what he is doing" (446) in the name of finding ever more parsimonious means for solving problems. In response, Blumenberg calls for a turn to rhetoric, on the grounds that it represents "a consummate embodiment of retardation [of time]. Circumstantiality, procedural inventiveness, ritualization imply a doubt as to whether the shortest way of connecting two points is also the humane route from one to another" (446).

Blumenberg's motive for turning to rhetoric here resonates with a theme that runs throughout Burke, who frequently expresses a skeptical attitude toward the Law of Parsimony and the "Occamite nonsense" (e.g., behaviorism and monetarism) that may arise from it: "For if much of service has been got by following Occam's law to the effect that 'entities should not be *multiplied* beyond necessity,' equally much of disservice has arisen through ignoring a contrary law, which we could phrase correspondingly: 'entities should not be *reduced* beyond necessity" (*Grammar* 324). For Burke, the modern age is characterized far more by crimes against the second law than against the first. If critical thinking implies an ability to solve problems efficiently through simplification, critical literacy implies an ability to generate complexity through reflection. Moreover, it also entails an ability not only to write clearly when one can, but complexly when one must, to defer to an audience's limitations when it serves one's aims and to challenge and expand those limitations when deference would defeat those aims. While the ends we seek in critical literacy are lofty indeed, and while we have reached no consensus about how best to achieve them, it's clear that teaching students how to write arguments is among the surest means of reaching them. In the process, the lessons students learn in an argument course undergirded by the principles of critical literacy are the surest to travel to other courses in the curriculum.

This last contention is borne out for many of us by our experience working in the area of writing across the curriculum. What many of us discovered when we spread out across the curriculum to help teachers in other disciplines improve their students' writing was that we were actually in the business of helping their students write better arguments. Or to put the matter more precisely, we were helping faculty in other disciplines teach their students how to *argue* like members of a discipline as much as teaching them how to *write* like members of a discipline. Teaching the formats for essays in psychology or physics proved to be relatively simple. But making students aware of the assumptions embedded in those formats, assumptions about the relative evidentiary weight different formats accorded to primary and secondary sources, experimental data, theory, anomaly, etc., proved to be a considerably more challenging task.

We, the agents of WAC, were in effect reprising the role of our Sophist ancestors; we were the *metics,* the foreigners passing through a territory, simultaneously handicapped by our outsider status and empowered by it. What may have struck a member of a disciplinary community as a demonstration of truth looked to many of us, with our new eyes, like a persuasive gambit. Like Moliere's Monsieur Jourdain who is surprised to learn that he has been speaking prose his whole life, many of our colleagues in other disciplines were surprised to learn that they had been using and teaching rhetoric the whole time. Once they achieved this awareness, many of these same colleagues became major proponents of a focus on argument not only in their own courses but in the writing courses we taught to prepare students for their disciplines. As we shall demonstrate in chapter two, the approaches used in contemporary argument courses, are eminently adaptable to other disciplines.

Argument and Identity

One of the more controversial aspects of critical literacy concerns the connections it draws between critical thought and identity. In urging students to become more reflective thinkers, proponents of critical literacy call attention to various forces in the world that undermine people's sense of agency and entice them to pursue ends inimical to a healthy sense of self and community. They call attention to ways in which the decisions we make on a daily basis, as consumers, workers and citizens, decisions about what to eat, how to advance ourselves in the workplace and who to vote for, both reveal who we are and reinforce, for good or ill, our self-understanding. Sellers of soap, management gurus and political consultants all have an interest not just in understanding who we are, but in shaping a self congruent with their ends, not ours. Students need thus to be reflective about these choices, made aware of the implications of some of their choices, and alert to the persuasive gambits common to those who encourage them to assume these identities.

This can prove to be a challenging task. Students are often strongly resistant to an emphasis on the relationship between who they are the everyday choices they make. They do not like the implicit suggestion that they might be the dupes of some shadowy group of "hidden persuaders," and they do not like the idea of having to pay so much attention to choices and decisions that heretofore have been effortlessly made. Aren't we making a mountain out of a molehill, they suggest, to shower so much critical attention on a lowly ad or a selection from a pop business book? Anyone who has taught a literature course will recognize the response. They are skeptical that anything so simple on the surface could have all this depth of meaning. The various concerns that students express about applying the lessons of critical literacy to their everyday life need to be taken into account. On the one hand, they are right to insist on their own resourcefulness and their own ability to keep their distance from the identities being proferred them by so many different interest groups. Many of them have thought critically about at least some of these choices and we always find a few students in every class who are in fact militantly on guard against external assaults on their identities. But on the other hand, many students underestimate how skillfully those who fashion off-the-rack identities for them manage to ingratiate themselves through the use of humor, irony, self deprecation and self-revelation, and numerous other devices designed to disarm them. In approaching the relationship between argument and identity, thus, it is important to respect students' position and experience in this area and to take it slowly at the outset. We like to begin the discussion of identity with a look at some of the most prevalent techniques used by those with prefabricated identities to sell, techniques to which none of us are invulnerable.

Consider, for example, one of most effective devices used by advertisers, political consultants and management gurus to disarm American audiences: the appeal to rugged individualism. Whether it is the politician who professes to ignore the polls and follow his gut, the manager who scoffs at conventional wisdom and dares to be great, or the male model dressed in cowboy garb who lights up a cigarette and laughs at death, Americans have long been susceptible to the charms of the rugged individual in all his many guises. Indeed, the easiest way to sell a mass American audience on behaviors or choices that have questionable consequences is to present that choice as an expression of rugged individualism. Rugged individualism constitutes what Perelman and Olbrechts-Tyteca call a *loci,* "premises of a general nature that can serve as the bases for values and hierarchies" (84). The premise represented by the model of the rugged individual is perhaps most economically summed up by the categorical imperative of the code hero: "A man's gotta do what a man's gotta do." One listens to one's inner manhood to intuit the best course of action and follows that guidance in the face of convention, popularity, lawfulness and personal risk. Like all loci, the model of the rugged individual draws its life from many streams, in particular, American history and American popular culture. A country born of revolution and nurtured on the "conquest" of a receding frontier, a country whose economic system is based on risk taking and competition, a country whose entertainment industry has provided a steady stream of cowboys, private dicks, rags to riches entrepreneurs and gang bangers in every medium—this is a country with rugged individualism buried deep in its DNA. Which is why the simple act of associating a brand, a product, a choice, a person, a candidate, or a proposal with rugged individualism has been so effective down through the years in forwarding the interests of its sponsor. But in the act of choosing whatever it is that the sponsor wishes us to choose, we further the hold of that identity on the national imagination, ensure its continued repetition and reinforce the rugged individual's status as a behavioral model.

But those who use the rugged individual understand that the ur-vision of the rugged individual—call it the John Wayne version—has limited appeal for denizens of various boxes on the psychographic grid and so they craft variations on the central model that speak most saliently to those to whom they are pitching their product. For some, the macho version of non-conformity is a turnoff and so they require a kinder, gentler version. Consider for example the charming, mildly amusing ad campaign for Apple Computing featuring personifications of the "MAC" and "PC" computer lines. Whereas the PC is personified as a plump, stuffy suit, with an exceedingly narrow view of his job description and a tendency to whine about his users' need to demand too much of him, MAC is personified as a skinny, hip, stylishly rumpled younger guy open to new possibilities, puzzled by PC's complaints about his users' demands and bemused by the PC persona. It is a classic conflict, albeit a soothingly muted one, between the staid "company man" and the edgy rebel, the bureaucrat and the innovator.

The current ad is a far tamer version of the classic Apple Super Bowl ad of 1984 introducing the Mac line of computers, featuring a woman eluding storm troopers to shatter a huge television screen where Big Brother is pontificating before an auditorium full of bowed figures. (While it might be tempting to see the advertisers' choice of a female figure for the role of rugged individual as a sign of advanced social awareness, it is more likely a reflection of their concern to hit a particular demographic.) The earlier version of the "rebel v suits" advertisement suggests that a good deal more is at stake in the choice between conformity and individualism and, by implication, between the choice of Apple and the unnamed establishment brand of computers. One's choice of computer is a political, not merely a practical or lifestyle choice. Given the outsider status of the Apple brand in 1984 when IBM dominated the market, the difference in tone is understandable. The ideological implications of the rugged individual stereotype in advertising tend to be ever more foregrounded the riskier the choice consumers are being asked to make (hence the Marlboro Man).

There is nothing inherently evil about Apple's imaginative use of stock characters from the American imagination to sell their product. Like all mythic simplification, it undoubtedly overstates the differences between the two products, not to mention the differences between two very large American corporations, but all advertising is understood to be delivered with a wink, and overstatement is hardly a sin. The mischief lies in the elevation of a questionable premise to an unquestioned assumption, and of a role that all of us are occasionally asked to play to an essentialist ideal that all should aspire to be. The mischief also lies in the constant reinforcement of individualist over communitarian values. If the values represented by "MAC" seem innocuous in the context of the ad, they may seem less so when extended to the realm of civic virtues. Rugged individuals, after all, do not play well with others. Their questioning of authority seldom appears to extend to questioning the authority of their own core values.

However much good they may do heeding the words of the bumper sticker, "Question Authority," they are ill-prepared by their credo for actually assuming authority themselves, for questioning the ends to which authority is best put, and for promoting collective action that secures a common good. Yet the ability or inability of politicians to sell themselves plausibly as rugged individualists has been an important predictor of political success in this country throughout much of the last three decades.

In the above analysis of the ad, we ourselves are making an assumption about identity that not everyone, certainly not all our students, may find agreeable. We assume that identity is what Burke calls "parliamentary" and variable as opposed to being unitary, essential, and fixed. In this view of identity, we play many roles and authenticity is not so much a matter of remaining true to a central self as it is a matter of consciously selecting the roles we play and being fully engaged in those roles. Rhetoricians' assumptions about human identity are as basic to the way they practice their art as the neo-classical economists' assumptions about identity—personified in neo-classical economists' default model of identity, *homo economicus*—are basic to their own practice. The literal truth of either discipline's assumption is always open to conjecture, though contemporary rhetoric's assumptions about identity appear to square better with those currently dominant in the fields of psychology, philosophy and psychology. The economists' assumption that human agents make decisions solely on the basis of rational self-interest, comports well with nineteenth century utilitarian assumptions about human nature, but appears often to be at odds with actual human behavior. Still, for all its admitted flaws, the model continues to work well enough to serve as a starting point for micro-economic analysis and continues to be used even by skeptics, albeit with increasing amendment and modification. While we are prepared to defend the validity of rhetoric's regnant model of human identity, we should not feel that we have to prove it beyond a doubt to our students or to colleagues in other disciplines. Like the economists' far more simplified model, it serves to explain a number of behaviors observed in rhetorical analysis and to provide a clear framework for rhetorical theory.

So just what are some of the implications of the "parliamentary," non-essentialist model of identity? First and foremost, the model implies a strong sense of agency on the part of every rhetorical actor.

The model assumes that people have the freedom to make choices, not just choices of behavior, but of identity, and that rhetoric is a primary means by which those choices can be systematically examined, made, and defended. The freedom assumed by rhetoric, can be seen from an essentialist standpoint as a curse, insofar as one is never quite "finished" and safe; like Sartre's existential hero, *homo rhetoricus* is "condemned to freedom." Hans Blumenberg contrasts human agents to other animals in this regard, noting that unlike other members of the animal kingdom, we are bereft of instincts that allow us to know or be anything *im-mediately.* Even self-knowledge or "self understanding has the structure of 'self-externality.'" A "detour" is required to acquire this knowledge, an act of mediation through the other—the phoros of an analogy, the vehicle of a metaphor, the second term of a ratio, the relationships we maintain with other human beings. In some cases we initiate this process of identity construction; in other cases we find ourselves selecting or resisting choices offered to or foisted off on us. In the latter case, rhetoric plays a particularly crucial role insofar as it "is not only the technique of producing . . . an effect, it is always also a means of keeping the effect transparent" (Blumenberg 435-36). This second capacity, the ability to interpret effects on ourselves as well as to produce effects on others, that makes mastery of rhetoric particularly crucial for our students at this moment in history when so many forces are at work conjuring up dysfunctional identities for them and marginalizing perfectly functional ones in the process.

Ethics and Argument

The model of identity that prevails in rhetoric, insofar as it stresses human agency and choice, ensures the centrality of ethics to our enterprise as well. As philosopher Charles Taylor has noted "selfhood and the good, or in another way selfhood and morality, turn out to be inextricably interwined themes" (3). We have failed to take proper account of this connection, he goes on to argue, mostly because of moral philosophy's fascination with "defining the content of obligation rather than the nature of the good life" (3). The good life, as that concept is understood by Taylor, is fundamentally social insofar as the self is fundamentally a social construct. I am who I am by virtue of my relationships with other humans and happiness cannot be understood apart from those relationships. It is a vision that flies in the face of those visions equating happiness with pleasure or maximization of utility, or, in the case of the rugged individualist, with complete self sufficiency. Unlike the neo-classical economists' model of the good life, a model that dominates the American popular imagination, social benefit is not an accidental byproduct of individual greed. For a social benefit to have ethical or rhetorical significance, it must be a product of intention. The good life is, in Kenneth Burke's homely phrase, "a project for 'getting along with people'" (*Attitudes* 256). Getting along with each other entails the collective identification of those "particular lived values that unite us and inform the institutions we cherish and wish to defend" cited by Stanley Fish. There is no universal standard that will dictate those values and institutions—or, more precisely, none of the various standards claimed by their adherents to be universal are universally subscribed to—hence the need to articulate them and work out the differences among them through the only means short of force we have to achieve this end—argument, or as some philosophers prefer, "conversation."

So long as one sees ethics not just in terms of individuals making the right choices, but also in terms of a society determining what options individuals have to choose among, and institutionalizing those choices through collective action, the study of rhetoric is tantamount to the study of ethics. That said, anyone who has taught argument will recognize the fundamental linkage between the two pursuits. Ethical questions arise out of all sorts of arguments, even some that seem at first glance far removed from sphere of ethical thought. The question is not whether we should attend to the ethical dimension of argument, the question is how best to go about teaching ethics in an argument class. Later on we will talk about ethical arguments per se when we discuss a theory of argument types known as stasis theory. We will talk about ethical arguments, that is those whose major claim constitutes an ethical judgment, as a special sort of evaluation argument and utilize some of the language traditionally used by philosophers when determining the "content of obligation" in a given circumstance and laying out systematic means for reaching ethical decisions. But at this point, we are talking much more broadly about the relationship between ethics and rhetoric. In what follows we will be concerned about the common features of ethical and rhetorical reasoning and about the ethics of arguing.

One way of underscoring just how much rhetoric and ethics have in common is to consider the question of where ethics might best be taught in a curriculum. The process of making a case for teaching ethics in a writing course focused on argument, makes eminently clear just how closely related the two pursuits are. Traditionally of course, ethics has been taught at the college level either in philosophy courses devoted to the consideration of ethical theories, their history and application, or in the case of some religious institutions in religion classes focused on practical application of religious principles and beliefs. Charles Taylor has pointed out some of the limitations of ethics at it is taught in philosophy courses insofar as it focuses on the "content of obligation" rather than the figuring out what a good life might entail. In pursuing various "thought experiments" built around moral problems, philosophers tend to help students understand the limitations of extant moral theories more clearly than they help them define for themselves a life worth living. Because writing courses in argument have no obligation to "cover" any particular set of moral theories, we are free to offer students the opportunity to pursue their own definitions. One of the most effective ways to start a conversation among students about their own notion of the good life—as opposed to the way that various philosophers have defined that notion—is to have them discuss Ursula LeGuin's wonderful short story, "Those Who Walk Away from Omelas." LeGuin's Omelas is an imagined utopian realm where it would seem the good life, by all the traditional measures, has been achieved. The only problem is that the continued bliss of the entire community is dependent on the continued suffering of one child who is kept in a basement and must never be shown any kindness. Every child in Omelas is told about the suffering child sometime between the ages of eight and twelve. Those who subsequently "walk away"—much to the puzzlement of the narrator—have apparently decided that the enormous quantity of bliss enjoyed by the society does not justify the suffering of one child. Their choice in turn reflects a belief in the parliamentary nature of identity, the belief that it is relational rather than essential, and that hence all who live in Omelas and know of the child's plight are implicated in its suffering and their ostensible good life is as flawed as their selfhood.

These days, of course, philosophy courses are far from the only place where the growing demand for ethics instruction is being met. As an alternative to philosophy courses, many disciplines today offer their own ethics courses emphasizing recurring ethical issues in the field and canons of behavior derived from the standards of the profession. However well intentioned such courses and however clearly they constitute an acknowledgment of the need for ethics instruction within the academy, they are, we would argue, problematic sites of ethics instruction precisely because there is no fundamental connection between the imperatives of the discipline and ethical imperatives. Moreover, whatever overt instruction in ethics students might receive in such courses must be balanced against tacit forms of ethical instruction they are likely to receive in other courses in their major. Like the obligatory "chapel" attendance that students at many church-affiliated liberal arts colleges chafed against throughout the last century, such courses have an unfortunate tendency to strike students as at best a quaint nod to moral correctness and at worst a distraction from their "real" courses of study.

Take the field of business, for example, a field that has most publicly taken it upon itself to emphasize ethics in recent years, thanks to a number of highly publicized business scandals. Given the regnant economic theories in America today, students are quite likely to be taught, directly and indirectly, in many different courses overseen by many different people, that markets are wiser than human agents. If one wishes to make a prudent decision about the possible consequences of a policy, one is advised to study the performance of the market in similar situations in the past. If one wants to know what has worked and is working, the only verdict that really counts is the one delivered by the market. A "fair" price, thus, is whatever the market will bear, while a "fair" wage is the least the market will allow one to pay. If one is in a position to fiddle the market a bit, allowing one to charge higher prices and pay lower wages, so be it, those sorts of adjustments are built into the market system, and as such are no more blameworthy than holding penalties in professional football. Against the backdrop of this near providential regard for the omniscience of markets, a single course in ethics introducing criteria foreign to the market dynamic into the decision-making process will likely have little effect on students' priorities or behaviors.

What is lacking in the one-off, business ethics course is the clear connection between "selfhood and morality." Any course starting with a hyphenated sense of selfhood, self-as-businessperson, inevitably leads to a truncated view of ethical obligation. Burke touches on the nature of the relationship between identity and ethical obligation in the process of defining his central notion of "identification."

> The human agent, *qua* human agent, is not motivated solely by the principles of a specialized activity however strongly this specialized power, in its suggestive role as imagery, may affect his character. Any specialized activity participates in a larger unit of action. 'Identification" is a word for the autonomous activity's place in this wider context, a place with which the agent may be unconcerned. The shepherd, *qua* shepherd, acts for the good of the sheep, to protect them from discomfiture and harm. But he may be "identified" with a project that is raising the sheep for market. (*Rhetoric* 27)

By the same token, corporate management may be consciously acting in interest of its stockholders to increase the return on their investment by performing acts that simultaneously "identify" them with the degradation of the environment their stockholders require to sustain themselves.

Even brief consideration of the connections between the modes of thought promoted by both ethics and rhetoric underscores the advantages of incorporating the teaching of ethics into an argument class One of the most important traits shared by ethics and rhetoric is their focus on process and procedural understanding—"how to"—over declarative knowledge—"what is." It is this concern with process that allows the two to involve themselves with "specialized activities" of every sort and to move easily between the personal and professional realms. In either case, the processes that ethics and rhetoric are both concerned with involve two stages: a process of *selection*—identifying the best argument/the most defensible choice—and a process of *communication*—formulating a justification for the argument or choice and/or promoting its wider adoption. According to most popular views of rhetoric, the first process ending in the choice, is all that is required. There is no further obligation to articulate one's reasons for making the choice or for sharing the process by which one arrived at the choice. But just as there are arguments for given ethical choices, there is an ethics of argument that requires one to make a case for one's choices. The difference here between ethical arguments and other sorts of arguments is one of degree rather than kind. While it's always useful to articulate reasons for one's choices and while it is prudent to do so whenever one is soliciting others' support of one's choice, one is compelled to do so when one's choice is ethical. The source of this compulsion lies in the nature of ethical choices. In evaluating, say, a college to people who are in the process of choosing a college, we would articulate our criteria in order to help them decide if the college is for them. But if we are making an ethical choice, about, say, justifications for torture, we are saying something much stronger. In making ethical choices we are choosing not just for ourselves in the here and now, but for others and for ourselves in future similar situations. When we term an act ethical, we are not simply saying "I did this," we are saying, "This ought to be done." If one, for example, claims that the American government is justified in using torture on enemy combatants, one is opening the way for a shift of the burden of proof from those who pronounce torture unjustifiable to those who support its use, and for the possibility that torture will be tolerated in a variety of other situations, including those situations involving the torture of American troops.

If one is first obliged under an ethic of argument to articulate a rationale for one's ethical choices, the second obligation one incurs is to ensure that one's rationale is candid. That is, for the rationale to be helpful, for it to guide further ethical acts, it must not only be truthful but extensive. One must be prepared to acknowledge the full range of choices—not necessarily every one, but all that might seem plausible or probable to those whom one addresses—that one considered prior to making one's selection. One's reasons for dismissing or subordinating likely alternatives and for selecting one's final course of action should be clearly indicated. The principles that guided one in evaluating those choices and the evidence in support of that evaluation should be clearly enumerated. The degree to which one is certain that one has made the best choice should be explicitly registered. (These caveats, along with the term "candor," are derived from Stephen Toulmin's treatment of argument to be more fully discussed in the next chapter.) While there is no formal code of rhetorical behavior under which one is obliged to offer a rationale that is both truthful and candid *in* one's argument, it is assumed that one could offer such a rationale if challenged to do so. Moreover, the failure to be candid *in* an argument may potentially render one's argument less efficacious. A competing argument that revealed what one had left unsaid or that called attention to alternative points one had glossed over could weaken audience adherence to one's own as readily as if it had shown a falsehood.

The process of selection in ethics is homologous with what rhetoricians sometimes call the invention stage. The process of discovering and evaluating choices comprises much of the *techne* of rhetoric and ethics alike. As we saw earlier, Hans Blumenberg has associated this process with the "retardation" of time, including a concern to account for "circumstantiality," the particular differences between one's given situation and others to which one looks for guidance. While we previously emphasized the cognitive rewards associated with this rejection of parsimonious means of understanding, we would here emphasize the ethical compulsions for such a move. Where automaticity prevails, there is no place for either ethics or rhetoric. One can only do or say "what a person's gotta do or say." Without hesitation. Ethics and rhetoric require choice and choice implies deliberation. In reaching this conclusion we do not reject the notion that the proper end of ethical instruction is to render virtue a habit. Ethical habits of mind, as opposed to mere knowledge of ethical theory and history, are certainly proper ends of ethical instruction. But that is not to say that such habits are best exhibited by the alacrity with which people make their ethical choices. One can construe the notion of habit more broadly, rejecting a behaviorist emphasis on habit as im-mediate response to a familiar stimulus; one can include under ethical habits of mind the inclination to seek out the ethical dimension of one's choices, the consideration of as many plausible alternatives as possible, and the thoughtful evaluation of those choices. By combining ethical instruction and rhetorical instruction with the latter's emphasis on "procedural inventiveness" and disciplined examination of alternatives we can hope to improve ethical choices by complicating and increasing the number of choices our students have to select from. Instead of focusing on the rightness of one's final choice, a rhetorically influenced ethic would emphasize the alternatives invented or discovered in the selection process and the unique responsivenes of the final choice to the particulars of one's ethical dilemma. It's here that the controversial nature of rhetoric is most obviously apparent.

For some, the test of ethical instruction lies precisely in helping students arrive in the most parsimonious manner possible at the Right Choice which is there and waiting for them; whatever detains one from recognizing and making that choice results from deficiencies in one's character. Only if one believes that the best choice may be a product of the deliberations rather than an *a priori* that pre-exists those deliberations can a "retardation" of time, a refusal to *"reduce* entities beyond necessity," be justified. At which point those who equate virtue with an unerring, quick twitch rejection of temptation will accuse one of relativism. For the moral absolutists—and certainly moral absolutism is an ethical position that significant numbers of people can and do take, however different their absolutes may be—the tests posed by Satan are true/false tests, not essay exams. One prepares for such a test by familiarizing oneself with the right answers, repeating them, memorizing them and then recalling them instantly when challenges present themselves. Only dullards have to deliberate and only infidels imagine that they might, by their own power of reason, come up with a better choice than the one prescribed by absolutes transmitted by some high priest's literal reading of holy writ.

The failure of absolutism from the perspective of ethics qua rhetoric is a failure of the imagination.[3] It's the failure to imagine a reading of holy writ other than the one offered by whatever authority happens to control the pulpit. It's the failure to imagine a ground of identification between oneself and whatever embodiment otherness has taken on. The failure of absolutism also involves a simple failure to notice things: The failure to notice that the answers derived from holy writ over the centuries change from time to time and from place to place, and the failure to notice that there is no court of appeal with binding authority to adjudicate differences among competing absolutes or to overturn the appeals of relativists. The major problem arising from the failure of ethical absolutisms is that they ultimately come full circle and return us to the place from whence ethics and rhetoric alike arise, the place where might makes right. Above all else, ethics and rhetoric share in their rejection of force as a means of resolving difference.

Rhetoric begins, as Burke argues, in acts of courtship, in the creation of a sense of identification between entities belonging to different classes—gender, socio-economic, political, etc. The obligations of ethics arise from the recognition of the self in others, the "thou-ness" of strangers toward whom one must act as one would wish to be acted upon. Absolutism creates a world of binaries—Us/Them, Good/Evil, Right Reading/Wrong Reading—and then offers no civilized means of overcoming those binaries. In fact absolutism counsels against parleying with, let alone identifying with, the Other. To maintain one's faith in an absolutist view of the world, one must remain always within the borders governed by those absolutes. To leave the kingdom of one's absolutes is to be challenged at every turn by strange ideas and customs and to have few resources for negotiating those differences. But we learned long ago from our Sophist forebears how to traverse multiple kingdoms and in the process multiple realities while hanging on to our sanity and our safety. If that most benign forebear of the absolutists, Plato, vanquished the Sophists in his dialogues, they in fact survived to argue another day and teach us how to do likewise. In a world beset by too much certainty about too many irreconcilable notions and too little willingness to set force aside and try courtship our students would be well served by ethical instruction infused by the spirit of the Sophists.

Notes

1. In using Perry's framework for this discussion of student development, we do not mean to imply an uncritical acceptance of his theory. A number of trenchant critiques of Perry's schema were mounted in the seventies and eighties, particularly by feminist scholars (e.g., Gilligan, Belenky, et al.) who noted the strong male bias of Perry's research and its failure to account for gender differences. Women's ways of knowing, we would acknowledge, are indeed different from men's ways, particularly when it comes to ethical matters. That said, the reactions of college students, particularly entry-level students, male and female alike, to the challenges posed by classes focused on argument, appear to track those anticipated by Perry's schema sufficiently well to use as a loose framework for the present discussion.

2. In the case of Fish v. Leo, we appear to be contradicting ourselves by declaring our preference for Fish's argument. But keep in mind, the nature of their disagreement is more in the nature of a "meta-argument" than a regular argument, and as such the reason for our preference goes back to the fact that Leo offers no reason to "listen" to opposing arguments, while Fish specifically calls for a dialectic approach to disagreement like the one we are supporting here.

3. Absolutism as we use the term here is a mindset rather than an ideology or belief system. Within any religion, thus, there are absolutists who pretty much act as advertised. There are also imaginative folk who manage to reconcile their religious beliefs with a concern for the well being of even those who fail to share their beliefs.

2 The History of Argument

Our goal in this chapter is not to present an exhaustive history of argument. Our goal is to construct a chapter about the history of argument that is optimally usable for contemporary teachers of argument. Certainly we have drawn from a number of many fine histories of rhetoric and of the teaching of writing, and our readers may consult our citations if they wish to explore those histories in greater depth. But in the brief space we have available for this discussion, we have aimed at economy over thoroughness, at usefulness over novelty. In order to make the following material as usable as possible, we have constructed a two-part chapter. In the first part we present a "slice" or core sample of pre-modern rhetoric in the form of two recurrent themes—or more precisely, recurrent *tensions*—that mark the evolution of argument theory. These tensions in fact survive into the present age and continue to animate current day controversies. The first tension centers on the ancient enmity between philosophy and rhetoric while the second focuses on rhetoric's not always successful resistance to ossification. After reviewing these tensions, stressing their applicability to current choices teachers of argument still face, we will proceed in the second part of the chapter, to offer a more in-depth discussion of several modern theories of argument which have either altered—or have the potential to alter—the way in which argument is taught. Because there has been a sharp break over the past fifty years in our understanding of argument, and over the past twenty-five years in our approaches to teaching argument, we spend more time on argument's recent history than on its storied past. In so doing we don't mean to scant the accomplishments of the Sophists, Aristotle, Cicero, Erasmus, Augustine, Campbell, et al. Indeed, as a number of contemporary theorists we cite have themselves acknowledged, the wisdom of our forbears shines through most strongly in the best work done in recent days. Insofar our goal in this chapter is to create a usable past by indicating the sources of our approach to argument, what follows comprises the heart of the book.

Philosophy vs Rhetoric

In one sense, everything discussed in this chapter can be understood through the lens of philosophy vs rhetoric. It's the ur struggle from whence so many of our skirmishes, then and now, have arisen. If early on most philosophers defined themselves through their differences with rhetoric, a number of more recent philosophers and critics, including Hans Blumenberg, Hayden White, Richard Rorty, Charles Taylor, Stanley Fish, Terry Eagleton, and others, have returned the favor and distinguished themselves from their peers by in some cases embracing rhetoric explicitly and in others by embracing ideas consonant with contemporary rhetoric. In the second part of this chapter where we highlight the contributions of contemporary rhetoricians, we will see that a number of them have their roots in philosophy. We will take up these more recent attempts to redefine philosophy through rhetoric later in the chapter. In the present discussion of the philosophy/rhetoric divide, however, we limit ourselves to those major themes that emerge from the ancient rupture of the two disciplines.

The ancient struggle between philosophy and rhetoric embodies many tensions, but our focus for this section will be on the central tension between and philosophers' bold claims to offer irrefutable demonstration of truths for ideal audiences, versus rhetoricians' more modest claims to persuade given audiences that a particular conclusion warrants their assent. The fact that even today, twenty-five hundred years after the debate began, prestige lies with those who claim to demonstrate truth to experts, versus those who claim to persuade general audiences underscores the uphill battle rhetoric faces in its struggle with philosophy to carve out a legitimate niche among the human sciences. Part of the problem lies in the fact that philosophy was long ago declared the winner in the struggle and subsequently the history of the debate was written from their point of view. As rhetorical theorist Susan Jarratt has suggested of the earliest rhetoricians, the Sophists, we have difficulty understanding them save through the lens of the ancient philosophers, in particular Plato and Aristotle, with whom history has sided for over two millennia. More recent history has been kinder to rhetoric, in no small part thanks to scholars like Jarratt, and consequently it has become possible to understand it on grounds other than those imposed by philosophy. Which is not to say that the above tensions have disappeared; they have simply been reconfigured as largely internal tensions within the field of rhetoric. One particular manifestation of the struggle, for example, may be glimpsed in attempts to "professionalize" the discipline of rhetoric, to transform it into a social science capable of delivering, if not irrefutable demonstrations, reliably data-based conclusions about the world, and to become more "autonomous" or less parasitic on other disciplines. Resistance to these attempts involves the aforementioned turn toward contemporary philosophers—who mostly reject philosophic traditions that demonize rhetoric—who espouse pragmatic and constructivist views and accept rhetoric as a trans-disciplinary activity without apology.

The tension between philosophy and rhetoric or demonstration and persuasion is sometimes also characterized as the tension between truth and effect. In simplest terms, this conflict is between those who view truth as independent of people's perception of it, and those who see audience-assent as a necessary condition of deeming something truthful. In our earlier discussion of Fish and Leo, whose meta-argument is in effect a contemporary revival of the ancient one we are now considering, we termed the former view "absolutist" in that it was non-contingent and non-relational. Philosopher Hans Blumenberg rejects such a view on the following grounds:

> In the dealings of Greeks with Greeks, Isocrates says, the appropriate means is persuasion, whereas in dealings with barbarians it is the use of force. This difference is understood as one of language and education because persuasion presupposes one shares a horizon, allusions to prototypical material, and the orientation provided by metaphors and similes. The antithesis of truth and effect is superficial, because the rhetorical effect is not an alternative that one can choose instead of an insight that one could also have, but an alternative to definitive evidence that one cannot have, or cannot have yet, or at any rate cannot have here and now. (435-6)

What philosophers suggested for centuries was possible is precisely what Blumenberg is here saying is not possible—definitive evidence for the truthfulness of their assertions in the here and now. Blumenberg's refusal to separate truth from effect points toward an acceptance of the fact that, as Burke puts it, we live in "Babel after the Fall" where the only alternative to force is to establish identification between speakers, a state that must be earned through considerable exertion and guile thanks to all those barriers of language, gender, class, and so forth that always already exist.

For Blumenberg as for Burke, only when speakers share a horizon does conversation, let alone persuasion and identification become possible. In a post-lapsarian world, truth is social. One is certainly free to assert that "definitive evidence" for one's point of view exists outside the awareness or understanding of those fallen souls with whom one converses, but that assertion itself carries no force absent others' willingness to grant it. A truth which has no effect, which gets nothing done in the world, is not much of a truth. A number of contemporary debates confirm the futility of appealing to sources of authority not granted by the targets of one's argument. The debate between creationists (or proponents of "intelligent design") and evolutionists, for example, is a clash of incommensurable languages and incongruent horizons. Not only is resolution of the question impossible to imagine, a meaningful conversation among the adversaries is difficult to envision. Whether my truth lies in a coherent theory buttressed by a century of empirical data or in the poetry of ancient holy text, it will not be received as truth unless our audience shares the horizon within which it resides. Even geometric proofs cannot be "demonstrated" unless the axioms on which they rest are granted. The incommensurable nature of various truths and vocabularies has of late given rise not only to rancorous and futile public debates, but bloody and violent clashes between incommensurable belief systems

The first great champion of the view opposed to the one attributed here to Blumenberg and Burke was Plato. The target of his scorn was of course the earliest school of rhetoricians, the Sophists. Ironically, Plato's stance toward the Sophists is articulated in a series of oratorical set pieces in which he deploys a range of rhetorical practices that bear an uncanny resemblance to the ones he charges against his adversaries. To make matters worse, Plato's practices are even less savory than those promoted by some of his targets. In particular, Plato's is a markedly "asymmetrical" rhetoric, to borrow a term from Thomas Conley (6-7). It is asymmetrical insofar as the speaker, Socrates in the case of Plato, is active, knowledgeable and has an agenda while his interlocutors, especially if they happen to be poets or Sophists, are typically passive, gullible and full of false knowledge. Ostensibly of course, Plato's Socrates has the best interests of his interlocutors at heart and the express goal of his interrogations is to educate them, to save them from the error of their ways by serving as a midwife who plucks truth from their unsuspecting consciousness. In theory, Plato has no designs on his audience and is the purest of persuaders. But even he cannot persuade his audience to acknowledge truths that lie beyond their horizons. Conversation cannot transport his audience to the unassailable truths he wishes to share. He must resort to the same sort of manipulative practices his foes are famous for using. Plato's genius lies not in his ability to craft logically airtight arguments but rather in his unmatched ability to disguise his asymmetrical rhetoric as dialogue.

In contrast to Plato's reliance on asymmetrical rhetoric, Protagoras is generally credited with developing a form of "antilogic" that renders dialogue open-ended, allowing the beliefs (*doxa*) of each speaker to play a role in the resolution of an issue.

> The Protagorean view . . . appears to be bilateral, in that the two sides of a question must be brought to bear on each other to effect some resolution of the issue at hand. Since neither side is privileged a priori over the other, and both are founded on the hearer's doxa, we may characterize the relationship between speaker and audience as "symmetric." (Conley 6-7)

Plato's manipulation of this form of dialogue makes clear how difficult it is to reconcile an absolutist faith in one's beliefs and genuine dialogue. If one privileges some beliefs a priori over other beliefs before a dialogue begins, one cannot hold out the possibility that those transcendent beliefs might be changed in the course of that dialogue. The only way that a dialogue might cause other beliefs to displace the a priori privileged beliefs is through some sort of chicanery. All of which takes us back to the Fish vs Leo debate in the previous chapter. Only "relativists" and those with dangerously "multiculturalist" leanings might hold out the possibility that genuine dialogue with one's enemies could be a good thing or that one's own views might actually be changed by such an exchange. The fact that the "absolutist" in the modern day version of the Sophist v Platonist debate fails to lay claim to any specific universal absolutes is symptomatic of the differences between the ancients' world and our own. Today's absolutisms, as M. H. Abrams once wryly noted, are sorely lacking in absolutes. Like Leo, most latter-day Platonists tend to rely on jeremiad as their primary vehicle of persuasion. By focusing their attack—and their audience's attention—on all the things that have gone wrong since approximately 1968 when the relativists took over the asylum, Leo and his ilk can avoid reference to any absolutes other than those that have sadly lapsed. The treatment of these universal values is in turn more of an exercise in nostalgia than in analysis.

Implicit in the opposition between ancient philosophers and rhetoricians, and their more recent incarnations, are different assumptions about the ends of reasoning. The ancient philosophers' rejection of effect as an aspect of truth is part of a larger difference between the two approaches. The end of reasoning for philosophy is some sort of discovery—of truth, of reality, or of the good—which will then be known and shareable. For rhetoric on the other hand, the end of reasoning is a choice; to be sure the choice may bring us closer to truth, reality or the good (and if any of the three are privileged by rhetoric it would be the latter, as we have indicated), but it is the act itself, performed in a particular time and place to bring about a particular outcome, not knowledge for its own sake, that motivates the process. Indeed, according to Blumenberg, the rhetorical situation is such that one "[lacks] definitive evidence and [is] compelled to act" (441), versus Plato who, according to Blumenberg, "institutionalized" the notion "that virtue is knowledge," thereby making "what is evident . . . the norm of behavior" (431). By Plato's lights once one possesses right knowledge one is compelled to act in virtuous ways, while rhetoricians hold that virtue must be compelled anew in each new situation, using incomplete information and means specific to that situation.

One of the major advantages possessed by philosophers promoting knowledge rather than action as the end of reason has to do with the need in some cases to reduce one's choices to two—the choice one recommends and all the alternatives one has passed over. As James Crosswhite has noted, this process can lend a reductive tincture to the products of rhetoric: "The need to take action, and thus the need for choice, sometimes forces bivalence—that is, demands a yes or no to the claims of arguments—but this should not be confused with the demands of reason" (36). What reason demands and what rhetoric is designed to produce is an expanded field of choices from which one can select, and more a clearer, more transparent, sense of criteria one might use in making that choice. Because philosophers don't necessarily have to act on the knowledge they discover, because the closest they have to come (cases of applied ethics notwithstanding) to choice and action is the occasional translation of principles into rules, they are saved the considerable grief that comes of wrong choices. History is littered, meanwhile, with winning, rhetorically superb, arguments that led to unsuccessful, unintended and even downright disastrous, consequences.

From rhetoricians' perspective, philosophers like Plato routinely flout the proverbial injunction against allowing the perfect to become the enemy of the good. While traditional philosophers have conjured perfect answers to life's most profound questions, they have needed to step outside history to do so and their answers seldom weather re-entry intact. Rhetoricians, on the other hand, have always restricted themselves to imperfect but workable answers to questions in the here and now. By refusing to step offstage into a golden past, a transcendent future or some unimaginable new paradigm, rhetoricians render themselves useful in the public sphere. Indeed, many of the earliest rhetoricians were public figures of some note who argued legal cases, helped pass legislation and helped define the values of their society. The great system-building philosophers of centuries past offered comprehensive frameworks that thoroughly explained the ways of the world and anticipated all life's important questions, though they seldom had significant impact (again, moral philosophers notwithstanding) on the day-to-day working of the world they lived in. Today, few philosophers presume to offer unified field theories of things. But that does not mean that their traditional role in the philosophy v rhetoric debate has disappeared; today it is filled by a class of thinkers, a subset of absolutists, sometimes referred to as ideologues.

While "ideologue" is a term sometimes used to designate a deviant person with biases and prejudices as opposed to a rational person free of subjectivist taint, our own use of the term here is more restricted. We don't equate rationality with objectivity and we do assume that everyone has biases, prejudices and beliefs that shape and limit their perceptions. ("A way of seeing," Burke reminds us, "is also a way of not seeing . . ." [*Permanence* 49].) We also assume that our beliefs and assumptions are corrigible, that they can and do change, and that while sometimes a change in belief is an epiphenomenon that follows a change in our experience, it is at other times a foreseeable outcome of an intentional and disciplined pursuit of novel views or disconfirming evidence, and of interchange with others. We assume in fact that the latter possibility represents an enabling condition of rhetoric. We also join with Aristotle in subscribing to the belief that it's easier to change minds a little than to change them a lot and that the readiest way of getting people to move toward unfamiliar beliefs is through familiar ones.

That said, we also acknowledge the existence of those who hold their beliefs with such single-minded tenacity and are so resistant to change that they deserve a special designation. In extreme cases they might be known as fanatics. But in the ordinary scheme of things the term ideologue seems more serviceable. They hold with remarkable tenacity to a handful of ideas that suffice to explain some piece of the world exhaustively and that contain at least the germ, they are occasionally emboldened to assure us, of a universal explanation. Ideologues are largely unmoved by arguments that oppose or evidence that disconfirms their beliefs. Faced with uncooperative facts or fatal counter-arguments, they may well choose either to mischaracterize or ignore the opposition. While they might grant the remote possibility that their beliefs could at some future date be shaken, the burden of proof they impose on their critics is all but unattainable. Their belief in God (not yours, theirs), the Free Market, Undecidability, or the New Paradigm is complete and any unfortunate consequences that may follow from acting in the name of their prime mover are brushed aside or rationalized. They view those who practice "antilogic" and promote symmetrical rhetoric as weak-minded and dangerously vulnerable to ideas that threaten our—which is to say, *their*—very way of life.

Which is why rehearsing some of Plato's major arguments against rhetoric proves to be sound preparation for arguing with today's ideologues and for anticipating arguments that our students' have imbibed from the numerous, well amplified ideologies available in today's clamorous marketplace of ideas. While some of today's most forceful ideologues argue their cases with the same sincerity that Plato argued his, others have made lucrative niches for themselves in media markets by becoming what we have come to refer to as "ideo-tainers," professional talking heads who offer their shrill, often outlandish claims, more to sell books and air time more than to advance a legitimate or even coherent position. With the mushrooming in recent years of all-news cable channels and Internet blog sites, the line between entertainment and news has all but disappeared, making stars of people who appeal to various carefully cultivated constituencies. The sort of faux ideologues who emerge in this market along with the various true believers who appear to operate mostly in the print market offer profoundly asymmetric models of argument to our students. Which is why learning the ancient skill of "antilogic," or dialectic, may prove to be a crucial survival skill.

The one figure from ancient rhetoric most worth lingering over in our highly condensed treatment of argument's history is Aristotle. Some would say that all one needs to know about argument is to be found in Aristotle. The rest are footnotes. While our admiration for Aristotle is great we also recognize a need to "discount" his treatment of argument for today's students. Moreover, we would suggest that a number of the modern day figures we touch on in this chapter, have done precisely that, expanding on Aristotle's understanding of argument's scope, setting aside some of his more parochial judgments about audience and recasting his insights so as to accommodate modern views about the effect of media on messages and the more active role that language plays in understanding.

Aristotle transcends the eternal struggle between philosophy and rhetoric, making rhetoric a respectable, if second tier sort of enterprise, useful for getting the world's work done. He is the first great systematizer of rhetoric, the first to offer a thorough analysis of its dynamic as well as a thorough taxonomy of its elements. He avoids the chronic philosopher's problem of allowing the pursuit of the perfect—represented by science and philosophy—to eclipse rhetoric's pursuit of the useful. He creates an intellectual space for rhetoric, calling for recognition of probable truths and acknowledgment of the impact that circumstances have on truth. He also makes clear that the proper power of rhetoric lies not so much in the design of winning arguments, as in the capacity to "see the available means of persuasion." An important element of that capacity lies in one's ability "to argue persuasively on either side of a question, . . . not that we may actually do both (for one should not persuade what is debased) but in order that it may not escape our notice what the real state of the case is and that we ourselves may be able to refute if another person uses speech unjustly" (I.1.12). Aristotle also made the study of audience into a primitive science.

While his early audience psychology probably strikes a contemporary reader as crude and stereotypical, a forerunner of "humors psychology," he makes a clear and convincing case for the importance of establishing a common ground with one's audience by attending to their beliefs and assumptions. Whatever the limitations of Aristotle's views on audience psychology, his willingness to take audience into account represents a major advance over Plato's disdain for the beliefs and assumptions held by his audience.

That said, Aristotle privileged the arts of dialectic and demonstration over the art of persuasion and was considerably less egalitarian than many of the early Sophists; he was also more suspicious of emotional and non-rational dimensions of truth. He appears to have shared the popular distrust of the Sophist tendency "to make the weaker seem the better cause" (II.24.11). In the latter case, he clearly had in mind the "unjust" use of antilogic by Sophists who after "arguing persuasively on either side of a question" elect the weaker case because it serves their interests, not those of the truth. But who is to judge finally which is the weaker and which the stronger case? Surely any argument which frustrates or weakens our own will appear to us weaker. Aristotle's argument here is perilously close to being circular: he presumes to know what can only be determined by testing arguments against one another. Setting aside Aristotle's occasional blind spots with regard to the Sophists, we now turn our attention to some of the reasons why Aristotle remains important, and more importantly how we might adapt his thoughts for use in the contemporary argument classroom.

Aristotle's distrust of non-rational means of persuasion is certainly understandable in the context of his time. Like Plato, he saw philosophy as a means of displacing the retrograde forms of reasoning inherited from the Greek myths, myths which the Sophists drew upon liberally as a source of doxa. As Susan Jarratt has argued, the early philosophers' hostility to rhetoric can be understood in part as a hostility toward any form of non-rational persuasion. She notes of Plato, for example, that he feared "the poetic transfer of crucial cultural information, because of its hypnotic effects [and] argu[ed] that it fostered an uncritical absorption of the dominant ideology" (xxi). While Aristotle's opposition was more muted than Plato's, and while he certainly recognizes a place for emotions in argument—at least so long as they are properly and exhaustively categorized and sorted into opposing pairs with virtue at the midpoint—he never seems completely comfortable with emotion and spectacle, two of the primary tools of ancient bards and Sophists alike, and offers only grudging acknowledgment of their significance. He includes spectacle, thus, as one of the six elements of drama in *The Poetics,* but deems it the least important element, dependent "more on the art of the stage machinist than on that of the poet" (VI) and chides those who rely on spectacle as opposed to the inner workings of the plot to create dramatic effect. In *On Rhetoric,* he takes to task the handbook authors (i.e., the Sophists) for their overemphasis on forensic or courtroom rhetoric: "for verbal attack and pity and anger and such emotions of the soul do not relate to fact but are appeals to the juryman" (I.1.4), and calls for a shift in emphasis to deliberative rhetoric with its more rational appeals. Implicit in Aristotle's reluctant attention to spectacle and emotion is a distrust of popular audiences, a distrust exacerbated by his tendency, in Burke's words, to view "audiences purely as something *given*" (*Rhetoric* 64) rather than in part a construct of the rhetor. In particular he reminds us several times about the limited abilities of popular audiences to absorb complex chains of reasoning.

The key to helping move beyond Aristotle's distrust of the non-rational is to move beyond his tendency both to typecast and disdain audiences. So long as audiences are understood to be creatures of their prejudices and emotions, non-rational appeals in argument will be viewed with suspicion. Students need to be exposed to more complex understanding of audience. In particular they need to understand that audiences, as various recent theorists from Walter Ong, Lisa Ede and Andrea Lunsford to Kenneth Burke, remind us, are both "addressed and invoked," catered to and created. Which is why we like to begin stressing from day one in our argument classes the metaphor of argument as conversation and the processes of collaborative invention. This notion of audience plasticity, which may be difficult for students to get their heads around as a purely intellectual concept, is much more understandable at the level of peer interaction.

A second useful element of Aristotle that needs to be recast for today's classroom concerns the sites of argument. He seems to imagine a limited number of venues and occasions where arguments take place (the legislature, the courtroom, the ceremonial occasion), while argument today is a good deal more diffuse. One can watch it play out on television or hear it on the radio, read it in the newspaper or download it off the Internet. Argument may go on over extended periods of time and come in staccato installments, sound bites and ripostes, attack ads and counterattacks. Often arguments in the public sphere will take submerged forms, supporting or critiquing a position by allusion to another position, or by championing an alternative without naming the position to which it is an alternative. Hot button public arguments don't so much evolve as metastasize as interested third parties to the dispute weigh in from talk shows, news programs, blogs, ads, editorials, leaked innuendo and so forth, offering new, not always reliable, "factual" revelations, and new lines of reasoning. Often such arguments will include more, sometimes many more, than two possible positions. In this regard, we have found it helpful to have students to keep journals in which they monitor ongoing controversies as opposed to focusing strictly on stand-alone, written arguments. It is interesting, in this regard, to observe how often new lines of argument appear in magazine pieces and editorials that are plucked out of the Internet ether and set down in print without attribution. (A recent example observed by one of our students following the Iraq War controversy concerned the abrupt, simultaneous appearance of an analogy to Vietnam—not an event war supporters had previously been eager to invoke—in the arguments of several conservative war-supporters who pointed to the almost immediate collapse of the South Vietnamese army after the American withdrawal. Like all analogies, this one suggests multiple possible conclusions including the one that says even if we stayed in Iraq for as long as we stayed in Vietnam and lost as many lives as were lost in Vietnam we would still not be able to assure the sovereignty of the Iraqi government. The war supporters unanimously rejected this possibility in favor of one suggesting that in withdrawing we would be responsible for whatever catastrophe ensued in Iraq.)

Finally, argument today relies much more heavily on visual elements than did argument in Aristotle's day. Particularly in the realms of advertising and marketing, an argument's appeal may be purely visual. In many realms, the visual medium provides a critical context for the textual message. In part, of course, this all has to do with the highly mediated environment we live in. Rarely do we attend a debate or hear an argument first hand. We are much more likely to learn of things through a highly manipulable medium that filters the message in very intentional ways. One can go on YouTube twenty-four hours a day and see countless imaginative takes on current controversies, highly edited and supplemented versions of public figures presenting arguments. These amateur videos can be at once both partisan and amusing. The other reason why the visual so often supplants the textual in the presentation of argument today has to do with a phenomenon that Aristotle himself understood: arguments that do not appear to be arguments often have a much better chance of slipping past our cognitive filters than more straightforward rational appeals. Such arguments may rely substantially or even entirely on the very "spectacle" that Aristotle disdained, on set design, backdrop, visual cues, camera angles, and so forth, offering few if any propositional arguments. Most current argument textbooks pay some attention to visual elements of argument—particularly in print advertising—and we highly recommend spending class time discussing and applying some of their lessons. That said, the specialized vocabulary needed for serious analysis of visual arguments, in their many different modalities, is so formidable that in writing classes focused on argument we can hope to do little more than sensitize students to the visual dimension of argument.

In sum, Aristotle's *On Rhetoric* remains an excellent source for understanding the production of persuasive texts and speeches, albeit one that offers little help in understanding how non-propositional events and behaviors function persuasively. Aristotle the philosopher privileges the rational, the occasional, and the textual elements of argument—and certainly these elements remain important to any contemporary discussion of persuasion—at the expense of the non-rational, mediated and visual elements of argument. Or to put the matter in Aristotle's own very useful terminology from Book II, the balance among his three "artistic" modes of persuasion (as opposed to various "inartistic" means such as torture), has shifted dramatically in recent years, from logos to ethos and pathos. In Aristotle's presentation of how these modes interact, ethos or the speaker's character—the rhetorical situation is invariably oral in Aristotle—is used to cast her remarks in the best possible light and thereby to gain an audience's attention; by awakening her audience's emotions (pathos), meanwhile, the speaker moves her audience toward action or sympathetic reception of the decision she calls for. Logos or logical argument is then used to make the speaker's case probable and alternatives improbable. Ethos and pathos here serve an important, but supplemental function in this scheme of things. The heart of the matter is the design of the argument's structure and the selection of reasons and evidence that will carry the most weight with the audience. Logos plays the same central role, for similar reasons, in Aristotle's rhetoric, as plot plays in his poetics; it is the soul of the piece, the driving force of the argument. But today, when ethos may be derived from celebrity as readily as from expertise or linguistic virtuosity, and when pathos can be invoked by a striking image and a poignant bar of music, persuasion can be earned with far less of the heavy lifting required by logos than in Aristotle's day and students need to be more aware of these "non-rational" dimensions of argument.

Rhetoric's Ossification Problem

The eternal struggle between philosophy and rhetoric has important implications for our second theme in the history of rhetoric, the recurrent devolution of rhetoric's imaginative powers into rigid systems and formulas. The question posed by rhetoric's perpetual ossification problem is this: to what extent can rhetoric be methodical without becoming inert. Kenneth Burke considers this question under the heading of the "Bureaucratization of the imaginative," which he deems "a basic process of history" (*Attitudes* 225) that can be slowed down, but never stopped or overcome. It arises when one of many possibilities generated by a principle or insight is carried out to the detriment of other possibilities. But of course for any possibility to be translated into actuality other possibilities must be ignored or less than fully exploited. We all experience this in our own lives as each choice we make about who we will be and what we will do forces us to set aside other choices. If dreams are to become reality, if politicians' promises are to become policies, if founders' visions are to become institutions, if inventors' schemes are to become products, if philosophical and religious beliefs are to become laws, other possibilities will have to be foregone or forsaken. Just as every way of seeing is a way of not seeing, every way of actualizing our vision is a way of not actualizing another vision.

But however inevitable and innocent the origins of this process, it can, over time, have more sinister implications. Originating insights gradually become orthodoxy and the systems they gives rise to become hierarchies that sort out and prioritize elements of the hierarchy according to the originating principle. Eventually the sometimes problematic hierarchy becomes a cumbersome bureaucracy, dedicated more to its own perpetuation than to the realization of the originating principle and the possibilities which the structure was founded to realize. Those atop the bureaucracy claim the orthodoxy as a possession to which they alone hold title and offer themselves as personifications of the principle to their underlings, at which point the "unintended by-products" (*Attitudes* 226) of their actions overwhelm the glorious possibilities that generated support for the originating principle. A classic example of bureaucratization involves the inversion of the Puritan doctrine of election, whereby the signs of election are converted into the causes of same and simultaneously whatever means the well-to-do "elect" used to earn their fortunes are divinely sanctioned while the lackluster fortunes of the non-chosen are attributed to failures of piety. A religious program to encourage humility and selflessness is thereby transformed into an apologetic for the status quo and various unsavory exercises in status enhancement. The basic logic of this three-hundred-year old canard can still be glimpsed in arguments from contemporary American political discourse. As Burke points out, all systems designed to actuate ideals eventually reach a point of diminishing returns when maintaining status within the system becomes the raison d'etre for the system.

Unfortunately, Burke's observations about bureaucratization hold true for all attempts at systematization, even for attempts to systematize rhetorical understanding. To adopt a *methodology* of invention means "that improvements can now be coached by routine. Science, knowledge, is the bureaucratization of wisdom" (*Attitudes* 228). Routine, to be useful, must be accorded axiomatic status. Or in Burke's homelier phrase, routine becomes a "cowpath" which "has been retained not because it has been criticized, evaluated and judged to be the best possible process, but simply because no one ever thought of questioning it" (228). Not even Burke's own methodology is excluded from his methodological critique. "Our formula, 'perspective by incongruity,' is a parallel 'methodology of invention' in the purely conceptual sphere. It 'bureaucratizes' a resource once confined to a choice few of our most 'royal' thinkers. *It makes perspectives cheap and easy*" (228-9). While this move entails some "deterioration" in insights yielded by the method, it also results in "a corresponding improvement in the quality of popular sophistication" (229) which to Burke's way of thinking at least, justifies the move. Perhaps the best known example of Burkeian methodology within the composition classroom involves the widespread use of his dramatistic approach, in the form of the Pentad—act, agent, agency, purpose, scene, and, sometimes, attitude—as a heuristic device. In our own view, most attempts to adapt Burke's dramatistic approach to writing classes results in undue deterioration of insights and loss of connection to the larger context from whence the approach originates. (The most notable exception to the latter caveat is David Blakesley's fine little introduction to the subject, *The Elements of Dramatism.*) Divorced from Burke's concept of "ratios," or relationships among the elements of the pentad, the pentad functions as little more than the old "Five W's" of the journalistic lead: Who? What? When? Where? Why? and sometimes How? But in the end, every teacher must weigh the gains in insight against the losses in "wisdom" entailed in the adoption of any classroom methodology.

This extended Burkeian preface to the subject of ossification is intended to put this issue into a perspective too often lacking when the subject of method is raised in the context of teaching argument. In the field of composition, the process whereby insights are converted into routines and heuristics become formulae is typically treated as capricious, avoidable and hence abominable. The value of democratizing a resource is subsequently overlooked and the mere presence of routine in a system will cause some to demonize it as "current-traditional." To be fair, there have been abundant examples in our history of cases in which pedagogies designed to help beginners master the art of rhetoric morphed into systems guaranteed to stifle people's imaginations, muck up their prose and alienate them from the subject we love. But unless we learn to tolerate a certain element of "bureaucratization" in our classrooms, we are in danger of turning rhetoric into an elitist (and essentially unteachable) art largely reliant on each individual's finely honed eye for the accuracy of representations—what in the eighteenth century would have been referred to as "taste"—rather than a rational, social, and replicable means of inventing meaning. The ossification problem, in sum, raises the most fundamental sort of questions about the teaching of argument, including the most fundamental of all—Just what *is it* we teach when we teach students how to write arguments?

Evidences of early ossification are apparent in disparaging references to the first "handbooks" of rhetoric, forerunners to today's textbooks. While some of this criticism is surely a function of philosophers' general disdain for rhetoric, at least some of it seems to have been merited. After Aristotle, according to George Kennedy, the urge to codify and systematize rhetoric grew apace with a general intellectual decline that overtook the ancient world.

> The acceptance of rules of art, of right and wrong answers, meant the beginning of that process of ossification which overtook all of ancient creativity. Practice within the art was controlled more and more by strict rules. The artist was more and more a virtuoso, exulting in the game and in its rules. The only place for enlargement was in the rules themselves, and thus we may expect to find the detailed working out of most of the subjects outlined in the early handbooks. . . . The development of rhetoric into a closed system was the prelude to a concept of life and thought as a closed system. (124)

While Aristotle elaborated the elements of rhetoric, explained its dynamic, and situated that dynamic within the context of other approaches to understanding, his successors too often contented themselves with the enumeration of elements, ignoring in the process Aristotle's larger concerns. Consequently they generated ever more elaborate terminologies ever more removed from everyday language and ever less applicable to practical concerns of the sort that early rhetoric emphasized. All one needed to know to argue successfully were the rules of argument and the parts of a persuasive speech. Each case was foreseen by the rules and categories of rhetoric while all "the mitigating circumstances of actual life" (Kennedy 267) were ignored in favor of plugging the case into the proper category and chugging out the solution dictated by the category. But the moment rhetoric gives up its concern for mitigating circumstances and the particulars of a given situation, it ceases to be rhetoric in any meaningful sense.

Put another way, this focus on the rules of rhetoric comes at the expense of attention to the uniqueness of each rhetorical situation, a concern the early Greeks termed kairos (timeliness). Kairos was particularly important insofar as it served as a tool for resolving apparent antinomies generated by the Sophists' antilogical approach to understanding. As Kennedy notes apropos of Gorgias' concern for kairos: "Any given problem involves choice or compromise between two antitheses so that consideration of kairos, that is of time, place, and circumstance . . . , alone can solve the dilemma and lead to the choice of relative truth and to action" (66). When laws and principles (or rhetoricians' rules) contradict each other, logic and ossified systems of thought will not help one out of the impasse. A priori hierarchies of value cannot help one decide which of two or more legitimate rules is more appropriate for a particular set of circumstances. Unless one can make such decisions one cannot act and rhetoric becomes a ceremonial activity virtually useless in the public sphere save as a degraded form of entertainment. If we learn nothing else about present practice from various historical versions of the ossification problem, it is the understanding that rhetoric is a "science of single instances," and that in the end, methods must accommodate circumstances.

Our tendency to forget the centrality of circumstance to understanding in rhetoric has been visible (literally) in writing classrooms for centuries. Anyone who has taught writing in college for more than twenty years will recognize in the current-traditional model of writing pedagogy a remnant of the "closed system" of rhetoric that prevailed more than two thousand years ago. Argument received little attention in such courses largely because once one consigns matters of critical literacy to other realms one is left with little of interest to say about persuasion save for promoting the five-part organizational structure that was considered the essence of good argument. Students were not encouraged to work with each other in such a course because the models and structures around which the course was built were visual and therefore readily available for replication by each individual; the invisible aspects of writing, conversation and all the processes that precede the product, were thus effectively abolished, and processes of invention were reduced to visualization exercises such as outlining and sentence diagraming.

For contemporary teachers of argument, the lesson to be learned from this centuries-old struggle is two-fold: we must on the one hand take great care in our teaching to guard against adopting or developing methods of teaching that make the construction of argument *too* "cheap and easy," reducing it to little more than an exercise in "plugging and chugging;" on the other hand, we must find ways of materializing and making available to beginners tools for producing insight and meaning. If we fail on the one side, our discipline will devolve back into a useless formalism; if we fail on the other side, our students will be denied access to the most powerful , least mysterious, "equipment for living" available to ordinary people.

Key Figures of Modern Argument Theory

Introduction to Kenneth Burke

The influence of Kenneth Burke on our approach to the teaching of argument, as should be clear by now, is enormous. We rely heavily on his terminology, his vocabulary of sometimes quirky terms, to articulate key ideas about both rhetorical and pedagogical theory. He is the lens that allows us to take both the short and the long views, to see the whole of the rhetorical enterprise and the role of argument within that enterprise. He is, we would argue, the one figure since Aristotle who sets out to encompass the full scope of rhetorical theory within the context of larger philosophic concerns. While he is not, we would also argue, a philosophic "systematizer," he is unwavering in his attention to the relationship between the general and the particular, the concept and the percept, the scene and the act.

Which is mostly how we have been using him up to this point. We've used his concept of "self interference" to sketch out a continuum of argument practices running from the audience-focused, advantage-seeking propagandists and advertisers to the act-centered, truth-for-its-own-sake-seeking pure persuaders. While allowing that in the world we occupy there is an element of advantage-seeking in every argument, Burke's general vision of argument practices shifts the emphasis away from winning over audiences to the search for more robust truths capable of encompassing initially antagonistic positions and "purifying" warfare into dialectic. We've acknowledged more than once his notion that a way of seeing is always also a way of not seeing, and that our instruments for seeing are "terministic screens," linguistic filters that render perception and evaluation simultaneous. It's this focus on language as an instrument of knowing that causes us in turn to place him in the company of those philosophers Richard Rorty calls "edifying," those whose aim is "to help their readers, or society as a whole to break free from outworn vocabularies and attitudes, rather than to provide 'grounding' for the intuitions and customs of the present" (*Mirror* 12).

The major question posed by Rorty's edifiers and by Burke is this: How do we avoid becoming victims of the very language we require to access the world? Or as Burke's "The Lord" remarks to "Satan" in the dialogue concluding *The Rhetoric of Religion:* "[W]here Earth People are concerned any terminology is suspect to the extent that it des not allow for the progressive criticism of itself" (303). For Burke, the key to achieving this sort of critical self-awareness is his dramatistic approach to understanding, what in his early work he refers to as "perspective by incongruity." Hans Blumenberg in his essay redeeming rhetoric for the late twentieth century, refers to something very much like Burke's perspective by incongruity when he cites "the procedure of comprehending something by means of something else" (Blumenberg 439). For Burke, to understand anything is not to understand it *as* something, a member of a category, but rather to see it *in terms of* something else. Hence the "ratios" of his dramatistic method. According to dramatism, there are five (eventually six) elements that contribute to a well rounded understanding of human motivation: act, scene, agent, purpose, agency and, later, attitude (which is an incipient act). In analyzing discourse to understand why something was done, or should be done, one would ideally consider all possible combinations of the elements, act-scene, scene-act, agent-act, and so forth. The relationship between any two elements is expressed as a "ratio." In any ratio, the second term functions as a sort of provisional essence for the pair. So, for example, in an act-scene ratio, the act is understood "in terms of" the scene which is in effect the lens through which act is understood. Various schools of philosophy are characterized by their tendency to privilege one of the terms, continually seeing all other elements "in terms of" the privileged element. Naturalism, thus, characteristically privileges scene such that human acts are understood primarily as a consequence of scenic conditions.

Burke's "paradox of substance" whereby a word "used to designate what a thing *is,* derives from a word designating something that a thing is *not* (*Grammar* 23) points us again away from the Law of Identity ("A is A") toward a more metaphorical mode of understanding. Finally, there is his notion of "representative anecdote" "itself so dramatistic a concern that we might call it the dramatistic approach to dramatism" (*Grammar* 60), whereby the whole is represented by one of its parts. To understand anything, we must understand it in its context, in the light of extrinsic matters and apposite terms that are *not identical to it,* but are rather *identified with it.* The basic relationship represented in language is thus metaphorical (Category Y is best understood by understanding Part X) rather than categorical (All that we need to know is that Part X is/belongs to category Y).

When our terminologies fail to allow for progressive criticisms of themselves, when we quit seeking perspectives by incongruity, we fall prey, among other things, to the earlier discussed tendency toward bureaucratization of the imaginative. While the bureaucratization of the imaginative is an inevitable process in Burke, our capacity for self-criticism allows us to stave it off and keep alive as long as possible our imaginative awareness of the originating principles that define the good life and animate our quest to realize it. If all this sounds far removed from the teaching of argument, let us return to the two essays we discussed in the first chapter by Stanley Fish and John Leo. Our criticism of Leo's position and our preference for Fish's can be traced directly back to their stances toward "progressive self criticism." Leo's rejection of "multiculturalism" as a front for anti-Americanism, is of a piece of his general rejection of attempts to understand the events of 9/11 in terms of "root causes" or "the need to 'understand' the terrorists and to see their acts 'in context.'" Any alternative way of seeing 9/11 "in terms of" something else threatens Leo's settled world view and is dismissed out of hand. Fish on the other hand sees the task before us precisely as getting past the various "false universals" that blind us to the world they name and "putting [our]selves in [our] adversary's shoes." Only by unsettling one's world view in this way can one stay alive to the animating principles of that world view, "the particular lived values that unite us and inform the institutions we cherish and wish to defend." The Fish v. Leo argument, in short, illustrates many of the basic principles of argument that Burke outlined so eloquently throughout his long career.

Burke's Realism. Burke offers perhaps the most economical characterization of his approach to rhetoric near the conclusion of the opening section to A Rhetoric of Motives, "The Range of Rhetoric." According to Burke, rhetoric "is rooted in an essential function of language itself, a function that is wholly realistic, and is continually born anew; the use of language as a symbolic means of inducing cooperation in beings that by nature respond to symbols" (43). Burke's "realism" here refers to philosophic realism as that term is understood in the medieval debate between the nominalists and realists. The foremost proponent of nominalism in that debate, William of Occam, is best known today for Occam's Razor, the proposition that "entities should not be multiplied beyond necessity" (*Grammar* 324). Burke's realism, meanwhile, requires equally that "entities should not be reduced beyond necessity" (324). When it comes to the needless multiplication of entities, the primary culprit for Occam is language when it is used for more than naming the immediate subject. All generic terms and abstractions are guilty of naming all sorts of superfluous entities. Such terms are viewed by nominalists as "conveniences of language" and not "real substances" (*Grammar* 248). But of course what Burke's paradox of substance suggests is that one can never use language simply to name an immediate subject. Every word designating what something is necessarily designates what it is not as well. Consequently, what a word connotes is as crucial to its meaning for Burke as what it denotes. Indeed, we have no access to the individual save through the symbolic or categorical: "Man, qua man, is a symbol user. In this respect, every aspect of his 'reality' is likely to be seen through a fog of symbols" (*Rhetoric* 136) As symbol-using animals, humans experience "differences between this being and that being as a difference between this kind of being and that kind of being" (*Rhetoric* 282). It is precisely this tension between the particular and the general, between the denotative and connotative functions of language, that lends language its symbolic resonance and enables us to see one thing "in terms of" another. Without that resonance and that capacity for "multiplying entities" beyond the here and now, language would be unable to induce cooperation among individuals who are themselves marked simultaneously by similarities and differences.

Again, this discussion of Burke's philosophic realism can seem at first far removed from the argument classroom. But it most assuredly is not. Take, for example, the notion of political correctness. While ostensibly a neutral term, it has been wielded in recent years most effectively by conservatives in national political debates. Squeamish liberals, so goes the argument, are incapable of "telling it like it is." They are forever inventing euphemistic expressions to paper over their various "agendas." Any number of gruff, "plain-spoken" conservative pundits make a living puncturing liberals' pretentious phrases and substituting a language "plain and simple as the truth," transforming "affirmative action" to "reverse discrimination" and so forth. (Comedian Steven Colbert of "The Colbert Report" spoofs conservative commentator Bill O'Reilly's pretensions to plain-spokenness with his "Word of the Day" segments, in which seemingly innocuous words and phrases are tortured beyond recognition by Colbert while an accompanying textual counterpoint silently undermines Colbert's earnest efforts at definition and lays bare his own partisan agenda.) These are people operating in the tradition of Occam, eager to reduce the unnecessary multiplication of meaning, and more recently in the tradition of Jeremy Bentham, who devoted his days to rooting out the insidious "question-begging appellative" (*Rhetoric* 92) that named more than one thing, placing the subject in a "eulogistic" or "dyslogistic" light thereby prejudging the subject in much the manner that circular reasoning anticipates the conclusion in its major premise.

Underlying the use of political correctness and the thinking of Occam and Bentham is the belief in a neutral, purely denotative language that names an "objective" reality, that in fact tells it like it *is* without hinting at what it's not. What Burke's definition of rhetoric immediately makes clear is that no such language exists. (Burke does acknowledge a "positive order of terms" [*Rhetoric* 183-84] that name things in the here and now, and recommends staying within such an order whenever possible. But beyond highly conventionalized terminologies, as in the sciences, that carefully avoid natural language and stipulate terms native to their discourse, opportunities for limiting ourselves to the positive order of terms are extremely limited.) Every word carries within itself the seeds of both eulogistic and dyslogistic meanings and in order to understand the term, it must be understood in use, within a context, and discounted appropriately. As Burke is quick to point out (*Rhetoric* 95), even Bentham's own utilitarian vocabulary granted certain terms eulogistic shadings regardless of usage, thereby running afoul of the very myth of neutral language he promulgated.

Burke's realism is not just a philosophical realism but an everyday realism as well. For all the power Burke grants to language, he also recognizes the considerable veto power that extralinguistic reality holds over words. However grand our visions and however persuasive our vocabularies, the failure of the material world to ratify our arguments is fatal for Burke. In this regard, Burke's linguistic realism must be distinguished from solipsism and the magical view of language. Burke explicitly rejects the belief that "the universe is merely the product of our interpretations," precisely because "the interpretations themselves must be altered as the universe displays various orders of recalcitrance to them" (*Permanence* 256). While language, our "fog of symbols," accounts for all that we positively know, the universe retains the power to negate and reform our interpretations. Indeed for Burke, the primary difference between false magic and the true magic of rhetoric has to do with the fact that practitioners of the former art promise to use symbols to induce motion in nature, while practitioners of the latter art use symbols to induce cooperative acts among people (*Grammar* 66). Judgments about the fitness of political and economic institutions are for Burke based not on some fixed idealistic standard, but on their capacity to meet the material needs of the people they purport to serve. According to Burke's realistic metric, such institutions have a "relative value [which] depends pragmatically, Darwinistically, on their fitness to cope with the problems of production, distribution and consumption that go with conditions peculiar to time and place" (*Rhetoric* 279). As we noted in our discussion of Burke's "bureaucratization of the imaginative," the important social role of rhetoric is to resist the conversion of imaginative possibilities that launch institutions into rigid dogmas resistant to the realization of those possibilities. While ideologues may turn a blind eye to the failures of their programs to "cope with the problems of production, distribution and consumption" in the here and now, rhetoric's task is to adapt the program to the situation, relying on the originating principles to plot new strategies.

Finally, Burke's realism is not just a philosophic or a common sense realism, it is also realism in the sense that the word is sometimes used in foreign policy circles. It is a realism of the sort that encourages us to pick and choose our battles, weighing the consequences of our choices against one another, as opposed to following our principles wherever they might lead us. It is a realism that recognizes choices of the rock-and-a-hard-place sort. It's this aspect of his realism that causes him to value someone like William James, whom Burke dubs "a meliorist" (*Attitudes* 3), a man who famously chose to "accept" rather than merely "protest" the universe, and who chose to believe on very pragmatic grounds that his faith "enabled him to have the sense of moving towards something better" (5). Burke's oft expressed skepticism toward perfectionism is the other side of this admiration for meliorism. Likewise, his dismissal of debunking as "perfectionism in reverse," (*Grammar* 100), a too thorough critique that cuts the legs out from under one's own position, is symptomatic of a balanced realism that forever finds elements of the people and systems he criticizes in his own person and beliefs. There are no simple oppositions in Burke's realism, no absolute Wrongs and Rights, no categorical differences. Every substance contains elements of substances extrinsic to itself. At every place on the various continua that Burke imagines, there reside elements of both extremes of the continuum. Burke accepts the fact that we live in a post-lapsarian world and that consequently rhetoric must, on occasion, pursue it subjects "into the lugrubrious regions of malice and the lie" (*Rhetoric* 23). Given that no perfect solutions are ever at hand, Burke's "scrupulous man will never abandon a purpose which he considers absolutely good. But he will choose the purest means available in the given situation. As with the ideal rhetoric in Aristotle, he will consider the entire range of means, and then choose the best that this particular set of circumstances permits" (*Rhetoric* 155).

Everyone who teaches argument should know something of Burke, if for no other reason to help them understand the place of argument and rhetoric in the larger order of intellectual enterprises and to remind them just how much is at stake in teaching it well. He offers us not so much a theory of rhetoric as a "way" of rhetoric, habits of mind that help us avoid simplistic modes of thinking and agonistic modes of arguing. Barry Brummett, in an essay that draws heavily on Burke's thinking, sums up our task nicely: "If we regard ordinary people (students) as the primary audience for rhetorical theory and its criticisms, then rhetorical theory and criticism's ultimate goal and justification is pedagogical: *to teach people how to experience their rhetorical environments more richly*" (658). To be sure, we also teach students how to "seek advantage" for their arguments and there is always an element of advantage-seeking in the purest of arguments. But by challenging them constantly to submit their terminology—or ideology if you will—to "progressive criticism of itself"we are challenging them to reconsider just what it is that they should seek advantage for. Rhetoric, Burke reminds us, is a realm in which "the tests of success are . . . to be tested" (*Permanence* 102). In the end, by enlarging students' capacity to find the available means of persuasion in a given situation and encouraging them to choose the "purest means available" we are teaching them to argue ethically as well as effectively.

Introduction to Chaim Perelman and Lucie Olbrechts-Tyteca

The New Rhetoric (*NR*) by Chaim Perelman and Lucie Olbrechts-Tyteca is a encyclopedic compendium of extremely useful rhetorical anecdotes, quotes, examples and strategems organized according to a system that is extremely fluid and flexible on the one hand, and extremely confusing on the other. John Gage likens the system to Burke's insofar as it comprises a "perspective of perspectives," treating argument not as a collection of a priori parts ala the syllogism, instead seeing its parts as "derived from a process of association and disassociation, linking and unlinking, rendering argument as a 'web' of parts in relationships of infinite variety" (13). On the negative side, Perelman and Olbrechts-Tyteca sometimes appear determined to name each and every one of the infinite relationships possible within their system using countless terms—sometimes invented, sometimes borrowed from obscure sources—that frustrate more than facilitate ready access to their system. Under the heading of "locus" for example, one may find twenty-four varieties listed in the index; and sixty-eight "traditional" figures are noted, mostly in passing, in addition to fifteen different sorts of presumably non-traditional figures. Perelman's short form version of the treatise, *The Realm of Rhetoric,* renders the system marginally more accessible by offering a skeletal version of the whole corpus, but to the detriment of the original's wonderful depth and diversity. (Perelman's 1970 essay, "The New Rhetoric: A Theory of Practical Reasoning," reprinted in Bizzell and Herzberg, represents an even more efficient miniaturization of the system.) Above all *NR*'s usefulness lies in the fact that it is a book of wisdom, of practical reasoning or *phronesis.* As such it is a book to read *in* more than it is a systematic treatise to be read seriatim. *The Realm of Rhetoric,* meanwhile, is much more helpful *after* one has read *NR,* and should never be read in lieu of its vast and mazy progenitor. Like Burke's system, Perelman and Olbrechts-Tyteca's lends itself to partial use, but in a very different manner. For all the complexity of Burke's thought, much can be done with a few powerful ideas that collectively comprise a "perspective by incongruity." In the case of *NR,* however, one may perhaps get best use of the book by in effect cannibalizing it, extracting useful ideas, strategies and quotes in much the way that schoolboys once ransacked commonplace books for promising ideas.

In order to render Perelman and Olbrechts-Tyteca's new rhetoric optimally useful to contemporary teachers of argument, we will approach it in two steps. In the first step, we will offer a brief overview of their approach and its place in the realm of modern argument theory. Then, by way of presenting their ideas in a more coherent, if less orthodox, manner, we will adapt some of their insights to a considerably less cumbersome approach to argument, stasis theory.

An Overview of The New Rhetoric. Like most philosophers who broke ranks and turned to rhetoric in the mid-twentieth century, Perelman and Olbrechts-Tyteca based their dissent on the rejection of the formal logical model of argument traditionally favored by philosophers, particularly the regnant logical positivists of the period. Citing Ramus' merger of dialectic with logic and its subsequent demotion of rhetoric to an ornamental art, Perelman reclaims dialectic for rhetoric and declares it complementary to demonstration defined as

> a calculation made in accordance with rules that have been laid down beforehand. . . . A demonstration is regarded as correct or incorrect according as it conforms, or fails to conform, to the rules. A conclusion is held to be demonstrated if it can be reached by means of a series of correct operations starting from premises accepted as axioms. Whether these axioms be considered as evident, necessary, true or hypothetical, the relation between them and the demonstrated theorems remains unchanged. To pass from correct inference to the truth or to the computable probability of the conclusion, one must admit both the truth of the premises and the coherence of the axiomatic system. ("Theory" 1390)

In distinguishing rhetorical argument from formal demonstration, Perelman and Olbrechts-Tyteca stress the following features. The starting point of an argument is not an axiom which is invariant and universal, but a premise or "generally accepted opinion" (*New* 5). The authors then distinguish between two kinds of premises "the first concerning the *real,* comprising facts, truths, and presumptions, the other concerning the *preferable,* comprising values, hierarchies, and lines of argument [*or loci*] relating to the preferable" (66). The premises are not objective or "impersonal" as in the case of logical axioms, but intersubjective or "personal" insofar as their force depends upon the degree to which one's audience accepts them as true, factual, coherent, plausible, and so forth. Because of the contingent nature of the premises, different audiences will offer them different levels of assent at different times and under different circumstances, a state of affairs the arguer must take into account. While the movement of the demonstration is to extend the reach of axiomatic truths to a particular truth and to compel assent to that truth, the movement of an argument is to increase the "intensity of adherence" (*New* 45) of one's audience to one's conclusion by sending one's premises "through a whole set of associative and dissociative processes" (65) that shape an audience's understanding of the relationship between the premises and the conclusion. Argument may increase the degree to which an audience accepts one's conclusion, but it can never "compel" assent in the manner of demonstration. While the end of demonstration is discovery of a truth, the end of an argument is to build on the "community of minds" ("Theory" 1388) that increased adherence to one's argument has created in order "to set in motion the intended action . . . or at least in creating in the hearers a willingness to act which will appear at the right moment" (*New* 45).

The starting point for *NR's* approach to argument, was not a theory of argument taken from philosophy, but a question about how people actually argue over values in the real world. Consequently the authors examined thousands of examples of values arguments taken from a variety of sources including political, legal, philosophical, literary, religious, and scientific works from every era. Whether or not the examination of those sources renders the authors' theory sounder is a moot point—but there is no doubt that their theory is richer for that examination. (Apparently Mme Olbrechts-Tyteca who was "well read in the social sciences and European literature" [Bizzell and Herzberg, 1372] deserves special credit for finding and selecting salient examples that render Perelman's theory significantly more useful and vastly more engaging than it would otherwise be.) In a sense, the examples overrun their theoretical framework making it impossible to reduce the theory to a handful of precepts. Subsequently the language of the new rhetoric is decidedly non-categorical, more nuanced and metaphorical than the typical language of mid-century rhetoric. A handful of key terms demonstrate this phenomenon. Instead of logical entailment, thus, the authors speak of "liaisons" among ideas; rather than contradictions, they talk of "incompatibilities;" rather than the certitude or even probability of a conclusion, they talk about its "reasonableness;" rather than audiences' agreeing or disagreeing with a conclusion, they talk about increasing or decreasing the intensity of their "adherence" to an argument. Perhaps most interestingly with regard to the possible effects of their methodology on their conclusions, the authors grant pride of place within their theory to the notion of "presence," the importance of bringing ideas before audiences in all their vivid immediacy. Fittingly, the greatest single virtue of New Rhetoric is the abundance of presence the book's numerous examples lend its theoretical framework.

In many ways, the movement of Perelman and Olbrechts-Tyteca away from traditional logic toward dialectic follows the path of Kenneth Burke, who also understands rhetoric as an expression of dialectical thought. Perelman himself underscores this connection when he cites Burke's notion of identification as the model for his own call to use rhetoric to form "a community of minds"and thereby "awaken a disposition to act" ("Theory" 1388) in an audience. In addition, the essential tension in *NR* between parts (examples) and whole (theory) is, as we've seen, a critical piece of Burke's approach to rhetoric as well. To understand one thing "in terms of" another thing rather than *as* another thing causes Burke too to seek out "representative anecdotes" (*Grammar* 523-25), rather than rules, laws or master narratives that exhaustively account for the whole. This same synecdochic manner of understanding would lead Burke to reject flat contradictions among ideas and to favor something like incompatibilities which he seeks to overcome through courtship rather than to abolish through debunking. Moreover Burke, like Perelman and Olbrechts-Tyteca, also emphasizes the inventive rather than the ornamental function of rhetoric. (While Burke further subordinates the persuasive to the inventive function of rhetoric, Perelman and Olbrechts-Tyteca, after acknowledging the importance of invention, continue to stress the persuasive function.) In both *NR* and Burke's *Rhetoric of Motives,* one is constantly reminded of the larger context that defines one's activities. For Burke, one's duties as a citizen always take precedence over one's duties as a specialist, no matter how much "occupational psychosis" may lead us to confuse professional and ethical obligations. Perelman and Olbrechts-Tyteca, meanwhile, ground their study of rhetoric on the notion of social justice and return to that emphasis throughout their treatise.

Finally, *NR*'s sometimes controversial notion of "universal audience" can perhaps be most helpfully understood in the context of Burke's notion of "pure persuasion." Just as there is no such thing as an actual instance of pure persuasion, there is no such thing in fact as a universal audience. Both are ideals that guide arguers away from "addressed" persuasion—"What will win this audience over to my position?'—toward the working out of the fullest possible understanding of their subject. The universal audience is not necessarily a more populous audience than a particular audience. When we write for well read, critical audiences in our specialty, their presumed skepticism and insight will push us toward our best, most reasonable arguments; advertisers pushing light beer toward white males between the ages of 18 and 29 doubtless set their sights considerably lower.

Stasis Theory and The New Rhetoric. In adapting NR to our own classrooms we have tried to identify simpler schemes that might serve as vehicles for selecting and organizing the book's many rich insights into a coherent whole of reasonable scope. The one scheme that best serves that function in our view is stasis theory. Originally, the stases arose in ancient Greek as a sub-category of forensic (or judicial) discourse, which along with epideictic (or ceremonial) discourse and deliberative (or legislative) discourse comprised the three forms of discourse. In recent years the stases have been revived and modified for use in the contemporary argument classroom primarily in recognition of the fact that, as Richard Fulkerson points out, they are "incredibly useful . . . because they are non-overlapping and sequentially progressive, and . . . , they can serve as generative heuristics to help students create the arguments needed in a paper" (40). The two scholars most responsible for the revival of the stases as an integral feature of argument instruction are Jeanne Fahnestock and Marie Secor. Their 1983 article in *College Composition and Communication*, "Teaching Argument: A Theory of Types" led many writing teachers to integrate the stases in their classes and many textbook authors to include a discussion of stasis in their books. The essay represents an exemplary case of contemporary scholars adapting ancient rhetorical tools to the writing classroom.[1]

Before we move on to demonstrate how one might use stases to organize strategies, anecdotes, and principles from *NR*, we'll offer a brief oversight of the scheme.

According to Aristotle, each of the three original categories of discourse that anticipate the stasis categories has a distinctive temporal focus. The deliberative dealt with proposals for the future, particularly legislative proposals; the epideictic with praise and blame presented on public occasions to reinforce community values in the present; the forensic—from whence the stases primarily come—dealt with verdicts passed on some past event typically in the legal sphere. Because of their early association with the law, ancient stases tended to follow the model of courtroom proceedings. Thus the prosecutor of a case would be required to make three sorts of thesis claims representing three points at issue or stases: that an accused person committed the crime in question (claims of fact), that the act committed constituted a crime (claims of definition) and that the act was not mitigated by circumstances (claims of value). The stasis taxonomy that will be drawn on for this particular exercise is derived largely from John Ramage, John Bean and June Johnson's *Writing Arguments.*

Ramage et al.'s five stases include: definitional (X is/is not an instance of Y), resemblance (X is/is not like Y—the authors posit two variants of resemblance claims, precedents and analogies), causal (X is/is not the cause of Y), proposal (X should/should not be done), evaluative (X is/not a good Y), and ethical (X is/is not good). (In more recent versions of the stases, Ramage et al. also draw a distinction between categorical and definitional stases depending on whether the criteria comprising category Y or the match between the criteria and features of a particular X constitute the focus of the debate. Here we continue to treat both stases under the heading of definitional.) The last three stases, it will be recognized, are derived from Aristotle's first two forms of discourse, the deliberative and the epideictic while the first two are derived from the forensic. The authors emphasize that each stasis is a type of claim as opposed to a type of argument (though most arguments feature a major claim which can be used to characterize the overall argument being employed), that would typically include numerous interrelated claims of varying sorts. The point of the stases is not to serve as a taxonomy of argument, but rather to help students understand the peculiar demands for reasons and evidence generated by each sort of claim, an understanding that can then be used to anticipate persuasive needs within their own arguments and to recognize places in others' arguments where such needs have or have not been met. The brief tag lines associated with each of the claim types are intended to represent the general thrust of the propositions included in the category. In actual arguments such claims often take on many different forms requiring in some cases some significant interpretation.

As noted in our earlier discussion of rhetoric's tendency toward ossification, there is always a tradeoff between the ease with which a given methodology may be applied and the danger that the conclusions of that application will be oversimplified. We argued at that time that the benefits of offering students a coherent approach to argument outweighed the dangers of ossification, but that one must keep in mind the Burkeian methodological imperative that "any terminology is suspect to the extent that it does not allow for the progressive criticism of itself.." In this regard, an important role served by *NR* in relationship to the stasis schema lies in its capacity to remind us of the larger contexts of argument as well as its ability to complicate our understanding of our task by identifying burdens of proof associated with each of the stases. To be sure, many of *NR*'s principles and strategies could be usefully applied in conjunction with all the stases. But in what follows, we set out to illustrate the role that *NR* can play in keeping the stases from devolving into formulae by focusing on a small number of issues centered on definition and resemblance claims on the one hand and evaluation and ethical claims on the other.

The careful distinctions drawn in *NR* between values arguments and logical demonstration reminds us of the limits of definitional and resemblance claims, and underscores the importance of carefully qualifying such claims and of supporting the more tenuous connections we are making. The section of *NR* which introduces the rule of justice ("Beings or situations of the same kind should be treated in identical fashion.") is devoted to "Quasi-logical arguments," a title that calls attention to both the apparent similarities and important differences between formal demonstration and substantive argument. The rule of justice fits into the description "quasi-logical" insofar as it is a formal rule or equation into which one can substitute many particular values. But quasi-logical arguments are less rigorous as a class than logical arguments insofar as the latter requires that "the objects to which it applies ought to be identical, that is, completely interchangeable. However, this is never the case" (219) in the realm of human values where "substantial" sameness, as Burke would have it, is the most we can hope for. In the end, one must make that most rhetorical of determinations: How much or how little are the objects in question alike and is their kinship sufficient to justify invoking the rule of justice.

In effect, thus, all claims of definition in *NR* could be considered claims of resemblance. While in principle we accept such an equation—if language is fundamentally metaphorical, all putative relationships of *identity* turn out on closer examination to be relationships of *identification*—we retain a distinction between resemblance and definition claims for pragmatic (what Burke might call "realistic") reasons. The distinction between definition and resemblance is part of ordinary language and names a very real distinction of degree if not, as implied, kind. While claims of definition blur differences between the terms being defined, claims of resemblance place those differences in the foreground. Consequently, the relationship between "beings or situations" for whom resemblance is claimed is more tentative, and the burden of proof is weaker than it is with regard to relationships established under claims of definition. (Conversely, the more tentative the claimed relationship of the terms being defined or likened, the less damaging an exception to the rule or counter example would be to whatever version of the rule of justice one's claim promoted.) It is pragmatic to retain the distinction for students, thus, both because the distinction is meaningful in the everyday world of natural language and because acknowledging the distinction leads students to recognize the significant differences in burden of proof they incur when they undertake one sort of stasis or the other.

A further distinction of the same sort can be drawn between the two different types of resemblance claim, precedents and analogies. In the case of precedents, the connection between the terms is sequential and, according to *NR*, "the terms brought together are on the same phenomenal plane" (293). Thus, for example, when we think of precedents we have in mind two or more legal cases, two or more historical situations and so forth. Once a precedent has been established, the extension of the rule of justice to the case at hand is thus reasonably clear cut. But no similar clarity exists in the case of analogies which may equate radically different entities. According to *NR*, analogies comprise "transfers of value" (381) from one term to another or "from phoros to theme;" but having claimed that two terms such as love and red roses are of approximately equal value, it does not follow that one can readily extend the rule of justice from one to the other and conclude that one ought, for example, to fertilize one's spouse or date a rose. In sum, in choosing among claims of definition, precedent or analogy preparatory to calling for an extension of the rule of justice from one term to another, one must take into account the level of support available for one's claim and must determine the degree of qualification appropriate to one's conclusion. While claims of definition, implying substantial sameness between the terms, require the most support, analogies. implying only shared values between the terms, require the least.

It is important for students to understand these distinctions among the claim types and the implications of those distinctions for the rule of justice. Many of the day's most important controversies in fact hang on matters of definition and resemblance and the differences between the two. Perhaps the clearest and most dramatic illustration of the importance of distinguishing carefully between claims of identity and claims of resemblance is seen in the tug of war among Supreme Court justices as they work toward a rule of justice that is workable in contemporary American society. Much of the court's deliberation could be characterized as ruminations over the degree of similarity between various cases, "beings and situations," and determining when they are sufficiently similar to invoke the rule of justice. Among the justices, some—the so called originalists or strict constructionists—accord claims of definition pride of place and hold them to be different in kind, not simply degree, from claims of resemblance. For these justices, the original definition of a term, as that term was understood by those who framed the constitution, is said to be immanent within the text and the only legitimate source of meaning. (On more than one occasion, justices have cited Sam Johnson's 1756 *Dictionary*—the only English language dictionary in existence when the American constitution was drafted—in an attempt to divine how the framers might have been using a particular term. Presumably, those same justices have opted not to cite Johnson's definition of "democracy" which he illustrates with a quote from Dr. Arbuthnot to the effect that "as the government of England has a mixture of democratical in it, so the right of inventing political lyes is partly in the people.")

Historically, the more literalist positions on legal interpretation prove to be difficult, if not impossible to maintain and hence the oft remarked phenomenon of justices "drifting to the left" toward a less rigid view of interpretation during years on the bench spent wrestling with extremely complex issues of definition and resemblance. (Perhaps unsurprisingly, the most notable recent exception to that rule, Justice Antonin Scalia, who after more than two decades on the court remains an ardent and unrepentant originalist, is the son of a formalist literary critic, formalism being literary theory's version of strict constructionism.) Among the factors that clearly influence justices who grow more flexible in their interpretive procedures in the face of protest from their originalist bretheren, are the changing historical circumstances that surround the cases. (Here Burke's axiom, "circumstances alter cases" is a useful guide.) For example, many years after the court had thrown out Jim Crow laws and other statutes implying that African-Americans somehow were categorically different from White-Americans and hence not entitled to the same rights and protections, laws against mixed race marriage were allowed to stand. Finally, in the wake of the Civil Rights movement of the sixties, the last of these statutes were struck down. While the principle of racial equality had been embraced a century earlier, the law was slower to extend the rule of justice to practices like miscegenation mostly because the "film of custom" made "anti-miscegenation" laws seem "natural," and it took a major historical upheaval to help the court achieve a new perspective on the issue.

The process continues. When the Supreme Court later struck down state statutes criminalizing homosexual practices, some argued, citing the earlier ruling on interracial marriage, that their ruling constituted a precedent for striking down bans against gay marriage. While some state courts—and several foreign courts—have indeed decided that similarities between the two phenomena are sufficient to extend the rule of justice from racial to sexual diversity, the Supreme Court has not. Fittingly enough, opponents of this extension, those sufficiently sophisticated to recognize a potential incompatibility in their position, use another of the many tools *NR* makes available to arguers working at "linking and unlinking" arguments as it suits their purpose. In this case, the device used by those who would draw a bright line between gay marriage and interracial marriage is the "philosophical pair." While ostensibly a device for categorizing similar phenomena, philosophical pairs inevitably elevate one at the expense of the other. The most notable of these pairs, the "appearance/reality" pair, originally designed to unlink sensory perception from truth-seeking, serves opponents of gay marriage in turn by deeming gay marriage a faux version of the real thing, heterosexual marriage.

Evaluation claims (X is/is not a good Y) and ethical claims (X is/is not good) may also be greatly enriched by borrowing from *NR*. Much of the book is in fact taken up with discussions of value and the authors are particularly helpful in articulating distinctions between ethical value claims and evaluation claims. Perelman and Olbrechts-Tyteca discuss values initially in the context of "types of agreement" among members of an audience that may be used as premises of an argument. Interestingly, the authors identify the unique characteristic of values that distinguishes them from other kinds of premises—facts, truths and presumptions—as being their *local* nature, thereby rejecting at the outset the notion of universal values of the sort that people like John Leo assure us exist. In a direct reversal of Leo's logic, in fact, the authors of *NR* contend that while the other forms of premise appeal to universal audiences, values claim "only the adherence of particular groups" (74). With regard to various claims to the universality of values such as "the *True,* the *Good,* the *Beautiful,* and the *Absolute*" (76) the authors offer the following response: "The claim to universal agreement . . . , seems to us to be due solely to their generality. They can be regarded as valid for a universal audience only on the condition that their content not be specified; as soon as we try to go into details, we meet only the adherence of particular audiences" (76).

By way of illustrating how *NR* can help one articulate the differences between evaluation claims and ethical claims we will consider surgeon and former senator Bill Frist's role in the Terry Schaivo case. The latter case, it will be recalled, involved a conflict between Florida woman Terry Schaivo's parents and her husband over whether her feeding tubes should be removed, thereby bringing about her death. A number of physicians attending Schaivo had declared her in a "permanent vegetative state," a condition which under Florida law permitted euthanasia. The state had intervened on behalf of the parents, the courts had ruled against them, at which point members of United States Congress attempted to intervene on behalf of the parents. Senator Frist went so far as to render a highly publicized judgment that Schaivo was not in a permanent vegetative state based on his viewing of a brief video clip.

With that background, consider the differences between an evaluative judgment of Frist's surgical abilities and an ethical judgment of his intervention in the case. Frist's excellence as a surgeon is best measured by standards of the medical profession generally and by the standards of his speciality (heart surgery) within that profession. "Compared to whom" is he an excellent surgeon? The judgments implicit in evaluation claims are always conditional on the answer to questions like this. In forming a response to such questions, it is always incumbent upon us to select the smallest applicable reference group and to derive our criteria and our weightings for those criteria from the function members of that group serve. Thus, while all doctors should have a comforting bedside manner and a reasonable degree of manual dexterity, family practitioners would be judged more by the former than by the latter. To the extent that people take issue with the functions of the class and the weights assigned to different criteria, the debate would necessarily go beyond members of the medical profession and their expertise. Those who disagreed would have to provide values from their own "local" store of values and bring them to bear on the medical profession

In the matter of Frist's opposition to removing Terry Schaivo's feeding tube, on the other hand, the judgment of his action is not conditional in the same way that evaluation claims of the preceding sort always are. The act he performs does not belong to a larger class of acts that brings with it criteria derived from the function of the class. The criteria for judging the quality of the act must come from the personal beliefs and values of those offering the judgment. This is the "local" dimension of ethical judgments alluded to by the authors of *NR*. The source of the judgment is local, while the implications of the judgment are universal. (Certainly there are cases, the case of the Nazis cited by John Leo, where the proportion of those agreeing to the judgment is so large as to be virtually universal. But few significant ethical issues would remain live issues if the assent to all judgments was so lopsided.) Thus, while only a certain number of people might agree with Dr. Frist that it is wrong to remove the feeding tube from a woman who has been in a permanent vegetative state for fourteen years, the claim implies that everyone *ought* to agree with that judgment. The fact that he happens to be a doctor, meanwhile, gives him little traction in the moral debate over euthanasia. Any argument he might offer to the American public, three-quarters of whom disagreed with Frist at the time he opposed letting Schaivo die, would have to be based on moral grounds. While at the general level, everyone might agree with Dr. Frist that a "culture of life" is a fine sounding idea, the Schaivo case required people to "go into details" of what that principle might mean, and as soon as they did, many dissented. Which is exactly what any reader of *NR* would predict.

In the context of Perelman and Olbrechts-Tyteca's theory, what might at first seem a straightforward task in the context of stasis theory alone is greatly complicated. According to *NR*, people do not subscribe to values monolithically. Individuals and groups hold values hierarchically, such that two individuals belonging nominally to the same group and subscribing to the same values may rank those values in significantly different ways. Two people, thus, who subscribe to "culture of life" values may agree that abortion is a very bad thing, while dividing over the role of embryonic stem cell research in that culture. In turn their differences over the question of stem cell research may reflect another value distinction discussed by Perelman and Olbrechts-Tyteca, the distinction between abstract and concrete values. However ardently someone might oppose the sacrifice of human life in abstract terms, they might make an exception for stem cell research if they had a loved one afflicted with life threatening disease that stem cell research showed promise of curing. Again, what *NR* teaches us about claims of value is that judgments about the goodness or badness of those values is driven by the local nature of the values in question. The values at issue are rarely seen as simply bad or good; they are better or worse than other values and the interaction of those values may diminish or intensify the judgments based on those values. Which is why one is more likely to decrease an audience's adherence to a value by invoking an alternative that is more esteemed than by attempting simply to discredit or debunk the contested value.

Stephen Toulmin

The last of our contemporary rhetorical figures, British philosopher Stephen Toulmin, is perhaps the most controversial. His approach has been called arhetorical—and certainly his unfortunate choice of illustrative cases lends support to such a charge—and too often classroom applications of his scheme veer off course, either into formulaic reductionism or total muddle. Some teachers describe the approach as too limiting, others complain that it's just flat confusing. Again, as with the other figures discussed in this chapter, one needs to be mindful of one's expectations when one applies Toulmin. What is it that you want from his approach? If one can answer that question with specific and modest expectations in mind, one will usually not be disappointed. In general, problems with Toulmin follow from unrealistic expectations. The authors of this book never rely primarily, let alone exclusively, on Toulmin's approach—too much classroom time spent converting lines of argument into Toulmin schema can be a most stultifying experience. We always remind students that their conversions will inevitably entail a good deal of interpretation and that, as the infomercials often silently confess in small print at the bottom of the screen, "Results shown may not be typical," when moving from potted illustrations to actual cases. It is best used in conjunction with an argument's major claim as a means of "checking" to ensure that the claim comes as close as possible to saying what one intends and to clarify the obligations one has placed oneself under in making such a claim. Consequently, we typically ask students to submit their major claim to Toulmin analysis after they have completed their rough drafts. Like *NR*, it works well in combination with a stasis approach, partly because both emphasize the claim. Whereas stases are particularly effective at expanding claims, Toulmin is particularly effective at sharpening and tightening claims. In the end, the peculiar strengths of Toulmin, the access it affords us to the inner workings of argument and the awareness it raises about an argument's linguistic nuances makes it worth the price of admission. That said, let us review the origins of his approach and its major terms.

The Toulmin Schema: The Un-Syllogism. Like Perelman and Olbrechts-Tyteca's NR, the point of departure for Toulmin's *The Uses of Argument* (UA) is formal logical demonstration. What distinguishes Toulmin's approach is the fact that he stays closer to the logical model, inventing a variation of the categorical syllogism to address the deficiencies of syllogistic reasoning—in particular its inattention to circumstances and its indifference to substantive as opposed to analytical truth—while retaining some of its strengths, in particular its ability to render arguments more transparent. Toulmin's approach, while narrower than the other approaches treated in this chapter, makes up for its lack of richness in its capacity to render arguments more coherent and more transparent.

In contrast to the categorical syllogism with its three terms (minor premise, Major Premise, conclusion) Toulmin, calls for six terms: (1) grounds or data; (2) warrants; (3) claims; (4) backing; (5) conditions of rebuttal; and (6) qualifiers. To illustrate a typical Toulmin scheme, we will borrow one of his own famously "arhetorical" examples. In a nutshell, the "argument," such as it is, goes like this: Petersen is a Swede, and since a Swede can be taken almost certainly not to be a Catholic, Petersen is almost certainly not a Catholic. The argument includes four of the six terms. "Petersen is a Swede" is the datum or ground, or "what one has to go on." "A Swede can be taken almost certainly not to be a Catholic," is the warrant, a generalization or rule that licenses the inference about the ground appearing in the claim—in this case, the claim that "Petersen is not a Catholic." The "almost certainly" represents the qualifier or the measure of confidence one may have in one's conclusion based on the "force" of the warrant and the strength of the data. One's argument may also include the other two items, "conditions of rebuttal" and "backing." The former name exceptions to the rule implied by the warrant. In the case of our friend Petersen, the possibility, say, that on his annual vacation to Italy he fell in love with a Catholic and converted to Catholicism in order to marry in the church. "Backing," meanwhile includes all assurances that the warrant we are using is acceptable; in this case statistical data showing the very small proportion of Swedes who happen to be Catholic.

It is not unusual to find Toulmin's schema reduced to three of the terms: Data—Warrant—Claim or as some argument textbooks would have it, Evidence—Reasons—Conclusion. While the latter trio of terms is probably less formidable for novices, when one "simplifies" his schema this way, one loses much of the precision of Toulmin's approach: Most warrants can be stated as reasons, but many reasons are impossible to convert to warrants. Moreover, reasons may also serve as grounds in a Toulmin schema. The simplification of Toulmin to three terms also entails a loss of transparency or what Toulmin calls "candor." The primary function of these terms, after all, is to tease information out of the elements of one's argument, information that might otherwise go unremarked. When students are required to supply qualifiers and conditions of rebuttal for their arguments, it provides a sharp reminder that they are operating in the realm of the probabilistic and the contingent rather than the categorical, and forces them to gauge carefully their degree of confidence in the claim and to acknowledge possibilities under which it might not hold.

More to the point, Toulmin's schema can "stand in" for a skeptical auditor, or what Toulmin refers to as a "challenger" to their argument. In this regard, *UA,* like *NR,* is strongly influenced by a judicial model of argument. Whereas the categorical syllogism ultimately represents an argument by authority—the system of logic itself offers one no way to question the truthfulness of the terms or to challenge assumptions—Toulmin's schema anticipates questions of truthfulness, raised by "opposing counsel," at every juncture. Put another way, the those "slots" in the Toulmin schema representing conditions of rebuttal and qualifier anticipate challenges that might be put to the adequacy of the grounds and the relevance of the warrant. The backing, meanwhile, anticipates a challenge to the legitimacy of the warrant. Given the difficulty any of us—but most especially students—have critically challenging our own arguments, Toulmin provides a systematic way of anticipating challenges and strengthening our arguments accordingly. (Not to mention, of course, critiquing the arguments of others.)

But Toulmin is also careful to delimit the challenges that might be put to arguments. If in theory all elements of an argument are open to challenge, in fact the vulnerability of those elements (his six terms) is limited by convention. That is, Toulmin accepts that many different fields of argument have in place agreements—some tacit, some explicit—about what constitutes sufficient and relevant grounds, legitimate warrants and authoritative backing and those agreements render challenges to many arguments moot. In fact, in some cases to name one's warrants and backing would be downright insulting to one's audiences. By convention then, the terms of a Toulmin model are less likely to be questioned than one might initially believe. Moreover Toulmin imposes a particularly stringent standard on backing, requiring it to have a "fact like" status, presumably to avoid the unseemly prospect of an infinite regress of justifications of justifications, of backings stacked like turtles "all the way down." Even within the most stringent of disciplinary conventions, however, the logic of the Toulmin model is nowhere near as necessitarian and narrow as that imposed by a categorical syllogism. As the work of people like economist Deirdre (nee Donald) McCloskey has clearly shown in recent years, even quantitative arguments in economics and other social scientific fields turn out to be much squishier, less objective and compelling, than their pseudo-syllogistic structures might lead one to believe. Finally, Toulmin's model has been freely and usefully applied to public policy and ethical arguments in which few terms carry stipulative definitions assented to by all or even most parties to the debate. Indeed the primary value of the model in such instances lies in its power to reveal the vulnerability of the premises (warrants and backing) upon which arguments rest and to provide a clearer sense of just how probable a given conclusion might be.

Toulmin Applied. To really illustrate Toulmin's approach requires us to move away from the sort of straightforward, uncontroversial claims that he uses to more controversial, open-ended claims of the sort students might actually use or encounter in persuasive discourse. To borrow a controversial claim from recent American political discourse, consider the following: "Some part of American workers' contribution to social security ought to be set aside in personal investment accounts." As is often the case, such a claim may arrive with a minimum of support or qualification. In order to assess the validity of the claim, we must inquire just what the arguer might have in mind for grounds, warrants, backing, qualification or conditions of rebuttal. In some cases, such matters will appear later in the argument. In other cases—such as this one—we will have to supply them or infer them from other statements made by the arguer(s).

The most prominent datum adduced to justify the above claim was something on the order of the following: "The social security system will soon be broke." Now, the first thing to notice about that particular datum is that it is itself a claim. In fact, the grounds of real world arguments are often themselves claims not immune to question, particularly when one is engaged in public policy issues as opposed to controversies within well defined fields where the rules for what counts as grounds are explicit and acknowledged by convention. Data seldom rise to the level of "facts" (keeping in mind once again that "facts" are here understood as a measure of audience assent, not of the correspondence between a proposition and an extraverbal reality) and are often open to challenge. It is, to be sure, a more widely accepted claim than the one that serves as the conclusion of the argument. But many people challenged the data on definitional grounds: What is the meaning of "soon" and what is the meaning of "broke"?

Both questions could only be answered by long range economic predictions which are notoriously shaky. That said, a consensus of economic opinion concluded that if nothing were done the system would start paying out more than it would receive in approximately 2017, and that it would have to reduce benefits by 20% to 30% some time between 2042 and 2052. (Other, more dire, predictions by the proposal's supporters were rejected on the grounds that the supporters used a different set of economic assumptions to arrive at their conclusions than they had used in making other long range economic forecasts.) The system was never projected to be completely bankrupt. (Indeed, economic analysis of several proposed solutions involving personal accounts indicated that in 2042 recipients would receive about the same or less compensation under those plans than under the worst case, "do nothing" scenario.) The term "broke," thus turned out to be a relative as opposed to categorical judgment. By the same token, opponents of the proposal emphasized that "soon" too is a relative term and asked a classic rhetorical question: "Compared to what?" is social security in financially dire straits, and "Compared to what?" is that threat urgent? As we saw in our earlier discussion of *NR*, the value of a given claim will be greatly affected by the claims that it is linked to or associated with by questions like these. Consequently, when opponents of social security privatization measured the dangers facing social security against dangers facing the medicare/medicaid system, the public found the condition of medicare/medicaid much more unsettling. Compared to the far greater impacts of the medicare/medicaid crisis, the problems of social security seemed eminently more manageable.

But whatever the problems with the adequacy of the data to the urgency and magnitude of the claim, the more interesting problems with the proposal from the perspective of the Toulmin schema concerns the warrant that might justify the move from the grounds—we will assume for now the adequacy of the data purporting to show the shaky financial condition of social security—to the claim. Just how does one get from "The social security system will soon be broke" to the claim that "Some part of American workers' contribution to social security ought to be set aside in personal accounts"? As is often the case in public policy issues, no such warrant was ever articulated, leaving the task up to those who questioned the claim. In imagining a warrant adequate to the task, the challenger needs to discern just how sure those making the claim are about the adequacy of their claim. In the case of the claim in question, the fact that it was seldom attended by qualifiers or conditions of rebuttal suggests the need for a warrant of considerable "force." That is, whatever rule or principle is adduced, it should make the conclusion highly probable, if not certain.

For the most part, inferring a warrant is a pretty straightforward matter once one has estimated the degree of certitude it ought to possess. Basically one is simply restating at a more general level the relationship between the grounds and the claim, something on the order of "Whenever G, then C," or "Whenever G, often C." In the pedestrian examples Toulmin provides in *UA,* the warrant seems self evident to the point of being superfluous. In the current case, however, the statement of the warrant can be at once self evident and controversial. There are, as it turns out, good reasons sometimes for not stating the obvious. In the case of the social security proposal, one obvious candidate for warrant might go something like this:: "When a public program is in trouble, privatizing at least a portion of the program is the best solution to the problem." All we've done is convert the grounds ("The social security system will soon be broke") and the claim ("Some part of American workers' contribution to social security ought to be set aside in private accounts.") into slightly more general versions of themselves and combined them. (The proponents of the plan dropped the terms "private" and "privatize" from their lexicon mid-debate because they judged the term too controversial; but by then they had been using the term for two decades or more to describe the very proposal they were promoting and the various synonyms they trotted out failed to stick.)

The advantage of restating things in warrant-like fashion is that it makes the reasoning behind the argument that much more transparent. In the process, it inevitably raises questions that might go unasked so long as one's focus is the particular case in question. In this case, warrants for proposal claims like the social security proposal imply a causal relationship between a problem and a solution ("Problem X, therefore Solution Y"). Establishing such relationships typically requires recourse to historical precedents ("Solution Y is very much like Solution Z that worked previously in a similar situation") and physical links ("Solution Y will work in the following way: A, then B, then C"), empirical concerns largely absent from Toulmin's nonproblematical examples where providing backing is a simple matter of looking up census data. In the case of social security, backing for the implied warrant that privatizing social security will cure its problems is necessarily less "fact-like" and more in the nature of a resemblance claim. ("Where X programs were in trouble, privatization saved them.") Toulmin's examples do not require such empirical support in part because of their formal similarity to categorical syllogisms. In categorical syllogisms, the major premise simply asserts membership in a category. In Toulmin's example, the warrant—"Swedes are seldom Catholics"—serves a similarly pedestrian function. While not, strictly speaking, a categorical proposition, Toulmin's warrant is sufficiently fact-like in itself as to render backing superfluous. The warrant for the social security argument is considerably less fact-like in character and would require significant backing to gain assent. Where privatization has been tried in the past, where has it worked and not worked and why? How is social security privatization like or unlike these precedents? Exactly how, step by step, would privatization bring about the salvation of social security? Various attempts to answer such questions proved unpersuasive to the vast majority of the American public. In fact, they ended up raising more questions than they answered. How could private accounts be supported without cutting contributions to the defined benefit portion of social security? What effect would the loss of trillions of dollars in contributions have on the financial soundness of the existing social security program?. In the end, proponents of private accounts backed away from their claim that it would help solve the social security program's problems and recommended them for different reasons.

Having an explicit warrant means in turn that we can now be more specific about the requirements for a proper backing. What evidence is there that *in fact* privatization is an effective means of fixing deficient public programs. Here the proponents could turn to a mixed bag of evidence, cases in which privatization has and has not been effective. One frequently cited precedent which might serve as backing for our warrant was the case of Chile, which totally privatized its system in the late 1970s. But even that precedent failed to provide the sort of rock solid, "fact-like" support for the warrant that the unqualified claim seemed to call for. The Chilean system had performed well overall, but most analyses suggested that it had worked out much better for middle class and wealthier participants than for poorer ones, most of whom would have been better off under the old socialized program. Since social security had been instrumental in cutting the poverty rate among America's elderly by two thirds (from about 30% to about 10%) since 1970, this was a particularly worrisome aspect of the Chilean experience. Moreover, the life of the Chilean program paralleled arguably the greatest run up of stock prices in the history of public trading markets, causing some to question its predictive value. (The Chilean program is, as this is written, being revamped dramatically in response to its tendency to shortchange the poorest members of the system.)

Today the proposal is mostly dormant after the administration withdrew it in the face of mounting criticism, but it remains a possible policy proposal. The bold, unmodified claims championing private accounts failed to win widespread support despite significant amounts of financial and political capital invested in marketing the notion. The more the public heard the proponents' arguments, in fact, the less support they expressed for the proposal. The weaknesses of those arguments could certainly be expressed without using Toulmin. But Toulmin's language offers up a particularly precise manner of expression for articulating problem areas. Working backwards from the general failure to qualify the major claim, one can readily recognize the considerable burden of proof assumed by the argument; in the context of that certitude, data supporting both the urgency and magnitude of the problem appear insufficient. Moreover, the mismatch between the problem (social security is going broke) and the solution (put some social security contributions into private accounts) was rendered more visible by laying out the argument. But most particularly, the lack of anything approaching "fact-like" backing for the warrant undercut public confidence in the argument.

All of which is not to say that the actual success or failure of an argument correlates strongly with their soundness as established through Toulmin. In the final analysis, the larger context, those circumstances within which the proponents were to "find the available means of persuasion," probably had a good deal to do with the argument's lack of success. A number of events of the recent past led people to be more risk averse, particularly with their retirement incomes. The stock market's sharp dip in 2002, followed by three years of weak recovery, rendered many people suspicious of any proposal that shifted their dollars to stock market accounts. Moreover, over the previous decade, many people had belatedly discovered that their private pension plans were insolvent or severely underfunded, on the verge of being abolished, or undergoing conversion from "defined benefit" programs with predictable returns to "defined contribution" plans whose returns were, once again, dependent on stock market performance. Finally, among the factors that led to the stock market troubles 2002 were the relaxed regulatory policies of the federal government that led to the spectacular failure of Enron and a number of financial services companies. Most arguments rise or fall on the basis of "substantial" matters such as these as opposed to "analytical" or formal weaknesses within an argument. But assuming that one has a grasp of the larger context and a familiarity with the relevant circumstances, Toulmin remains a powerful tool for checking that their argument is the best possible expression of those factors.

Summary

So what might contemporary teachers of argument take away from this brief historical survey of argument? From the early struggles with philosophy we can learn to embrace the very "realistic" basis of our enterprise, to accept the fact that we cannot promise certainty or even truth with a capital T as an outcome of argument. We can, however, offer a means for achieving a fuller, more complex understanding of the world and an increased likelihood that this understanding will be translated, however imperfectly, into actions and decisions. We can celebrate the fact that the first full scale book of rhetorical theory, Aristotle's *On Rhetoric* is a primer for citizen participation in Greek democracy, and that from our inception we have prepared non-specialists to fulfill their obligations as citizens. We can without apology offer systematic means for inventing and testing arguments even as we remain ever wary that those means do not degenerate into facile ends. We can, in the wake of philosophy's "linguistic turn" whereby language's power to construct as well as to represent reality has been acknowledged, accept responsibility for helping people "to break free from outworn vocabularies" and to ensure that whatever terminology they may use is capable of "progressive criticism of itself." Once language is understood as fundamentally metaphorical and value-laden rather than literal and value-neutral, once understanding is presumed to be an act of seeing one thing *in terms of* another (identification), not an awareness that one thing *is* another (identity), interpretation ceases to be an exercise in disambiguating badly crafted language, and becomes a basic requirement of all understanding, a translation of a general understandings into specific, circumstantial ones. By the same token, the relationship between general rules or principles and particular cases is such that the principles are no longer presumed to explain the cases, on the model of covering laws explaining physical phenomena. Rather the relationship between principles and cases is two-way; while principles provide a means for interpreting cases, cases challenge and modify those very principles. In sum, the major shifts in philosophy over the past century have moved rhetoric from the disciplinary margins into the disciplinary center and transformed the major foci of rhetoric, argument and interpretation, from ancillary activities, symptoms of a breakdown in the "clean machine" of communication, into essential operations.

In terms of actual classroom practices, rhetoric teaches us that the lessons of history are best turned to the task of helping us get beyond history. The ancients and early moderns, the great systematizers of the previous centuries, can take us so far and then we have to adapt their general principles to the circumstances we find ourselves in. Traditionally rhetoric was viewed—too often through the distorting lens of philosophy—as a second rate version of logical demonstration, inquiry for proles. The sphere of argument was carefully delimited and the model of persuasion was the occasion, a formal, usually oral presentation given in a limited number of venues. Little attention was paid to the media through which messages passed and their possible effects on those messages. Audiences were viewed as givens who were to be strategically "addressed" according to an understanding of human nature that resembles a crude version of the elaborate psychological grids that today's propagandists and advertisers rely on to manipulate their audiences.

In translating the broader lessons of history to the classroom, several useful generalizations apply. Clearly contemporary arguments seldom play out in a single venue or a single medium. They advance on many fronts through numerous media, each of which puts its unique demands on the arguer. In particular, the effects of those media extend beyond the text, written or spoken, to the manner of presentation, the filters through which messages must pass en route to audiences, the way in which cameras and microphones, lighting and settings and so forth call attention to some features of the text and deflect attention from others. We must attend to the ways in which the genres of presentation—political speech, newspaper editorial, letter to the editor, talk show banter, print ad, TV ad, and so forth—affect our understanding of a text. Often times the non-rational—not to be confused with the *irr*ational—aspects of argument play a larger role than the rational factors in determining the efficacy of a given argument and we have to learn how to read those factors. We need to give our students opportunities to work with argument in its many guises and not limit their exposure to anthologized collections of essay-length arguments, often aimed at a very limited range of audiences.

In adapting contemporary argument theory to the classroom, our challenges are more specific. How might one organize a writing class focused on writing around the diverse figures discussed above? Without being too doctrinaire, we encourage something like the following. Read *in* Burke, most especially his *Rhetoric of Motives,* and Perelman and Olbrechts-Tyteca, most especially their *New Rhetoric,* by way of developing a conceptual framework within which to teach argument. Meanwhile, the most adaptable and useful day-to-day approach to teaching argument in our view, remains the stasis approach. It is loose and baggy enough to accommodate any subject, lends itself well to both invention and analysis of argument, and offers novices a reasonably simple language for discussing individual arguments. Finally, we recommend careful, limited use of Toulmin in conjunction with the close reading of major claims in student arguments. The application of Toulmin can be particularly useful at the second draft stage of writing, when students know their argument well enough to sense its strengths and weaknesses, and are sufficiently committed to it that they will be challenged by, but not defeated by, the severe interrogation of a Toulmin schema.

Notes

1. The contribution of Fahnestock and Secor's essay to contemporary argument theory is exemplary both in terms of its important impact on the field and its particular approach to theory. Much of the best work that has been done by rhetoric and composition scholars dealing with argument in recent years has involved adapting earlier approaches or retrofitting approaches from other fields to the needs of contemporary argument. (In addition to Fahnestock and Secor's contribution, John Gage's imaginative working out of the enthymeme for writing students exemplifies the first sort of contribution, while Richard Young, Alton Becker, and Kenneth Pike's adaptation of Carl Rogers's psycho-analytic approach to the realm of argument exemplifies the second.) A number of interesting and useful books and articles about argument have been written by rhetoric and composition scholars in recent years (several of those are cited in our bibliography), but we have not seen the development full fledged theories of argument to rival those developed in recent years by scholars in communications and philosophy. While we find these latter theories of limited usefulness in the writing classroom (see below, chapter three), we appreciate the rich and sometimes passionate exchanges about argument regularly conducted within those fields.

3 Issues in Argument

In this chapter we will examine four related controversies that frame our understanding of argument and its value in the classroom. First, we will critique the traditional practice of teaching "informal fallacies," paying particular attention to the slippage between the formal models of fallacy and their actual application. Second, we will extend that critique to the influential "pragma-dialectical" school of argument theory and its attempt to construct a framework within which fallacies may be defined and evaluated more precisely. Third, using Richard Fulkerson's recently updated taxonomy of composition practices, we will look at the major alternatives to the teaching of argument in writing classes and the place of argument teaching among those practices. Finally, we will consider the pros, cons and challenges of teaching about propaganda in a writing class devoted to argument.

The Fallacy Debate

The treatment of informal fallacies in writing classes focused on argument is a hardy perennial. Despite the best efforts by many within the field to end the practice, and over the protests of some textbook authors who would like to have discussions of the fallacies removed from their texts altogether, the fallacies remain. There is, it appears, a sort of inherent appeal to the fallacies, something like the appeal of prescriptive grammar in other writing courses. In a field so fluid and complex, the fallacies are finite, concrete and offer practitioners the tantalizing prospect of rendering thumbs up or down judgments, of being able to pronounce arguments not merely weak or strong, but flat out wrong or right. Thus, just as the beleaguered writing teacher worried about justifying a grade to a student may welcome the opportunity to note faulty tense agreements and non-parallel constructions ("No arguing with the handbook, my friend."), the distraught critic of a particularly leaky student argument may be equally pleased to point out the utterly unambiguous presence of the argument *ad hominem, tu quoque* variety ("No arguing with Latin, my friend"). While helping students understand that a thesis is self-evident or vacuous or that their evidence is irrelevant to their claim can be difficult and time consuming, penalizing them for fallacies and grammar mistakes takes less time and requires less justification.

To be sure, some who use informal fallacies in the teaching of argument have higher motives. There is a long tradition in the field of teaching the fallacies going back to its very beginnings. The genesis of the fallacy approach can be traced to Aristotle, who primarily in *De Sophisticis Elenchis* (as well as *Prior Analytics* and *Rhetoric*) treats fallacies as a collection of intentionally misleading arguments dreamed up by Sophists to bewilder and outflank their opponents. Some of the thirteen fallacies he enumerates are entirely dependent on linguistic trickeration while others are said to be independent of language. But the problems of murkiness that have beset fallacies down through the centuries are present here at the very beginning in this distinction. As noted by the authors of *Fundamentals of Argumentation Theory,* Aristotle's examples of linguistic and non-linguistic fallacies are not particularly enlightening. In fact, many modern day students of fallacy are hard pressed to find any that aren't dependent on evasive, charged or ambiguous use of language. Consider the following sophistic argument taken from Plato's *Euthydemus* which is cited as an example of a language-independent fallacy: You have a dog; your dog is father to puppies; your dog is your father (qtd Eemeren et al. 58-59). Laid out like this, the argument would appear to be prima facie absurd and unlikely to deceive even the most credulous interlocutor. Even in its original dialogue format it seems painfully transparent. By Aristotle's lights, it is a language independent fallacy resting on an "an illegitimate shift of an attribute from an accidental property of a subject . . . , to the subject itself or vice versa. . . . what Aristotle here means by 'accidental' is not clear" (59). Even if we could figure out precisely what Aristotle had in mind by designating an attribute "accidental," most of us would find his explanation unnecessarily circuitous and complex. Just because a dog is a father to some puppies does not make him father to everything else under the sun, any more than designating someone a wife entails designating everyone else under the sun her husband. That's a major category mistake of the sort people in real life just don't make. The only grounds for terming this a "language-independent fallacy" would seem to lie in the fact that it is so spectacularly clumsy that few people are likely to be fooled by the linguistic sleight of hand that turns "your" and "father" into universally applicable properties. Indeed many of today's paradigmatic fallacy examples are as self-evidently wrong headed as the ancient examples. Unsurprisingly so since many of them appear to have been lifted from previous generations of textbook fallacy examples.

Still, the fallacies continue to be a staple item in writing classes devoted to argument, despite the fact, as Richard Fulkerson has pointed out, "there has never been an agreed-upon definition or a usable classification of fallacies" (*Teaching* 96) and the actual number of fallacies cited in argument textbooks varies widely with many of them bearing multiple names. In an attempt to render the study of fallacies more useful to writing teachers, Fulkerson cites work done in the informal logic movement, in particular a definition of fallacy developed by Howard Kahane. According to Fulkerson's analysis of that definition, a fallacy is present if one cannot answer yes to the following three questions:

1. Are the premises—both explicit and implicit—acceptable?
2. Is all the relevant and important information taken into account?'
3. Does the form of the argument satisfy the relevant rules of logic? (97)

Fulkerson sets aside the third question on the grounds that it speaks to the rules of formal deduction which makes it difficult to apply apart from extensive time spent teaching logic, time which could be better spent on more substantive concerns. Moreover, problems in formal logic seldom occur in real world arguments. He then goes on to cite eleven major fallacies that he terms "substantive" in the sense that they are non-formal and fall under the first two questions posed by Kahane's definition.

Fulkerson's discussion is useful and clear and anyone determined to teach fallacies in argument should refer to it. As Fulkerson makes clear at the outset and throughout his discussions of the fallacies, the "fallacy of fallacies" as it were, is to mistake a substantive for a formal defect. To presume, as many do, that "any argument lacking the identified fallacy is a good argument" (15) is akin to presuming that any argument without factual errors is sound. Their absence does not guarantee persuasive argument in the same way that the absence of formal errors in deduction guarantees a sound argument. By the same token, to find a particular argument laid out in the same fashion as a fallacious argument does not ensure that the argument in question is fallacious. In the case of a "slippery slope" argument for example, if someone argues that doing A will lead to B, which will lead to C, and so forth, that argument may or may not be defective. Some slopes, after all, are indeed slippery and some causal chains, even quite lengthy ones, are airtight. Just because an argument follows a pattern often followed by arguments that turn out to be fallacious, does not render the argument in question fallacious. The error one makes in thinking so is akin to the fallacy of *post hoc ergo propter hoc* ("after this therefore because of this"). Linking events in serial order is merely a symptom of causation, and until one can actually show a causal link, one has not proven anything. So it is with supposedly fallacious arguments. In the end, one must always show, on substantive grounds just why they are fallacious. Having shown conclusively that a particular line of reasoning is fallacious, one has typically only weakened an overall argument, not overturned it.

But as the preceding objections to the fallacy approach suggests, some useful insights can emerge from looking at an argument through a fallacy lens. Viewed as a heuristic or a symptom that raises pointed questions about a given argument, rather than an algorithm that classifies and evaluates an argument, a fallacy may lead us to a fruitful line of inquiry. At least several of the fallacies do indeed show up regularly in real world arguments in recognizable forms. For example, those fallacies cited in conjunction with causation, the venerable *post hoc, ergo propter hoc* and "slippery slope" fallacies show up commonly, particularly in conjunction with policy/proposal arguments. Unlike arguments in the sciences which because of stricter rules of evidence, more precise means of measurement, and a tradition of carefully qualified claims tend to produce fewer controversial causal claims (or at least fewer that spill out into the public domain), causal claims in the public policy arena tend to be both harder to quantify and easier to manipulate for political ends. In the case of educational testing, for example, the establishment of high stakes exams in primary and secondary schools is taken as evidence that something is being done to better the educational system and, better yet, to ensure that "no child [will be] left behind." In that context, bumps of three or four points on the test scores are taken as validation of the "accountability movement."

•

But a rise in scores that comes "after the test" guarantees neither that the higher scores are "*because* of the test," nor, more importantly that the test measures actual learning or proficiency. What the test results may very well indicate is that teachers are getting better at teaching to the test and students are getting better at taking tests or that the tests are being dumbed down. When results on state tests used to measure student progress are contradicted by the results of national tests designed to measure student proficiency at grade, tests not tied to funding or school accreditation, the "progress" on the state test needs to be reexamined. As a number of critics of the testing movement in education have pointed out, testing in and of itself does nothing to improve student learning. Or as some critics have colorfully suggested, "You don't fatten a hog by weighing it."

One can find examples of fallacious reasoning of this sort in numerous public debates and, truth be told, they are not unknown in our professional journals. Having the fallacious patterns in mind may potentially help one recognize the symptoms of fallacious reasoning when one comes across them and organize one's response to the arguments they underwrite. The decision about whether or not to discuss informal fallacies in a writing class has less to do with the prevalence of the problems they articulate or the usefulness of the fallacies in detecting those problems than it does with the pedagogical challenges they pose. For one well versed in the fallacies, real ones are readily distinguishable from apparent ones. To novices, on the other hand, the form is easily mistaken for the substance. Someone on the lookout for "*post hoc, ergo propter hoc,*" arguments may come across an argument that makes a properly modest claim for causal relationship based on statistical correlations that are highly persuasive and still assume the whole argument is fallacious.

There are further pedagogical problems with the fallacies approach. Philosopher Michael Scriven, an early leader in the critical thinking movement, has, according to the authors of *Fundamentals,* opposed "the use of fallacies for the purpose of argument criticism, contending that doing so requires building into the argument-identification process all the skills that are needed anyhow for analysis" (182). Why teach students the vocabulary of "fallacy talk," Scriven wonders, when determining the actual status of the argument can be done so in the "natural language" of *claims, evidence, reason* and so forth, used in standard rhetorical analysis? Learning the Latinate language of fallacies is in Scriven's view an unnecessary step. The all purpose "hasty generalization" fallacy, for instance, offers nothing new in the way of a tool for assessing how well an argument has been supported. Skimpy evidence is not just a fallacy, it is a basic weakness of many arguments. One is well advised to judge the adequacy of support within the context of the understanding and degree of skepticism any given audience brings to the argument. Generally, thus, we share Scriven's skepticism about the usefulness of fallacy talk in our classes. But by the same token, we try always to offer at least brief exposure to a selected group of fallacies like those dealing with causality that do crop up in the real world and that can be rendered more recognizable by use of the fallacy vocabulary. In our experience, at least a few students find the approach helpful.

The Pragma-Dialectical Approach to Fallacies

The brainchild of the International Society for the Study of Argument (ISSA), based at the University of Amsterdam and consisting mostly of European and Canadian linguists, philosophers, rhetoricians and communication theorists, this approach deserves attention if for no other reason than the leading members of ISSA have published prolifically on the subject and are frequently cited by American students of argument. (The extremely useful *Fundamentals of Argumentation Theory* which we've been citing is the product of ten ISSA members, and the book's two lead authors, van Eemeren and Grootendorst, are founders of the approach.) In some sense, the pragma-dialectical (P-D) approach represents an attempt to rescue the fallacies approach from the sorts of criticism offered above and to carry on the promising work begun by the informal logic and critical thinking movements in the 1970s and 1980s.

Most American students of argument will find the name of this approach at least mildly puzzling. The pragmatic tradition of American philosophy which infuses the work of many American rhetoricians and many contemporary American philosophers supportive of rhetorical approaches to argument, goes considerably beyond what the P-D advocates seem to have in mind. For American pragmatists, an adoption of a pragmatic approach entails certain assumptions about the centrality of language to an understanding of the world and, consequently, models for constructing knowledge such as Oakeshott and

Rorty's "conversation of mankind" and Burke's "parlor." It entails a rejection of formalistic and systematic approaches to philosophy in favor of "edifying" and interactive approaches. The ends of philosophy for pragmatism lie not in increased stores of knowledge or greater certitude about The Truth, but in decisions and acts that move one incrementally closer to a vision of "the good life," a vision that pragmatists continually interrogate and modify in response to changes on the ground. The P-D movement, meanwhile, seems to identify "pragmatic" mostly with the act of taking into account unexpressed premises of arguments according to "standards for reasoned discourse" (*Fundamentals* 14). The pragmatic part of pragma-dialectical thus licenses one to consult "contextual information and background knowledge" (15) in assessing the validity of an argument and speech-act theory in determining the function of given claim. This more modest understanding of pragmatic can be traced to the point of departure for the P-D approach, the traditional deductivist approach to argument based entirely on internal rules for well formed arguments. Compared to the latter approach, the willingness of P-D analysts to consult extra-verbal, non-formal elements of the argument and to take motive and purpose into account can be seen as significant, however minimal its resemblance to more robust understandings of pragmatism by American students of argument.

By the same token, the "dialectical" portion of P-D analysis is, when compared to American uses of the term, similarly modest in scope. Burke's dialectical approach to understanding, as exemplified by his dramatistic method, is for example, a major engine of understanding. Seeing one thing—say "act"—in terms of another thing—say "agent"—results in a unique understanding of the phenomenon in question. Reversal of the pair in question or substitution of different terms may result in a radically different understanding. It's a means of understanding the world that resists closure and certitude, that is above all heuristic. The P-D understanding of the term, meanwhile, rests on the assumption that "all argument goes on between two (or more) discussants who are engaged in a mutual, synchronous interaction aimed at resolving an issue." (Fulkerson 15). It's a high-minded understanding of argument—according to the authors of *Fundamentals* more an exercise in "joint problem solving"(277) than in persuasion—and, not incidentally, one seldom encountered in the real world. While P-D proponents would cheerfully grant that few arguments realize their ideal—"For various reason, argumentative reality does not always resemble the ideal of a critical discussion" (295)—they would defend the model on the grounds that it provides a useful standard by which to evaluate real world arguments.

Which takes us back to where we began the discussion, the P-D attempt to rescue fallacies. What was missing from traditional approaches to fallacy they argue was a standard for distinguishing those arguments that resemble fallacious arguments from those that are truly fallacious. While their own standard is, they would concede, quite stringent, it is not unrealistic. They may be right. The major obstacle to using the approach for most American students of argument, trained in rhetoric as opposed to philosophy or linguistics, is the formidable complexity of the model. If one is to use P-D in one's class, one must be prepared to use it alone because much of one's semester will be spent elucidating the elements of the system and illustrating those elements with extremely simple examples far removed from the sorts of controversies that students actually encounter in the world. In the sense that P-D is helpful in rendering the presentation of an argument more candid, it resembles Toulmin's approach. But in that it requires the acquisition of a much more extensive vocabulary prior to translating natural language arguments into proper P-D layouts it is more like Toulmin squared. Perhaps cubed. Consider the elements of the system: there are four theoretical principles from whence are derived norms for the study of argument; there are four stages of "difference resolution"; there are ten rules for critical discussion; there are five types of speech act used at various stages to help reach resolution (thirteen possible uses of the five speech acts at the four stages are listed on page 289); and forty three possible rule violations are noted in a chart on pages 304-06. Whether or not the extraordinary lengths P-D advocates go to clarify when an argument is not just formally but substantively fallacious lead to more effective analysis of argument is open to debate. For most teachers of argument, the failure of the ends to justify the means is, it would appear, less arguable. To the extent that P-D is a tool of argument analysis, it is for now probably best restricted to professionals.

Alternatives to Focusing on Argument in a Writing Class: Critical/Cultural Studies

In a *College Composition and Communication* essay, "Composition at the Turn of the Twenty-First Century," Richard Fulkerson sets out to establish the lay of the land in composition studies, contrasting the current landscape to the landscape he found in 1990 when he attempted a similar topographical feat in "Composition in the Eighties." What Fulkerson discovers in his latest perusal of the field is that it "has become a less unified and more contentious discipline early in the twenty-first century than it had appeared to be around 1990" (654). He identifies three alternative axiologies or theories of value that give rise to three distinctive approaches to composition. (A fourth approach, the seemingly impossible-to-kill current-traditional approach, is reluctantly acknowledged but little discussed by Fulkerson.) The three axiologies include the "social-construction" view that gives rise to a "critical/cultural studies" (CCS) approach, an expressive view that gives rise to expressivism, and a "multi-faceted rhetorical" view that gives rise to what he terms "procedural rhetoric" (655). The latter approach, meanwhile, is further divided into three forms of procedural rhetoric: "composition as argumentation, genre-based composition, and composition as introduction to an academic discourse community" (671). By Fulkerson's lights, in today's "less unified and more contentious" environment, selecting any one of these approaches may well constitute a controversial act.

We agree with Fulkerson about the divided state of the discipline, a state perhaps best captured in his citation of Gary Olson's contention that composition studies is on the verge of "the new theory wars" (681). We are also sympathetic with his clear preference for procedural rhetoric in general and an argumentation emphasis in particular. We are, however, generally less critical of the alternative approaches than he appears to be and in some cases our grounds for preferring an argument focus over other approaches are different. (Part of these differences can doubtless be traced to the inevitable foreshortening of perspective Fulkerson must manage in order to construct a readable map. As he acknowledges, all of these approaches are more complex and heterogeneous than can be credited in the scope of an overview.) Moreover, it is also not clear to us that an emphasis on argument is pedagogically, as opposed to ideologically, incompatible with some of these other approaches. (In our chapter on "Best Practices," in fact we look at a number of different pedagogical approaches to the teaching of writing that seem perfectly compatible with an argument focus.) At any rate, in today's environment, the decision to focus on, or in some quarters merely include, argumentation in a writing class is a politically charged choice that one had best be prepared to defend against advocates for the other approaches. In those programs where curricular decisions are largely made collectively, one may well find oneself pulled into the debates rehearsed here in very immediate, sometimes painful ways.

Certainly the major shift in emphasis in composition over the past twenty years involves the rise of CCS approaches. Championed most notably by James Berlin, this approach encompasses a number of different emphases, including feminism, service learning or community service and critical pedagogy (not to be confused with the determinedly neutral critical thinking approaches of the 1970s and 1980s). Fulkerson is critical of CCS primarily for focusing too much on issues of social justice and "'liberation' from dominant discourse" (660) and for its tendency to privilege student empowerment over improved writing as a course outcome. He is also suspicious of its focus on the interpretation of texts and cultural artifacts as opposed to strategies for invention and revision of student text. He sees an uncomfortable similarity between CCS courses and the "popular and durable literature-based composition courses. In both types, students read texts judged important by the teacher. They write about those texts, and their work is evaluated on how well it shows that they understand and can perform the interpretive approach" (662-63). Such courses, Fulkerson suspects, are motivated in part by what he dubs the "content envy" (663) of writing teachers.

Our own preference for argument-based writing courses over a CCS approach does not imply an outright rejection of content-rich writing courses, even when that content is compatible with the content taught in a typical CCS course. Offering students a common set of texts and/or artifacts to read and discuss does not preclude direct instruction in argument or writing. Moreover, in a collaborative or cooperative learning based environment, common texts and subjects can be extremely useful in the promotion of discussion and negotiation of meaning. That said, we do share some of Fulkerson's reservations about what all too often *actually* happens in content-rich courses, particularly when the content in question is a passion of the teacher. Discussion of the selected texts and artifacts may come at the expense of discussion about students' own texts and time devoted to invention and revision of their work. Few of the textbooks apparently designed for use in CCS courses offer much in the way of instruction about invention or revision and fewer still discuss rhetorical principles in any serious way. Much of what is demanded of students in such courses is argument-based writing, yet there is little explicit instruction on how to write arguments or how to think about them and the assignments, qua argument assignments, are not always clearly focused. Certainly many teachers who use this approach create their own primary source materials for the course for reasons not unrelated to their commitment to a CCS focus. But in any case, anyone using a CCS approach who wishes to ensure a balance between a content focus and a focus on student writing should be prepared to do some fairly heavy pedagogical lifting.

In some cases, CCS courses built around a single theme may feature texts and artifacts that echo a common point of view and point in a single direction, discouraging reasoned dissent from and critical reflection on the works in question. Even courses putatively designed to inculcate critical consciousness may hinder the development of that capacity to the extent that they ignore Burke's methodological imperative—"any terminology is suspect to the extent that it does not allow for the progressive criticism of itself." In debunking and critiquing the vocabularies of others, it's important that we remain aware of our own vocabulary's limits, limits that will be cited and protested by many students whose political outlooks may be decidedly different from those of the typical CCS advocate's.

To repeat, we do not think that CCS courses *necessarily* fall prey to the above faults, any more than we believe that argument-based courses necessarily fall into empty formalism or Panglossian notions of pluralism. Certainly, as we made clear in the first chapter where we discussed critical literacy in a more generic sense, we share many of the liberatory goals enunciated by CCS advocates. We believe that students can be empowered by writing courses and that they can become more conscious of the ways in which dominant discourses and ideologies short circuit critical thought. We believe they can do this even as they become better writers. But, we would argue, one may achieve such goals without focusing exclusively or even significantly on the materials commonly featured in CCS courses. Indeed, in some cases, students may be more likely to achieve the ambitious goals set by CCS advocates in an environment that places greater stress on students' own processes of reading, thinking, writing, talking, and listening than on the primary and secondary materials typically assigned in the course.

Any course that hopes to combine successfully a focus on CCS materials and better student writing must make clear the close working connection between students' interpretation of texts and artifacts and students' construction of their own texts about such material. Here again, our perspective differs from Fulkerson's. While he tends to treat interpretation as a separate activity that detracts from the development of students' writing abilities, we tend to see the two activities as complementary, and hold with Ann Berthoff's reversible dictum that "How we construe is how we construct." In the context of a writing course, interpretation can become an invention activity, a means of generating original text. But it can only work that way if it is clear to students that there is not One Right Way to read the material and if multiple ways of reading text are modeled for them by the teacher, by their peers and by the materials they interpret. If we are tempted to scant students' development as independent thinkers in the name of right-minded conclusions we may wish to nudge or even prod them toward, we would do well to remind ourselves once again of Michael Berube's concept of "reversibility" and of our inability to foresee the ends to which our students may put the intellectual means we place in their possession.

Expressivist Pedagogy

Fulkerson's critique of expressivist approaches, which "despite numerous poundings by the cannons of postmodernism and resulting eulogies, is, in fact, quietly expanding its region of command" (655), suggests that they comprise "a consciousness-raising and coming-to-voice class" (666) that in the name of psychological health commit many of the same sins against composition instruction committed by CCS advocates in the name of political liberation. The fact that Fulkerson devotes less than half the space to critiquing expressivism that he devotes to critiquing CCS or procedural rhetoric appears to reflect his somewhat dismissive view of expressivist approaches. In the one extended example he offers of a scholar defending an expressivist curriculum, he rejects, justifiably it would appear, the author's basic premise that the curriculum is in fact expressivist on the grounds that "[t]he inclusion of a single autobiographical narrative in the first course is a perfectly standard practice and doesn't warrant labeling the course 'expressive.'" (668).

Our own view of expressivism is again more positive than Fulkerson's. In fact we see a particularly compelling case to be made for asking students to compose personal narratives in writing classes focused on argument and for teaching students how to read personal narratives as a form of argument. While we view argument-based courses as better designed to meet the ends of rhetoric and, in the long run, to serve both the developmental and cognitive goals of students, we accept the importance of engaging the personal in writing courses and we acknowledge the contributions of latter day feminist and expressivist scholars in helping us achieve that engagement in ways that help further all our ends. While Fulkerson's critique of expressivism is well taken, he ignores some interesting work being done by "second generation" expressivist scholars and relegates one of the most powerful and egalitarian instruments of persuasion to secondary status. To be sure, a good deal of work needs to be done developing means of evaluating, interpreting and responding to personal narrative to realize its full potential in argument classes. But some contemporary expressivist scholars have already started down that road and in what follows we offer some of our own observations designed to identify some of the pitfalls of persuasive personal narratives and some ways of addressing those pitfalls.

In this regard, we cite Candace Spigelman's "Argument and Evidence in the Case of the Personal" as an exemplary instance of situating the expressive in rhetorical tradition (specifically, an Aristotelian tradition) and contemporary theory and of making a case for the personal in the context of persuasive writing. Spigelman uses personal writing "to refer to the ways in which writers make sense of their lives by organizing their experience into first-person stories" (65). Regardless of their length, these stories "serve ends beyond pure expression of opinion or cathartic confession" (66). One of the most important ends these personal narratives serve is evidentiary. What counts as evidence, Spigelman points out, is whatever an audience is willing to grant as evidence. In traditional disciplines, this means that only those forms of evidence recognized by experts in the field will count. Which means in turn that outsiders to those traditional disciplines—often women—whose personal experiences gainsay the conclusions of the experts will have a difficult time being acknowledged by those experts. Personal narrative thus "stands as 'a significant and subversive act,' giving voice and authority to women's claims to knowledge by naming their experiences as relevant and admissible data." (66)

While narrative surely still fulfills an important role in lending authority to outsiders' knowledge claims, it may no longer seem so subversive. In the wake of such developments as "thick description" in anthropology and new historicism in literature and history, not to mention the work of numerous theorists from Paul Feyerabend to Michel de Certeau, narrative today serves an evidentiary function for many insiders as well as outsiders. (To be sure, as Spigelman points out, some "post-modernists question [personal narrative's] representation of subjects as individuals"(69), but such complaints are more commonly directed to the manner in which the representation is constructed than to the legitimacy of personal narrative as such.) Certainly many of our students will encounter personal narrative and various forms of ethnographic research in the university and should be prepared to respond to it critically and to reproduce it intelligently. As Fulkerson notes, our own field has embraced "a vaguely interactionist constructivism" (662) over the past twenty years, and in the process legitimated, even privileged, first person narrative evidence in our research. Predictably, Fulkerson is not sanguine about this development. After we briefly consider his concerns about expressivist scholarship, and our own significantly amended version of those concerns, we will return to Spigelman's defense of personal narrative both as a scholarly tool and as a persuasive tool and consider ways in which that defense might be expanded upon to make personal narrative more readily usable in writing classes focused on argument.

Citing research performed by CCS scholars, Fulkerson notes that "The pedagogical claims, although sometimes based on ethnographic case studies, are never said to be generalizable but always local. Their epistemic status is that of sophisticated lore. 'I saw this happen,' or 'I did this and it helped my students'" (662). Fulkerson's complaint here strikes us as a bit backwards. The primary flaw of ethnographic research, he argues, is that it can't be generalized. But of course, it *can* be generalized, if not by the author, by the audience. In fact such research often *is* generalized either by those who conduct it or by those who cite it. Our concerns about the use of case studies center on the fact that it is not clear just how far or in what direction the generalizations derived from them may take one, since explicit limits are seldom acknowledged or articulated within the studies themselves.[1] In this regard, ethnographic researchers are no different than many other purveyors of personal narrative who either intentionally or unintentionally leave unclear just what function their narrative serves or what rules or generalizations might be legitimated by the evidence they present. Indeed, audiences for literary narratives would consider such commentary intrusive, unnecessary and even downright insulting. By way of clarifying the function and truth status of narrative cases in research, we return to Perelman and Olbrechts-Tyteca and their discussion of the confusion over the three different functions "particular cases" (350) might serve: as *examples, illustrations* and *models.* The particular case they cite is that staple of American magazines, the celebrity profile in which magazines

> describe the career of this or that big businessman, politician, or movie star without explicitly drawing a lesson from it. Are the facts retailed just a contribution to history or a sidelight on it? Are they examples suggesting a spontaneous generalization? Are they illustrations of well-known recipes for social success? Or are the central figures in these narratives put forward as remarkable models to be emulated by the public? It is impossible to be sure. Probably a story of this kind is meant to—and often does indeed effectively—fulfill all these roles for different classes of readers. (351)

Given the differences in scope of the generalizations legitimated by the different types of particular cases, the mischief that follows from recounting a case and then studiously avoiding "drawing a lesson from it" may be significant. Is the case in question primarily an *example* that hints at a larger pattern even as it helps establish the existence of such a pattern? Or is it a *model,* an unquestioned ideal that audiences should aspire to? Or perhaps it is an *illustration* of a settled pattern that is accepted as such? To leave this question in doubt is to leave one room to offer up an ostensibly unique event for an audience's entertainment that eventually morphs into a rule imposed on one's audience.

While we acknowledge some of the dangers of employing particular cases and personal narratives in research, we believe that those dangers are outweighed by the value of personal narratives. Personal narratives are a useful research tool and a powerful persuasive tool—indeed, it is the power of personal narrative that makes its abuse so dangerous. Instead of turning students away from personal narrative, thus, we argue that they ought to be taught how to construct and critique them. We need to share with them the very sorts of concerns that were articulated above. That said, we return now to Spigelman's essay and to some of the concerns she shares about the dangers of narrative and some useful metrics she develops for evaluating personal narrative in the context of persuasive writing. We will then attempt to build on what she began sketching out here.

Spigelman is particularly concerned with "the problematic of validity testing in experiential research" (79) and cites a question that Richard Flores raises about his own work: "How are my evaluative peers to assess my scholarly work that is fastened to my experience of growing up in south Texas beneath the watchful eye of those whose views of Chicanos were blatantly racist? Could my peers write in their reviews that my account is incorrect and that I must reconsider my experience?" (79). To answer the question Flores raises, Spigelman turns to two personal narratives about writing, one by a community college writing instructor, the other by short story writer Raymond Carver. The contradictory conclusions reached by the two writers illustrate the "problematic of validity testing" at least for those who read the narratives hoping to glean insights into their own teaching as opposed to those who read for pure entertainment. In the case of the community college instructor, the major generalization or claim that emerges from the story points to the futility of commenting on student writing. The claim is based on a discussion the writing teacher has with her husband about a high school essay for which he received a grade of ninety-five with no comment. In the case of Carver, meanwhile, the major generalization or claim that emerges from the story concerns the value of strenuous feedback and evaluation based on classes he took with novelist John Gardner. How is one to evaluate these two apparently contradictory conclusions drawn from personal experience?

Spigelman turns to James Raymond's approach derived from Aristotle's discussion of example and enthymeme. He directs students' attention to the assumptions underlying the narrative and to the question "What would a reader have to believe in order to find the arguments persuasive?" (80). Spigelman then extends Raymond's analysis by turning to Walter Fisher's narrative paradigm and his assertion that "All narratives may be evaluated and critiqued for the validity or 'rationality' by applying principles of '*narrative probability,* what constitutes a coherent story,' and '*narrative fidelity,* whether the stories they [audiences] experience ring true with stories they know to be true in their lives" (80). In assessing narrative probability, one is advised to pay particular attention to the appropriateness of characters' words and actions insofar as that standard of appropriateness is derived from characters' earlier words and actions and the values they imply. Narrative fidelity, meanwhile, demands that we examine the assumptions underlying a writer's claims about the significance and meaning of their story and test those assumptions against our own assumptions and those we share with others. When she applies this metric to the two stories, Spigelman finds that the community college instructor's story ignores many possible variables that, based on her own experiences as a teacher/researcher, might better account for her lawyer-husband's eventual writing fluency than the "95" with no comments that he got on his sophomore English paper. Carver's essay, meanwhile, seems more consistent with the assumptions about the teaching of writing that she shares with many in her field and is hence said to possess greater narrative fidelity. Spigelman's ability to evaluate the two essays on non-impressionistic grounds underscores her point that one can teach others how to approach the task. Furthermore, as she further stresses, "uninterrogated and unevaluated personal narrative is seductive, and consequently dangerous," (83) and we cannot afford *not* to teach rhetorically informed personal writing in our classes.

We find Spigelman's essay suggestive and, as far as it goes, persuasive. But, as she readily concedes, considerable work remains to be done in the area of assessing claims derived from personal experience. While we will always be able to assess claims (almost always explicit) in expository essays with greater certainty that we can assess claims (usually tacit) arising from personal essays, we can surely attain a greater degree of confidence in our assessments than the current state of the art allows. Perhaps the best way to begin setting out the work that remains to be done in this area is to note some of the limitations in Spigelman's evaluative criteria. First, consider her primary reason for faulting the teacher's personal narrative—its lapse in narrative fidelity. The teacher draws conclusions from her experience about the unimportance of feedback that do not square with Spigelman's values and beliefs or those of her community. The teacher appears "to ignore twenty-some years of composition research in favor of the quick grade" (80). But Spigelman does not cite any of the "twenty-some years of composition research" that substantiates the consensus about the importance of comments on student essays and that lapse is significant. To be sure, there is a loose consensus about the importance of revision and feedback, and there is scholarship supportive of the consensus; but a) the scholarship in question is less unanimous than Spigelman suggests both on the question of where teachers ought to direct their comments and the optimum amount of feedback to offer, and b) little if any of that research is very recent.

Perhaps the most frequently reprinted and cited essay on responding to student writing, Rich Haswell's 1983 *College English* essay, "Minimal Marking," while it does not encourage zero response, does argue for an economical response to student writing. More to the point, the values and assumptions in Haswell's piece are a far cry from those that motivate Carver's ten revisions of one short story and Gardner's careful responses to each (79). Haswell's essay appears to assume that few teachers of undergraduate writing would have the time to offer all their students the level of attention that Gardner lavishes on Carver and that even fewer students would have the savvy and commitment to take advantage of that advice in the way that Carver does. (In fairness to students, few of them would possess the sort of technical vocabulary required by Carver to process Gardner's meticulous responses to his work.) In short, Carver's story would seem to function more as a fascinating example of an apprenticeship relationship between two supremely talented writers than as an exemplar of a student-teacher relationship replicable in undergraduate writing classes.

Moreover most of the research on revision and feedback is twenty or more years old in no small part because of the earlier alluded to "personal turn" in composition research. Whatever its flaws—and we recognize many—empirical research did provide members of the composition community a basis for consensus on basic matters of pedagogy such as revision and feedback and today many of us, including those among us scornful of empirical research, continue to rely on it as the basis for an informed consensus as opposed to "sophisticated lore." Perhaps the one piece of scholarship that most clearly articulates that consensus, George Hillocks's essay "What Works in Teaching Composition: A Meta-analysis of Experimental Treatment Studies," is over twenty years old. It could not be replicated today precisely because there wouldn't be enough empirical studies of what does and does not work in composition to reach any meaningful conclusions.

Just as the personal essay by the teacher ignores certain important variables that might better account for the husband's development as a writer, Spigelman's comparative analysis of the two narratives also ignores certain features that could play a significant role in her final evaluation. First, in discussing narrative fidelity she treats the standard of judgment—"the stories [we] know to be true in [our] lives" (80) and the values and beliefs shared by our community—as relatively unproblematic. She spends little time justifying that standard and focuses her evaluation on the failure of the values implicit in the teacher's story to match up with the standard she brings to bear. But as Fulkerson's essay makes clear, our own community is considerably less homogeneous than it has been and today few of us would feel confident that our own practices, values and beliefs resonated with a majority of those in the field. In lieu of such a consensus, critics of a personal narrative must rely more heavily on the stories they know to be true in their own lives as the basis for judgment. To counter objectionable claims implicit in a narrative, they are probably well advised to situate their counterclaims in narratives based on their experiences, something Spigelman does not do, and perhaps wisely. While not necessarily a bad thing, the practice of answering narratives with narratives means that our claims will be endowed with less certainty and our evidence with less authority than if we could invoke a consensus view.

A second unremarked feature of Spigelman's analysis concerns the disproportion between the authoritativeness of her two sources. One cannot help but wonder about the role that ethos plays in her evaluation of the two accounts and our own response to her judgment. The personal account of a community college writing teacher about her husband is contrasted to the personal account of one of the leading lights of late twentieth century American literature and his equally illustrious mentor. In some sense, Carver and Gardner are the sort of people—"models," in Perelman and Olbrechts-Tyteca's vocabulary—whose actions are self-authorizing insofar as they define ideals that mere mortals strive to meet. If a community college teacher violates a putative community norm, we are less likely to question our norm than we are the person; but if a major figure violates the same norm, we may well be moved to question or ignore that norm. The ethos we ascribe to writers of stature like Carver and Gardner is a function of more than their bona fides.

The ethos of these writers, like the ethos of every writer, depends greatly on the quality of their writing exhibited in the particular text being assessed. The quality of Carver's prose is very fine indeed, featuring deceptively complex stories told in a straightforward almost offhanded manner. While we tend to agree with Spigelman and others that the quality of Carver's prose owes more to conscious labor and attention to craft (witness his ten revisions) than to mysterious gifts, we also note that few writers, for whatever reasons, produce work of comparable quality. Many do try to write personal narratives with models like Carver in mind. In fact, many more people feel called to write personal narratives than feel compelled to read them. The gap between authorship and readership has to do with the deceptive promise that personal narrative holds out to people weary of laboring over impersonal, expository prose on subjects not of their own choosing, written in languages not of their own making, following scripts not of their own devising—which is to say much of the writing that is done in the world each day. Turning to personal narrative promises people an opportunity to say what matters to them about subjects of their own choosing, in their native tongue, following scripts so thoroughly imbibed over the years that they don't feel like scripts. But, as the gap between readership and authorship for personal narrative suggests, the promise often proves illusory. While personal narratives are relatively easy to write, readable personal narratives are difficult to write and engaging personal narratives are devilishly difficult to write. Cautionary examples of flawed personal narratives are all around us in our scholarship, in our classrooms, and even on bestseller lists. They are, to be sure, flawed in different ways. The worst of our students' personal narratives tend to be not-quite-coherent, not-quite-plausible re-enactments of popular myth, 750-word scripts for a MasterCard ad. The worst of our colleagues's personal narratives, meanwhile, tend to read like religious homilies, earnest, plodding and predictable tales ending in an admirable, if obvious, moral. Reading these works, one is reminded that the freedom of personal narrative is purchased at a significant price, and a big part of that price is the obligation, in Henry James's famous dictum, "to above all be interesting." Lest we grow discouraged from reading our colleagues' and students' worst efforts, reading the best of our colleagues' and students' works—not to mention those of people like Raymond Carver—will remind us why it is so important to keep trying.

These are but a couple of the many perplexities we confront with setting out to assess claims arising from personal narratives. With Spigelman's help, we have only begun to sort out the challenges. Whatever standard may eventually be developed to help us render sound judgments, we are convinced that a reasonable standard can be developed. Develop it we must. There are some truths that can only be discovered or properly justified through personal narrative. Those are the sorts of truth too important to be filtered out of writing classes in argument in the name of avoiding a turn from writing instruction to therapy.

Procedural Rhetoric

As is so often the case when three possibilities are explored by a composition scholar, the third one, whether because of a devotion to Nestorian order or because of racial memories of Goldilocks getting things "just right" on the third try, is the privileged position. Clearly Fulkerson is most comfortable discussing and elaborating his own tertium quid, "procedural rhetorical approaches." Hence he begins discussion of the approach by citing a document from the Council of Writing Program Administrators (WPA), a document "officially approved by the organization of people who actually direct programs" (670). The WPA "Outcomes" statement, he points out, for the most part excludes the goals of CCS and expressive approaches from its desired outcomes and emphasizes traditional rhetorical goals. He goes on to maintain that the inattention to procedural rhetoric in our leading journals has more to do with its settled nature as the status quo approach than it does any inherent flaws in the approach. As he suggests, argumentation would appear to be one of the dominant approaches actually taught in the classroom. In addition to argumentation, he cites two other rhetorical emphases under this general heading: "genre-based composition, and composition as introduction to an academic discourse community" (671).

Contemporary genre-based approaches to composition do indeed receive a fair amount of scholarly play. Not to be confused with older genre approaches or their near relatives the dreaded "modes" (narration, description, process, and so forth), the genre approach is considerably more fluid and theoretically sophisticated. Derived in part from Bakhtin *(Speech Genres and Other Late Essays)* and anthropologists such as Clifford Geertz ("Blurred Genres"), the approach has been adapted to work in composition by a number of communication and composition theorists. In particular, Carolyn Miller's1984 essay, "Genre as Social Action" is frequently cited by scholars in our own field, along with subsequent work by Carol Berkenkotter and Thomas Huckin, Aviva Freedman and Peter Medway. Miller's definition of genre, developed to describe oral genres specifically, is "contextual/situational . . . in contrast to the older idea of a genre as a form/formula" (164). The relationship among members of a given generic class is conceived to be familial rather than homogenous. The genre approach assumes that most writing occurs in recurrent situations. The similarities in these situations concerning such matters as purpose and audience gives rise to roughly similar discourses, adapted to the specifics of the situation.

In all this, we are a long way indeed from the modes, which are first and foremost structural forms. One has little sense what might motivate a description paper or a process paper or who one's audience might be for such discourse; mostly what one knows is what goes where. While genre-based approaches don't necessarily exclude formal considerations, they reverse the order of traditional modal-based approaches. Instead of starting from the assumption that form motivates writing, they start by looking for those recurrent situations out of which writing arises and consider the formal choices—along with numerous other choices—writers make in such situations to determine what "family" of formal choices might be appropriate. Because their focus is on recurrent situations, the "typical" audience for a given genre will have certain expectations about appropriate response and writers must work with those expectations, satisfying them or artfully disappointing them for maximum effect.

Like CCS approaches, genre approaches stress the importance of close reading textual models of the genres students are asked to produce. Like CCS, they "presume that texts are socially constructed and intertextual" (165). To understand one instance of a genre requires not merely formal information about the genre, but substantive understanding of the important or paradigmatic models that writers and audiences can be expected to have in mind when the construct and construe any particular instance of the genre. While genre approaches face some of the same dangers that CCS courses face when it comes to balancing attention to texts and attention to student processes, the rhetorical focus of the approach assures that the interpretive activities carried on in the class should translate more directly into the students' construction of text.

As it turns out, the genre-based approach is perhaps the easiest of the alternative approaches to meld with a focus on argument. A genre-based understanding of argument is built in to virtually every major approach to argument and every major argument textbook. Stasis theory is in effect a genre theory as that theory is understood by most contemporary theorists. The major stases are inductively derived from recurrent sorts situation and recurrent aims of rhetors in those situations. The value of stasis, like any genre-based approach, is not that it dictates a particular structure, but that it allows us to anticipate audience responses and points of emphasis in the construction of an argument. It's not so much a pre-fab form that arises out of our awareness of the stasis at issue—though depending on the context of the argument, a given form might be strongly called for—as it is a series of moves, adapted to the particulars of the situation.

Teaching an argument-based writing course using a stasis approach, also allows one to adapt most readily to the final alternative approach to writing, the introduction to academic discourse communities. In this regard, Fulkerson cites Gerald Graff's position in *Clueless in Academe* "that all academic discourse is argument characterized by certain preferred intellectual 'moves' that should be shared explicitly with students" (672). A student who understands argument as a similar series of moves made in response to a stasis calling for an evaluative or a causal claim should have little difficulty adapting to an approach that stresses the particular manner in which a sociologist understands evaluation or a chemist understands causation.

That said, the introduction to academic discourse communities approach is problematic for a number of reasons. As Fulkerson notes, the approach has been criticized for valorizing certain values and standards that favor middle-class white students and indeed have been under increasing attack within disciplines in recent years. Moreover, the practical difficulties of introducing students to generic academic discourse poses some challenges for the teacher. Undoubtedly the best place to learn academic discourse is within a community that uses a specific variant of that discourse. Why spend time worrying about what skills and capacities might transfer to another discipline? Let those in the disciplines teach students how to write in the appropriate manner. To learn how psychologists, physicists or political scientists writer, we would need to learn the vocabulary, methodology and rules of evidence acknowledged by members of each community, an impossible task in a single class. In fact, to the extent that one sees the primary function of first year composition to be the introduction of students to academic discourse, requiring a first year composition course appears to make little sense. Members of the so-called "abolition" movement, a movement calling for the abolition of first year writing requirements and in some cases first-year writing classes, consistently cite the absence of disciplinary norms and conventions in such classes as a reason for abandoning them.

While we do not have the time or space here to present a full case for the teaching of argument in writing classes as an antidote to the various maladies cited by the abolitionists, we would note that the underlying argument of abolitionists encounters the same difficulties that Kenneth Burke foresees befalling all debunking arguments, as exemplified by flaws he finds in Thurman W. Arnold's *The Folklore of Capitalism:* "In order to knock the underpinnings from beneath the arguments of his opponents, he perfects a mode of argument that would, if carried out consistently, also knock the underpinnings from beneath his own argument" (*Philosophy* 171). So it is, that if one rejects the relevance of first year writing to writing done in all other college courses, one would, on the same grounds, be compelled to reject the relevance of rhetoric to arguments in all other disciplines. Indeed, what is most striking about the revival of rhetoric in recent years is the extent to which its study has caused people in other fields, notably biology and economics, to reassess their own argument practices. By the same token, the importation of rhetoric to other disciplines through WAC programs caused many teachers in other disciplines to reassess their approach to the teaching of writing. While obviously writing and rhetoric are always to some extent parasitic activities, best understood as writing *about* something or as the rhetoric *of* something, that truism does not gainsay the trans-disciplinary nature of writing and rhetoric, the existence of powerful resemblances and overlaps among their varied applications, and the capacity of rhetoric and writing to alter that to which they attach themselves. Moreover, even if abolitionists were correct in their views about the irrelevance of basic writing to writing done elsewhere in the academy, there remains a powerful rationale for the teaching of writing as "civic discourse," a capacity that will prepare them to discharge their duties as citizens as opposed to preparing them to write elsewhere in college.

To Teach or Not to Teach . . . Propaganda

For many years, writing teachers have been understandably reluctant to invoke the term "propaganda" in the classroom, let alone to teach students what the term might mean. In ordinary usage it is purely a pejorative rather than a descriptive term. Virtually the only time one hears the term invoked is in the context of a partisan dismissal of an opponent's case: "They" use propaganda while "We" offer up reasonable arguments. The term seems too alarmist for everyday analysis of persuasion. The current climate is not entirely healthful when it comes to dealing with loaded issues like propaganda in the classroom. In our own state of Arizona, for example, a bill currently before the state legislature would forbid high school and college instructors from uttering partisan political sentiments in the classroom. While it remains unclear just what a "partisan" comment might entail, students would be encouraged to report what they perceived to be offenses to authorities who would then sort out the matter with the accused. The bill is apparently patterned after similar bills put forward in various other state legislatures in the wake of protests by people like David Horowitz, Dinesh D'Sousa and Ann Coulter claiming that liberal "brainwashing" is commonplace in America's public schools. Little wonder that in such an environment people might be reluctant to examine particular acts of political speech as being possibly propagandistic.

But that said, propaganda describes a very real set of persuasive practices, practices that are to some degree present in many apparently non-propagandistic arguments. As we saw earlier in our continuum of argument practices, there is no such thing as pure persuasion in the real world, and some element of the worst persuasive practices can be found, however faintly, in the best. Our ability to detect those practices at work in any argument, and to confront them in the worst of those arguments is increasingly critical. There is little doubt that we are at present ill-prepared to deal with propaganda in any thoughtful way, largely because the dynamic of propagandistic persuasion is not widely understood—worse yet, that dynamic is widely *mis*understood—and receives little attention in the classroom. More to the point, the use of such practices has arguably increased in recent years as media have taken on new forms optimally suited to the dynamic of propaganda, the temptation to use it has been intensified in an increasingly "winner take all" society, and resistance to it has been weakened by a public education system ever less committed to teaching critical literacy and ever more committed to teaching to various standardized tests.

Before we begin examining just what propaganda is, we will take a moment to say what it is *not.* We do so in the belief that the popular misconceptions about propaganda we alluded to earlier remain one of the major barriers to a contemporary understanding of the phenomenon. One of the most persistent of these misconceptions is the belief that propaganda is for the most part a tool of a totalitarian state. Nazi Germany, Communist China, North Korea, the former Soviet Union, Iraq under Saddam Hussein—in the popular mind, these are the models of propaganda use. In the name of controlling its population, state-run media monopolies feed a constant stream of "official truths," uplifting music and personal messages from "dear leaders" to its people. "Documentaries" featuring various triumphs of the state are artfully constructed so as to merge the political leaders with their myths. Omnipresent billboards and posters feature images of leadership and patriotic quotes from past heroes. Citizens are required to attend state "celebrations" built around displays of military might. Those unreceptive to the propagandistic messages are sent off to state run facilities to be "rehabilitated." The borders are hermetically sealed to prevent citizens from seeking their own truths abroad and to prevent "outside agitators" from telling alternative stories. While this model may be historically accurate, and in a few cases—(e.g., North Korea)—may still be in play, it is today simply too expensive to maintain even for the most determined dictators. Moreover, with the advent of the Internet, it is all but impossible to police. Today propaganda is simultaneously more widespread and less obvious than in days past.

What Is Propaganda? Burke and Ellul

At the end of this section we will lay out in abbreviated form some of the major features of propaganda in order to help people recognize it and better understand its negative impacts. But at this point we will step back and take a broader view of propaganda, using as our guides two thinkers who in our view offer the most thoughtful rhetorical analyses of the phenomenon: Kenneth Burke, particularly his 1941 essay "Rhetoric and Hitler's 'Battle,'" and French social philosopher Jacques Ellul. Perhaps the most useful starting point for this analysis is Burke's distinction between realist rhetoric and magical rhetoric touched on in the first chapter. In making that distinction, it will be recalled, Burke emphasizes the *realistic* capacity of rhetoric to "induce cooperation" among people as opposed to the *magical* power of language to "induce motion in things" (*Grammar* 42). Burke rejects this magical view of language on the realistic grounds that the extraverbal realm, while it depends on language for its comprehension and understanding, is independent of language insofar as it retains the power to thwart our linguistic designs on it. Mere saying, for Burke, does not make it so.

Propaganda can be understood in this context as an attempt to reduce audiences to the state of thinghood and to "induce motion" in them that suits the needs of the propagandist. To that end, the propagandist enterprise is a highly reductive one: reduce the audience to the lowest common denominator and appeal to the basest elements of the human character; infantilize the audience by stressing the godlike omniscience of the propagandist and the audience's dependence on him for security; limit the audience's access to disconfirming information and counter-arguments by excluding them from propagandistic persuasion, by mischaracterizing them, and by limiting opponents' access to audiences. The result of all this, according to social philosopher Jacques Ellul, is what he calls "orthoproxy." Like its etymological cousin, orthodoxy, orthoproxy refers to a more or less unreflective set of beliefs, but insofar as orthoproxy names a largely unconscious motor response to stimuli that "short circuit all thought and decision" (27) it goes well beyond orthodoxy. Ideally, orthoproxy is best achieved by making "the individual live in a separate world; he must not have outside points of reference. He must not be allowed a moment of meditation or reflection in which to see himself. . . ." (17). As we've already suggested, the traditional means of achieving this end, given the massive amounts of money and manpower required to effect it, are no longer seen as viable by most governments. But these days, as we shall see, less draconian versions of it can be achieved relatively easily with much smaller investments of resources.

While at this point in our study Burke requires no introduction, Jacques Ellul most probably does. His major work, *Propaganda: The Formation of Men's Attitudes,* was written more than four decades ago in 1962, but it remains arguably the most thorough and thoughtful treatment of the subject available to students of rhetoric, particularly for its explanation of how modern social forces interact to render us more vulnerable to propagandistic appeals. Indeed, a number of the trends that he cites in that study as responsible for the rise of propaganda up to the mid-twentieth century, seem if anything even more pronounced today. In particular, he suggests that an education system that teaches people how to read, but not how to think critically is a prerequisite for the spread of propaganda. In part this is so simply because a literate—but not critical—population is required for the formation of a mass media that serves as the most efficient transmission of propaganda. In this regard, Ellul's critique of education anticipates Paolo Friere's 1970s critique that helped lay the groundwork for the critical literacy movement. One of the major differences between the two, and the point at which we find ourselves parting ways with Ellul, concerns the latter's skepticism about "mass education" and its ability to reform itself. In general, Ellul's attitudes toward "the masses," mark him very much as a man of his time and his place.

So just what is propaganda? Ellul offers the following, not overly helpful by our lights, definition:

> Propaganda is a set of methods employed by an organized group that wants to bring about the active or passive participation in its actions of a mass of individuals, psychologically unified through psychological manipulations and incorporated in an organization. (61)

While we will not linger over this definition, we would offer one observation about it. Ellul's definition, it seems apparent, could be extended to include such matters as the indoctrination of consumers by advertisers and marketers. But his study focuses on political propaganda and our discussion of him follows suit. We do so even though, as we shall argue shortly, the practices and techniques of propagandists and those of marketers increasingly overlap, more and more propagandists emerge from the fields of advertising, marketing and public relations, and relentless persuasion in the consumer sphere surely renders people more amenable to propagandistic appeals in the political sphere. All that said, the aims and impacts of those who offer pitches on behalf of products and those who offer pitches on behalf of political causes are significantly different.

The major difference between the two spheres has to do with the fact that the sphere of consumption, at least at the level of individual choice, is essentially amoral, while the political sphere is, at all levels, inherently moral. The kinship between the political and the moral spheres has received extended attention most recently from George Lakoff, who begins from the premise that "political perspectives are derived from systems of moral concepts" (41), and exhaustively explores the implications of that assumption for contemporary American politics. Behind questions about health care, abortion, social security, taxation and so forth lie fundamental questions about fairness and happiness and the sanctity of life. To the extent that we bracket off moral questions from political issues and conceive of choice on the model of selecting from among competing brands of beer, we trivialize those issues and potentially alienate citizens from the political process. Lakoff's larger point, however, is not so much that the moral dimension of politics has been ignored in recent years, it is that the moral dimension of politics has been grossly oversimplified in order to manipulate audiences in a manner that by our lights appears to be propagandistic. For moral questions to properly inform political issues, the prevailing moral view must be sufficiently inclusive to ensure that every major moral position gets a hearing and that a moral consensus emerges from some sort of dialectic process. To the extent that political discourse in the public sphere is dominated by a single set of moral beliefs intolerant of dissent, and to the extent that those beliefs are in turn not seen as ends in themselves, but rather as means of controlling those who subscribe to them and achieving interested political ends, the quality of our political decisions and the acuteness of our moral sensibilities will suffer accordingly.

But while Ellul's definition of propaganda acknowledges the use of "psychological manipulations" such as those we've just described as part and parcel of the propagandist enterprise, it does not automatically extend to the practice of lying. Indeed, the belief that a message must be intentionally untruthful to qualify as propaganda is one of the most important barriers to its recognition. While propagandists may on occasion resort to the spread of "disinformation," the risks of being caught out in an outright lie are sufficiently great to discourage grand scale lying. The ideal propaganda message would be full of accurate facts saturated in speculative innuendo, repeated constantly over an extended period of time until the innuendo takes on the character of fact. In the language of early advertisers, "Repetition is reputation," a formula that works largely because of our tendency to mistake familiarity for certainty, the "film of custom" for truth.

To borrow again from Lakoff, propaganda is more a matter of "framing" information so as to induce people to draw desired conclusions than it is a matter of feeding people faulty information and insulating them against truthful information. Framing is typically conceived of as the careful selection of a vocabulary that prejudges the issues under discussion. The tacit metaphoric implications of word choices will tilt the audience in the desired direction. To use one of Lakoff's favorite examples, to couch a discussion of tax policy in the rubric of "tax relief" as opposed to "tax cuts" implies that taxes are an oppressive burden on the taxpayer; while there may be a limit on how much one may wish to "cut" taxes, there is no limit on how much one may seek "relief" from taxes.

But for our purposes, framing may be extended from matters of vocabulary and metaphor to the medium through which a message is received. In today's highly sophisticated media, issues are often literally framed by the scene in which they are presented. To cite one contemporary example, "Hannity and Colmes," a long-running Fox TV News program, features a conservative point of view (Hannity) "balanced" by a liberal point of view (Colmes). But even a cursory viewing of the program will convince some that a heavy thumb disturbs the balance. Hannity has the look of a network anchorman; he's a vigorous, blustery fellow, full of certitude who dominates his supposed liberal foe Colmes, a sepulchral fellow with the look of a small market weatherman and a tendency to mumble, who often offers up arguments with an air of wistful hopelessness. Colmes appears seldom to score many points in their exchanges, let alone come away with many wins. No "lies" need be told in such a format because ineffectual truths work just fine.

In framing information, propagandists may distort its significance, exaggerate or understate its future implications, obscure or disguise the intentions of the speaker, or attribute doubtful motivations (usually the propagandist's own, least presentable, motivations (Ellul 58) to their adversaries. Like some popular TV shows, propagandists love "stories ripped from the headlines," converting current events, particularly spectacular events that conform to popular myths (45), to crises demanding the attention of the masses. In Ellul's words,

> Obviously, propaganda can succeed only when man feels challenged. It can have no influence when the individual is stabilized, relaxing in the midst of total security. Neither past events nor great metaphysical problems challenge the average individual, the ordinary man of our times. He is not sensitive to what is tragic in life and is not anguished by a question that God might put to him; he does not feel challenged except by current events, political and economic. Therefore, propaganda must start with current events. (44)

To repeat: we do not share, here or elsewhere, Ellul's disdain for "the ordinary man of our times," but his contention that news is a constant source of propagandistic fodder seems, if anything, truer today in the age of the 24/7 news cycle than when he made it more than four decades ago. Some distortions of current events are, to be sure, inevitably introduced in the reporting of those events by mainstream news media. But such media represent a dwindling share of what passes for news today. For most of the serious propagandizing taking place today, we can look to the rapidly growing segment of news broadcasting that is "secondary" to journalistic news. This is the world of "Hannity and Colmes," of pundits and political consultants, bloggers, editorialists, and foundation policy wonks who spin and interpret the news, through various forms of infotainment that are far cheaper to produce than actual news coverage. One way to gauge the propagandistic slant of such programs is to note the extent to which they are conducted "in the language of *indignation,* a tone which is almost always the mark of propaganda" (Ellul 58). In extreme cases—think "talk radio"—such programs appeal to the crudest feelings such as "hate, hunger . . . pride" (38) and fear to stir its audience's passions.

Burke echoes many of the above points in his discussion of Hitler, whose rhetoric is a model of "impure" rhetoric on Burke's continuum.

In the introduction to his review of *Mein Kampf*, the occasion of his essay, Burke simultaneously calls attention to the impurities of Hitler's rhetoric and the responsibility of rhetoricians to articulate the dynamic of that rhetoric. Reviewers have an obligation to analyze "exasperating, even nauseating" (*Philosophy* 191) books like Hitler's. He likens a hasty, dismissive review of *Mein Kampf* to burning it on a pyre, ala Hitler himself. In so doing, Burke argues, we miss an opportunity to discover how Hitler has managed to concoct a medicine so gladly swallowed by many millions of people, and thereby to "forestall the concocting of similar medicine in America" (191). Burke goes on to point out that while Americans might believe that our virtues will protect us from Hitler's spell, it is in fact "the *conflict among our vices*" (192), the parliamentary wrangling of our differences—that is, rhetoric itself—that protects us from the charms of Hitler's "perfect" system, his unified field theory of human nature.

One of the themes in Burke's analysis echoed twenty-five years later in Ellul's is the association between modern propaganda and the techniques of marketing and advertising. Modern propaganda, as opposed to its earliest manifestations as "agit-prop" or invective used to stir up partisan fervor, is considerably more subtle and scientific. As Burke notes of Hitler, he possesses the "'rationality' of a skilled advertising man planning a new sales campaign. Politics, he says, must be sold like soap—and soap is not sold in a trance" (216). Ellul, by the same token, characterizes the propagandist as "more and more the technician who treats his patients in various ways, but keeps himself cold and aloof, selecting his words and actions for purely technical reasons" (25). What was characteristic of propaganda in the mid-twentieth century seems today to be paradigmatic. Thanks to technological advances, the convergences between propaganda and marketing are even more pronounced in today's highly mediated environment. The line between the two activities is ever less bright and ever more frequently crossed by an "occupationally psychotic" core of people who spin candidates, policies, wars, and sport utility vehicles with equal aplomb using many of the same techniques.

One of the most important lessons propagandists learn from advertisers concerns techniques for carefully dividing one's audience, an art perfected by legions of demographic and psychographic researchers employed by marketers. Propaganda is, to use Ellul's social scientific term, "partitioned" (212), or to use Burke's more traditional rhetorical descriptor for "advantage-seeking" rhetoric, propaganda is "addressed." In a famous speech Burke gave in 1935 to the American Writer's Congress, he described the propagandist's parasitic relationship to his audience as follows: "As a propagandizer, it is not his work to convince the convinced, but to plead with the unconvinced, which requires him to use *their* vocabulary, *their* values, *their* symbols, insofar as this is possible" (Simons 271-72). Which is why propagandists, like advertisers, study audiences so closely, so that their messages will be expressed in the appropriate vocabularies, values and symbols that will find their mark with finely discriminated groups whose needs, desires and fears are scrupulously mapped.

In a closed, homogeneous society, like Hitler's Germany, this means that propaganda can be channeled through a single medium to appeal to a massive group of "ins," whose needs, anxieties and aspirations, not to mention their myths and fantasies, are exhaustively understood, at the expense of the minority "outs" who represent the ins' worst fears about themselves. But in a pluralistic society like America, this means that propaganda, to be effective, must have access to multiple outlets for custom-crafted messages targeting diverse constituencies. Ironically thus, our apparently free and robust press, and the countless channels of information it provides, may prove as invaluable to propagandists as it has to advertisers in dividing and conquering audiences.

As this last remark suggests, however invaluable a free press may be to combating propaganda, it is only a necessary, not a sufficient condition for resistance. As Ellul points out, "All propaganda has to set its group off from all other groups" (212) which is done by ensuring that every group has media outlets devoted to its beliefs. "They learn more and more that their group is right, that its actions are justified" (213) while rival groups are repeatedly affirmed to be wrongheaded and wrongly motivated:

> This criticism of one's neighbor, which is not heard by that neighbor, is known to those inside the group that expresses it. The anti-Communist will be constantly more convinced of the evilness of the Communist, and vice versa. As a result, people ignore each other more and more. They cease altogether to be open to an exchange of reason, arguments, points of view. (213)

More than forty years later, with the advent of digital and satellite TV offering hundreds of channels of information, the Internet with its numberless portals and blog sites, not to mention talk radio, Ellul's critique would seem to be even more salient. We truly do live, as Burke suggests, in "the state of Babel, after the Fall," and to the extent that modern media multiply and harden divisions among a citizenry, they render the rhetorical antidote to such a state—something like Rorty and Oakeshott's conversation of mankind—that much less efficacious.

The partitioning problem described above is compounded when one takes into account the indirect effects of media on those elected to represent the citizenry. Because of ever escalating cost of winning elections, due primarily to the high cost of buying media time and producing political ads that themselves exhibit increasingly propagandistic tendencies, office holders are more and more beholden to special interests willing to subsidize their campaigns. Fealty to special interests in turn makes it increasingly difficult for representative bodies to transcend their partisan wrangling and harmonize their interests in the name of the public good. The oft remarked decrease in comity and productive conversation in the American Congress is a sign that Ellul's partitioning model has been extended from the electorate to our elected bodies. Indeed, Burke suggests that this has always been the case and that the changing nature of media may have simply exacerbated a chronic affliction within elected bodies.

Burke's conclusions about the underlying causes of legislative divisions come in the context of his discussion of Hitler's psychology, a discussion conducted in the language of Freud. Burke argues that Hitler's own "parliamentary self" was deeply riven by conflicts among the id, ego and superego. Hitler in turn projected the prodigious inner struggles besetting his personality onto the world, in particular the deeply divided parliament of the collapsing Habsurg Empire. Imposing his totalitarian vision on the world represented a magical cure for his inner divisions. All evidences of heterogeneity, of difference, hence became for Hitler symptoms of "democracy fallen upon evil days" (200). The inevitably messy democratic political process with its emphasis on debate, compromise, and consensus is converted by Hitler into a "Babel of voices, and by the method of associative mergers, *using ideas as images,* it became tied up in the Hitler rhetoric with 'Babylon,' Vienna as the city of poverty, prostitution, immorality, coalitions, half-measures, incest, democracy (i.e., majority rule leading to 'lack of personal responsibility'). . . ." (200). On some of the more rabid talk radio programs, one can hear similar analyses conducted in similar tones of righteous indignation and moral outrage by today's news fabulists. According to Burke the newspaper editorialists of his day followed the form, if not the pitch of Hitler's rhetoric, a remark that seems still to resonate:

> Every conflict among the parliamentary spokesmen represents a corresponding conflict among the material interests of the groups for whom they are speaking. But Hitler did not discuss the babel from this angle. He discussed it on a purely symptomatic basis. The strategy of our orthodox press, in thus ridiculing the cacophonous verbal output of Congress, is obvious: by thus centering attack upon the symptoms of business conflict, as they reveal themselves on the dial of political wrangling, and leaving the underlying cause, the business conflicts themselves, out of the case, they can gratify the very public they would otherwise alienate; namely, the businessmen who are the activating members of their reading public. (201)

The net result of the above scenario is to weaken public faith in government. Insofar as rules, institutions, principles, and traditions of government may limit propagandists' power or impede a particular program they wish to enact, they would not view this as necessarily a bad thing. Hence Ellul's declaration that insofar as citizens are "uninterested in political matters" they (the state and/or those who control it) will be left with a "free hand" (191). But at the same time, there is a point of diminishing returns beyond which continuing to weaken public confidence in government may not be in the self interest of those who control, or wish to control, levers of governmental power. If public dismay about government deepens without check, propaganda "has absolutely no effect on those who live in . . . indifference or skepticism" (190). How then do political propagandists simultaneously undermine confidence in government as an institution while expanding those governmental powers that serve their ends?

The trick, according to both Burke and Ellul, is to personalize government, identifying it increasingly with the personality or personalities of its leadership. According to Ellul, "The cult of the hero is the absolutely necessary complement of the massification of society" (172). Through the hero, Ellul argues, the average person "lives vicariously" (172), whether the hero happens to be a movie celebrity or president. In the political realm, Ellul sees this theme play out most clearly in the political parties, whose propagandists (or PR people if one prefers) exploit "the inclination of the masses to admire personal power. . . . by creating the image of a leader and investing it with attributes of omnipresence and omniscience. . . ." (217). To buttress his contention here, Ellul cites the 1952 American presidential race in which Eisenhower successfully exploited this inclination at the expense of Adlai Stevenson, the quintessential aloof intellectual, who viewed his ideas, not his persona, as the key to his claims on the presidency.

Ellul, in passing, notes how Fascism repeatedly claimed to have "restored Personality to its place of honor" (172), a point that in turn looms large in Burke's analysis of Hitler's propaganda. In particular, Hitler is skillful at "spiritualizing" or "ethicizing" the material bonds linking different strata of society by "personalizing" such links, making it "crass to treat employers and employees as different *classes* with a corresponding difference in the classification of their interests. Instead, relations between employer and employee must be on the 'personal' basis of leader and follower. . . ." (217). (By the same token, those who today point out inequities among social classes are charged with instigating "class warfare," while the general populace is inundated with books, tapes and seminars on "leadership," a mystical quality that is rewarded with ever more fabulous sums of money.) The vocabulary Hitler uses in effecting such magical transformations is the prestige terminology of religion, a terminology he hijacks with impunity.

> Here again is where Hitler's corrupt use of religious patterns comes to the fore. Church thought, being primarily concerned with matters of the "personality," with problems of moral betterment, naturally, and I think rightly, stresses as a necessary feature, the act of will upon the part of the individual. Hence its resistance to a purely "environmental" account of human ills. Hence its emphasis upon the "person." Hence its proneness to seek a noneconomic explanation of economic phenomena. (201)

This personalization of all relationships within the Nazi state is eventually extended to the image of the state itself. In the interest of achieving peace and harmony "the wrangle of the parliamentary is to be stilled by the giving of *one* voice to the whole people, this to be the 'inner voice' of Hitler, made uniform throughout the German boundaries, as leader and people were completely identified with each other" (207). Hitler thus offers the German people "the *bad* filling of a *good* need" (210), by perverting the religious desire for ultimacy. In effecting this unification Hitler turns to criticism of a peculiarly propagandistic sort. "Not criticism in the 'parliamentary' sense of doubt, of hearkening to the opposition and attempting to mature a policy in the light of counter-policies; but the 'unified' kind of criticism that simply seeks for conscious ways of making one's position more 'efficient,' more thoroughly itself" (211). The world Hitler creates through propaganda, censoring opposition, excluding contradiction, identifying the essential unity of the state with the "blood" of the Aryan race, is Ellul's propagandistic dystopia, a hermetically sealed world in which the individual has no "outside points of reference."

For all that propaganda is ordinarily identified with rhetoric, both Ellul's and Burke's understanding of the term renders it more of an anti-rhetoric. What happens to propaganda in Hitler's Germany and Ellul's Western democracies is what happens to any term allowed to become too "thoroughly itself." In Burke's language, it succumbs to the paradox of purity and becomes different in kind from every instance of the term from which the ultimate definition has been built. It simply reverses the process by which we earlier arrived at the concept of pure persuasion, eliminating every hint of sacrifice and standoffishness, of dialectic and invention, until it is purely "addressed" and every potential interlocutor has been transformed into a motion.

To better understand just why propaganda may have become a more pervasive force in our advanced democracy supposedly immune to its charms, we return to Ellul and an important point he makes about the workings of Western democracy. "For the average Westerner, the will of the people is sacred, and the government that fails to represent that will is an abominable dictatorship" (129). In order for any democratic government to maintain its legitimacy, it must maintain popular support in the form of public opinion, electoral support or both. But public opinion, as anyone who follows polling data knows, is famously fickle. Support for an administration's or party's economic or military policies waxes and wanes depending on how good or bad the news may be on the economic or military front. Yet to be effective, policies must be stable and policy makers need to take the long view; if the news runs against them—and inevitably it will run against them for a time—they must modify or even reverse their policies, accept political defeat or persuade people that their policies are either actually working or just about to work.

The conundrum for politicians is neatly captured by Ellul, who notes that every administration, whatever the party affiliation, "gives the impression of obeying public opinion—after first having built that public opinion. The point is to make the masses demand of the government what the government has already decided to do" (132). In some cases we may—at times correctly—attribute a sinister motive to these clandestine attempts to influence public opinion. The policies being promoted may in fact benefit special interests at the expense of the public good. But even those policies which are in the public interest will face many of the same difficulties as those faced by corrupt practices. The fact that civically sound practices may be easier to defend on rational grounds does not guarantee their popularity or gainsay the need, at least in the eyes of their proponents, to utilize propaganda on their behalf. Hence the inevitability of propaganda.

Propaganda, thus, is not something we can hope to eradicate or, in Burke's parlance, debunk. We can slow its spread and push it toward more legitimate forms of persuasion by critique and questioning. Like advertising and marketing practices with which it is so intimately linked, propaganda too can be more or less pure, but only if it fails in its cruder forms—advertisements disguised as government press releases touting the benefits of controversial programs, industry-sponsored faux research selectively cited by government officials to support dubious policies, fake journalists lobbing softball questions to government officials, real news commentators offering paid testimonials in support of programs and policies without acknowledging that their support is paid for, and politicians holding "town hall" meetings in Potemkin village settings with carefully selected participants asking scripted questions-—thanks to real journalists doing their work and/ or because sophisticated audiences have learned how to "discount" suspicious claims and how to critically question symbolic actions.

To assist in this regard, we offer the following brief summary of propagandistic practices.

Propaganda in a Nutshell

Before we consider the symptoms and dynamic of propagandistic practice, we offer the following caveat: The differences between propaganda and other more legitimate forms of rhetorical practice are differences of degree. Every rhetorical practice is more or less pure or impure and none of the following can be applied categorically to a given act. If one were to reduce the whole thing to a soundbite, our view of propaganda might be dubbed "Advertising on steroids for political causes." Many of the following conditions characterize ordinary political discourse as well as propaganda. Determining when ordinary political discourse becomes propaganda requires "parliamentary wrangling" among people of various political persuasions. Consequently one is perhaps best advised to think of these conditions as conversational gambits rather than taxonomic traits.

1. The dissemination of political propaganda requires that one own *a* stage if not *the* stage. Without a stage, one is powerless not only to disseminate one's message to a mass audience but to frame the debate so as to undercut competing messages. While not all who disseminate a message need be card-carrying members of an organization or even privy to a plan to engage in the spread of propaganda, those who originate and craft a propagandistic message must do so consciously in the name of a belief system. In the present scheme of things, propaganda often spreads like gossip in an oral culture, through uncritical amplification of consciously crafted propagandistic messages that originate in mass media and then proliferate over the Internet, on talk radio, call-in TV shows, letters to the editor and so forth. Increasingly, the direction of that movement is reversible, as enterprising bloggers initiate propagandistic messages that mimic the messages of the "official" leaders.

2. Like advertisers, propagandists are exacting "partitioners" of markets whose messages often reflect extensive research into the psychological and demographic makeup of their audience. They rely heavily on Burke's "cunning" in seeking advantage for their ideas, speaking to the fears, wishes, and desires peculiar to their target audience in an attempt to circumvent rational consideration and to induce "motion" in those they address.

Their appeals rest less on evidence and reasons than on "common sense" that "goes without saying." Also like advertisers, propagandists are adept at persuading large audiences ("You") that they are speaking to them individually (*you*) and persuading them to hew to a party line in the name of thinking for themselves.

3. However much the techniques used to create and market propaganda are borrowed from advertising, crucial differences remain. Advertisers by and large purchase their stage in straightforward cash transactions. Propagandists, meanwhile, by and large use the public media, in particular the news media, to disseminate their message. Also, advertising is typically presented overtly as advertising, while propaganda is rarely presented as propaganda. To the extent that an audience knows a message is propaganda, the effectiveness of the message is likely diminished. At times, propagandists will go to extreme measures—(e.g., planting fake news stories in mainstream media or creating faux third party organizations, and so forth) to deliver their message while disguising their intentions.

4. The text of the propagandistic message is typically derived from current events. Often it focuses on a problem or crisis that grabs public attention by virtue of its spectacular nature and/or its conformity with a popular mythic theme—(e.g. A Rugged Individual [David] takes on Big Government [Goliath]). The material consequences of the problem are less important to propagandists than its symbolic resonance. (In some cases, in fact, the problem is manufactured in order to divert attention from other problems that are of considerably greater public consequence but which are less tractable and/or reflect less well on those doing the propagandizing.)

5. By hooking on to a problem that has already aroused public attention, propagandists can amplify the themes that animate their message. By framing the meaning of problematic events in keeping with their ideological themes, they can persuade the public that their interpretation of a singular event is in fact a confirmation of an underlying order. Assuming a solution is posed for the problem—as opposed simply to blaming another ideology for the problem—it will reflect the propagandists'

ideology more clearly than it will fit the problem. Often the problem will be reframed as a moral problem and the proposed solution will be more spiritual or moral than pragmatic in nature. Consequently propaganda will shift our attention to the personal dimension of the problem and away from the environmental causes of the problem. In its most virulent forms, propagandistic solutions call for the punishment, exclusion, or impeachment of scapegoats whose behaviors justify the tone of indignation or moral outrage favored by propagandists.

6. Propagandists evidence faint enthusiasm for "self interference" or "proving opposites." Their arguments are often constructed in secret with little input from diverse sources; they distort, demonize, or entirely exclude opposing views on the topic at hand; they speak to the lowest common denominator in their audience. If propagandistic arguments run up against inconvenient facts or persuasive counter-arguments once they are loosed on the world, those who propose these arguments will not waver, nor will they offer justification. They will repeat the argument endlessly, displaying a heroic fixity of purpose that passes for leadership in some quarters. (Burke notes that Hitler refused to alter a single item of his original 25-point, Nazi platform because he "felt that the fixity of the platform was more important for propagandistic purposes than any revision of his slogans could be, even though the revisions in themselves had much to be said in their favor"[212].)

7. Whereas propaganda in closed societies is often fashioned around a "cult of personality," propaganda in open societies tends to be fashioned around a "cult of celebrity." The biographies of those who speak in the name of an ideology will be tortured to fit the myths that underlie that ideology, and they will come to personify the ideology in much the way that movie stars often come to be identified with the characters they play.

8. The more agitated an audience, the more effective propaganda can be. For its reception, propaganda requires an unsettled, anxious, even fearful audience. A sense of crisis, of being under attack, renders an audience more tolerant of one-sided arguments and reduction of one's opponents to cartoon figures. Propagandists may invent crises, but more typically they simply

> gin up actual problems of finite proportions into apocalyptic problems of gargantuan proportions. Internal critics of their propagandizing are then readily lumped in with their amorphous enemies.

That then, is propaganda in a nutshell. In the interest of ourselves being "fair and balanced," we like to invite our students to apply the above observations not just to the practices of the present administration, but to the films of Michael Moore and to shows on Air America as well.

Notes

1. One of the best known recent examples of the phenomenon cited here whereby a researcher relies heavily on anecdotal and narrative evidence to establish quantitative categorical judgments about her subject involves the work of Deborah Tannen. While most of her peers in the field of sociolinguistics support the "direction" of her findings about differences in the ways males and females communicate, a number take issue with the quantity of impact and universality of those differences. To conclude from the finding, say, that males are five or ten per cent more likely than females to respond to a particular situation in a particular way that there are categorical differences in their responses (i.e., that they exemplify male and female "styles" of response) appears to overstate the matter. For a fuller rhetorical analysis of Tannen's methodology, see Ramage's *Twentieth Century American Success Rhetoric: How to Construct a Suitable Self.* Carbondale: Southern Illinois UP, 2005. 167-85.

4 Introduction to Best Practices

In this chapter we will review some approaches to the teaching of writing that either feature argumentation or may be most readily adapted to feature argumentation. While those who focus on, say, liberatory rhetoric in their writing classes may not think of themselves as proponents of argument pedagogy, their approach lends itself to an argument focus and indeed requires some attention to strategies of argument to be successful. Any approach that both facilitates the teaching of argument and involves an innovative approach to teaching writing will be included here under best practices. But before reviewing those practices, we offer the following brief overview of principles basic to any successful writing course and of the practices themselves.

What Works in Teaching Writing

As we have previously suggested on several occasions, few researchers in the field of rhetoric and composition continue to focus their energies on empirical evaluation of classroom practices. In denominating a particular approach a best practice, thus, we are not so much commenting on the pedagogy necessarily associated with the practice or the results achieved by the practice. In fact, we know little about the results obtained from these practices other than those reported anecdotally by their proponents. We favor some practices over others mostly because they resonate with our own rationale for teaching writing in the first place and because they don't conflict with basic principles of teaching that in our view underlie any sound writing class.

In articulating our rationale for teaching writing and our principles of instruction, we would cite two works that have particularly influenced our thinking. The first, James Crosswhite's *The Rhetoric of Reason: Writing and the Attractions of Argument,* offers an extended philosophical brief for grounding writing courses in argumentation.

Drawing on the work of a wide range of philosophers including Plato, Aristotle, Heidegger, Perelman and Olbrechts-Tyteca, Levinas, Cavell, Habermas, Schrag, and Gadamer, Crosswhite develops the concept of a "rhetoric of reason" and positions it as an alternative to the radical skepticism of deconstruction as exemplified by Derrida and de Man. (In process, Crosswhite also points out places where Derrida may serve as a support as well as foil for a rhetoric of reason). The book recommends itself to teachers for a number of reasons. It makes a strong case for the efficacy and importance of general education in contemporary American higher education, it establishes a framework for understanding argument primarily as an act, a means of addressing practical problems and making choices, as opposed to a set of propositions, and it sets out a way for squaring non-essentialist views of truth and identity with a sense of responsibility for one's choices. Crosswhite's book addresses a number of the theoretical, philosophical, and pedagogical issues touched on briefly in this book in a much more comprehensive way. While there are distinct points of difference between our viewpoint and that of Crosswhite's (in particular we demur from the book's starkly pessimistic conclusion), it offers something of a macro-view of our rationale for the teaching of argument in writing classes.

George Hillocks's *Teaching Writing as Reflective Practice,* meanwhile, offers a more fine grained, micro-view of our pedagogical philosophy. While Hillocks and his methods for understanding writing instruction are currently out of season among many in the field of rhetoric and composition, the conclusions he draws from his work and his humane application of the principles he derives from it remain relevant to our enterprise. As noted earlier, many who scorn Hillocks's work and methods continue to hold assumptions about how best to teach writing that are grounded in and most readily justified by his work. Indeed, over the years when explaining and defending the function of our writing programs ("Why don't you stress grammar and the 'fundamentals' of writing more in your courses?"), and securing resources for those programs from upper administrators, academics whose backgrounds are largely in the sciences and social sciences, Hillocks's work resonates in a particularly powerful way. At the risk of oversimplifying that work, we enumerate the following principles of classroom practice derived largely from that work or from the extension of his principles to our own situations.

1. *Active learning is much more effective than passive learning.* Some of the entailments of this principle include the following:

a. *Keep lecturing (what Hillocks refers to as "presentational mode" of teaching) to a minimum.* If you must lecture, and there are times when most of us feel such a need, keep it short, fifteen minutes or less. As much as possible ensure that your lecture grows out of your students' questions rather than an a priori agenda based on your need to "cover" all relevant material.

b. *Build the course as much as possible around inquiry rather than the assimilation of information or free expression.* In the case of argument-focused classes this may well mean more attention given over to local issues that allow students to deal with primary as well as secondary sources. Inquiry-based learning focuses on "basic strategies of inquiry [that] appear in every field" (100) rather than specialized strategies of inquiry. In the case of an argument-based course, an inquiry approach would stress the following: making an inventory of prior knowledge and assumptions about an issue; forming a hypothesis, a "warranted assertion," or tentative major claim; testing that tentative claim by gathering new information through reading, questioning, surveying, and so forth, and by critical discussion of one's claim with peers in the class.

c. *Stress peer group learning and independent study in the classroom.* Inquiry is something that should be going on inside as well as outside the class. Hillocks uses the term "environmental teaching" to designate "teaching that creates environments to induce and support active learning of complex strategies that students are not capable of using on their own" (55).

2. *Transparency is as important to good teaching as it is to good government.* Make clear your expectations and goals for each class, and for every assignment—papers and inquiry activities alike. Encourage the wide sharing of drafts and activities throughout the process. When possible, present earlier student responses to the assignment to clarify expectations and criteria. Offer feedback that is specific and at the same time global (e.g., tell them they have not offered sufficient evidence in support of a particular reason, or their warrant for the reason is unacceptable to their audience v. "There's faulty parallelism in sentence three.").

3. *Set high expectations and create mindful processes that help students realize those expectations.* One of the theoretical mainstays in Hillocks's approach is Vygotsky, in particular his notion of the "zone of proximal development" (ZPD). The ZPD defines the area between one's actual capabilities and those potential capabilities that are achievable with thoughtful guidance. In this case, "thoughtful guidance" would include classroom activities; in particular, opportunities for invention work both oral and written, intermediate peer and teacher feedback on written work, and sequences of drafts based on that feedback.

4. *Practice what you preach; be a learner in the classroom.* Hillocks encourages teachers to practice an inquiry-based approach to their own classroom. In communicating your objectives to students prior to undertaking an assignment or activity, you are in effect offering an hypothesis about what will work in achieving your end. Pay attention to what actually happens and test your hypothesis. When something does not work, figure out why and rethink your assumptions.

5. *Accommodate students' different learning styles and intelligences as best you can.* Use multiple channels for gathering, assimilating and presenting information. If you don't have a computer-mediated classroom, do what you can to encourage the use of visual media and computers outside the classroom.

6. *Play to your strengths as a teacher.* (This is not so much from Hillocks as from our own experiences.) Just as we do what we can to accommodate our students' diversity, we need to respect our own uniqueness. Some of us are indeed brilliant lecturers—though in our experience, fewer than think so. Some of us structure wonderful group assignments and activities. Some of us are marvelous working with students one on one. Whatever you do best as a teacher, whatever made teaching exciting for you in the first place, find a way to use your strengths.

Best Practices

What follows is by no means an exhaustive list of ways to incorporate argument into the classroom. It is a compilation of best practices. First and foremost, this section is meant to help teachers use argument as a means of engaging the world. Anyone who has ever taught a class that asks students to write arguments knows that there is no one "best" way to go about structuring the class. There are many ways, and we seek to enumerate a number of them.

For instructors who are new to the field of argument, this section offers a map of the pedagogical terrain. For more experienced instructors, it offers a reserve of ideas on how to re-structure existing classes. If we implore our students to constantly question their assumptions about their arguments, we must also be willing to question our assumptions about how we teach argument.

The entries that follow represent an eclectic approach to rhetoric and argument as different means of viewing the world and not as ends that can be achieved by merely exercising some formula (although at times scholars who advocate for their use do suggest very formulaic processes). Some best practices emanate from the desire of instructors to help their students move beyond the isolated position of self and locate themselves within the larger context. These identity-based social endeavors include liberatory rhetoric, feminist argument and service learning.

Liberatory rhetoric is an educational movement that arose as a reaction against passive student models of education. It was instrumental in bringing to the forefront issues of representation in the classroom and acknowledging that education is not a neutral process—ideology is always being transferred along with knowledge. When incorporated into the argument classroom, liberatory rhetoric openly politicizes the classroom, places the culture at the center of discussion, and calls on students to critically question the course content and the experiences that they bring to the table as well as the ideologies that they hold as writers. Writing is a vehicle that is used in multiple ways to prepare students to engage critically with the world around them.

Feminist argument also challenges the status quo. By seeking to replace the zero sum, winner/loser construction of argument with a more ethical approach, feminists call us to use less aggressive and more cooperative strategies, especially focusing on the importance of listening, understanding, and dialogue in argumentative exchange. In the classroom, feminist approaches to argument can be implemented incrementally and don't require wholesale adoption.

The next entry, service learning, sees language as a social activity that is at once interpretative and constructive. In much the same way that liberatory rhetoric aims to help students become self-actualized, service learning seeks to foster an early appreciation for civic engagement. In many cases, this manifests itself in a linking of writing classes with on-site, project-based interactions with local businesses or organizations; however, this is not a necessity for service learning. Prolonged engagement with and research on a local issue could be substituted. Service learning offers students an embedded way of experiencing rhetorical situations with real exigencies and constraints to consider. It also exposes students to a side of academia that is not walled in by disciplinarity.

Much like service learning, Writing Across the Curriculum (WAC) has as its goal the softening of disciplinary boundaries. It holds as its central principle that students learn more when they grapple with course content in writing. For instructors who are not in the field of English, WAC provides a rationale for why writing should be utilized across the disciplines. WAC posits that argument is the cornerstone of a university education. Disciplines are distinguished primarily by the forms of argument and rules of evidence they favor. In fields not traditionally viewed as writing intensive, writing activities can be used to reinforce disciplinary principles and acquaint students with the methods of inquiry that are validated by their field.

The rapid increase of technological possibility has forced teachers to reassess the role and impact of writing technologies on argument. Computers and writing is an incorporation of a new writing technology into the field of argument. Since contemporary students have been reared at the keyboard, it is important to take into account the literacies that they are bringing to the classroom. The technology can also expand the bounds of what is meant by writing, especially when hypertextual writing is used in the classroom to re-envision argument. Advances in technology have also impacted research methods. The reliability of sources and authorial ownership of ideas are among the issues fraught with controversy.

Visual rhetoric also focuses on ways that technologies are impacting our lives. Visual rhetoric attempts to broaden discussions of argument to include consideration of the visual images that increasingly accompany or displace words. Even though visual images are more memorable and thus more resonant than words, their impact often goes unremarked. There are embedded messages in visual media, and recognizing those messages require us to rethink the way we process information. Through exploration of production and consumption of visual texts, students can become more aware of the subtle ways that images convey persuasive messages.

Why should argument, and to a greater extent rhetoric, be deemed worthy of this level of attention in the classroom? We should teach rhetoric to protect ourselves from rhetoric. Persuasive messages are all around us. They make up the amalgam of our collective selves. The better we—and our students—are able to identify the messages that we receive for what they are, points of view and not as monolithic truths, we will better be able to function in the world of "Babel after the fall." This best practices section will be most useful if it is used as a jumping-off point to further exploration of what these theoretical, pedagogical positions have to offer in the context of a particular class. These summaries of practices highlight the diversity among practitioners. Texts that best demonstrate how these practices intermingle with argument have been included in the "for further reading" sections that follow each best practices topic; those of particular relevancy have been annotated for you.

Liberatory Rhetoric

The concept of liberatory rhetoric, also commonly referred to as critical pedagogy or critical rhetoric, has been defined in composition studies in a number of ways. The idea of liberatory pedagogy springs from the work of Paulo Freire. Freire, a Brazilian educator, believed that the "banking system of education"—a model of education that depicts students as empty vessels needing to be filled by knowledgeable teachers (*Pedagogy* 72)—contributed to political oppression by conditioning people not to question. The central role of a liberatory rhetoric is to help students recognize the inherently political nature of education. This approach assumes that the world is unjust and that the various means by which power is accrued, maintained, and distributed are unmarked and often unremarked. Thus, education is not neutral; teachers and students possess assumptions, expectations, and values of the "dominant ideology" that often go unaddressed in the classroom (Shor and Friere 13). Because political opinions are intentionally and unintentionally transferred from teacher to student during the learning process, students need to assume responsibility for understanding the enculturating nature of educational systems for interrogating the assumptions behind received knowledge. Freire's *Pedagogy of the*

Oppressed grew out of work with illiterate Brazilian peasants, a truly oppressed group, and located the space for a true liberatory education in grassroots efforts—outside of the control state sponsors of literacy. Consequently, Freire's ideas must be modified with the needs of contemporary American college writing students in mind.

Throughout the late 1970s and early 1980s, Friere's work was influential in the field of rhetoric and composition, as teachers tried to incorporate progressive theory into the seemingly apolitical work of writing instruction (Bizzell 319). The most useful component of Friere's theory for teachers of argument is his stress on critically examining problematic interactions on a local level (Shor, *When* 46). Instead of focusing on the abstract dialectical interactions of ideas, values, and concepts, Freire calls for a focus on "generative themes," the focal points of discussion that ground the abstract. The subject matter comes directly from the everyday artifacts of the specific community within the given culture (Freire 97). In the case of Freire's Brazilian peasants, this meant starting with the perceptions of drinking water rather than the concept of social justice.

For contemporary American teachers of writing, Freire's generative themes might involve sustained interaction with issues that interest students, such as tuition increases or representations of race on television. Such focus allows students to act upon ideas rather than passively consuming the ideas of another and fosters an environment where education is about self-actualization. As Ann Berthoff argues in "The Intelligent Eye and the Thinking Hand," it is important to "[teach] composition as a mode of thinking and a way of learning" and to "avail ourselves of that incomparable resource, the minds of our students . . ." (41). Stated another way, "subjectivity is a synonym for motivation . . . material that is of subjective concern is by definition important to those studying it" (Shor, *Freire* 24). Thus emphasis on critical thought about local issues will likely eliminate uncritical rehashing of hackneyed topics, such as abortion and the death penalty, and tap into the imaginations of students as a starting place for rhetorical invention (Berthoff 42).

Liberatory rhetoric is not without its critics. Some scholars question whether overtly politicizing the classroom necessarily empowers students. Elizabeth Ellsworth's "Why Doesn't this Feel Empowering?: Working Through the Repressive Myths of Critical Pedagogy," offers a comprehensive critique of liberatory pedagogy. Central to her argument is the belief that most courses touting liberatory goals have unstated political agendas behind the call for "critical consciousness," thus also creating an environment where a particular political ideology is advanced at the expense of others. David Lazere questions another premise of liberatory rhetoric, asserting that

> leftists err grievously in rejecting . . . a restored emphasis on basic skills and knowledge which might be a force for liberation—not oppression—if administered with commonsense, openness and to cultural pluralisms, and an application of basics toward critical thinking, particularly about sociopolitical issues, rather than rote memorizing. (9)

Lazere's qualm is relevant; if one is to overcome the systematic power of society, presumably, s/he must be able to use the discourse of power properly to communicate with whomever has authority. Even ardent supporters of liberatory rhetoric see potential problems with its proposed ends. Patricia Bizzell, for example, is critical of the suggestion that the awareness of inequality "automatically also awakens a desire for progressive political change" (320). Acknowledging the agency of students necessarily affords them the power to remain static, especially if they realize that their own privilege is challenged when the status quo is upset.

Despite the divergent views about the worth of liberatory pedagogy, many scholars still see value in locating ideological struggle in the writing classroom. However, in practice, liberatory rhetoric can take multiple shapes depending on the instructor and course materials. Ira Shor begins with everyday artifacts since these are within the "generative universe" of students. This can best be exemplified with his "World's Biggest Hamburger" activity (Shor, *Critical* 162-69). On one occasion, Shor took a hamburger to class for students to examine using the three-step Description-Diagnosis-Reconstruction method:

> The burger is the nexus of so many daily realities . . . It's not only the king of fast foods, the lunch/snack/dinner quickie meal, but it's also the source of wages for many students who work in the burger chains . . . So, I was able to hold in my hand a weighty interstice of mass experience . . . I brought a burger to class and interfered with a major uncritical flow of mass

> culture . . . Close up, on reflection, many of the students found the hamburger repulsive . . . When I read back to the class a composite of their descriptions, the burger took a strongly negative shape. I next asked people to attempt a Diagnosis of this object. The obvious problem suggested by our work so far was: If the burger is unattractive, why do we eat so many of them? Why are there so many fast food restaurants? Why are so many things put on top of hamburgers? Are they nutritious? What did we do for restaurants before the fast-food empires began pushing burgers? (169)

After the students more fully considered the hamburger as a problematic theme of inquiry, they were charged with the task of reconstructing it—different classes approached this in different ways. One created healthy alternatives, while another recreated the entire production and distribution process to unveil the complex relation of food to culture. It is Shor's contention that activities of this sort are powerful because they cast everyday objects in unusual roles, which allows students the opportunity to re-envision the ordinary. Teachers of argument should consider exercises of this kind because they are overtly argumentative. Students will inevitably have differences of opinion about the nature of ordinary artifacts in their lives; if framed properly, they can see that their attempts to describe, diagnose and reconstruct are actually personal constructs bound together with political positions (169).

Another shape liberatory rhetoric takes is exemplified in James A. Berlin's, *Rhetoric, Poetics, and Culture* under the heading "social epistemic rhetoric." One assignment sequence

> begin(s) with an essay from the *Wall Street Journal* entitled "The Days of a Cowboy are Marked by Danger, Drudgery, and Low Pay," by William Blundell . . . its codes are at once so varied and so accessible to students . . . Students first consider the context of the piece, exploring the characteristics of the readership of the newspaper and the historical events surrounding the essay's production, particularly as indicated within the text. The purpose of this analysis is to decide which terms probably acted as key signifiers for

> the original readers . . . The meaning of *cowboss* is established by seeing it in binary opposition to both the cowboys who work for him and the owners who work away from the ranch in cities . . . [these] binaries suggest others, such as the opposition of nature-civilization . . . and cowboy-urban cowboy. Students begin to see that these binaries are arranged hierarchically, with one term privileged over the other. They also see how unstable these hierarchies can be . . . Students analyze, discuss, and write about the position of the key terms within these socially constructed narratives . . . [and] discover that the essay attempts to position the reader in the role of a certain kind of masculine subject. They can then explore their own complicity and resistance in responding to this role. (125-27)

This method suits Berlin's objective, which is to alert students to the way that "narratives"—the signifying practices that appear natural and not constructed—shape their lives. The writing associated with this sequence is focused on "the position on key terms within the socially constructed narrative code" (126). For example, while individuality and freedom are terms commonly associated with cowboys, the article also depicts cowboys as respectful of authority and submissive to the cowboss (126). Once the initial narrative structure is teased out, more thorough analysis of the same sort will allow students to situate each narrative within larger economical, social and political frameworks.

Robin Muksian Schutt suggests grounding course content in social spaces:

> The benefits of specific cases as text seem to have resurfaced recently with the emerging concept of "contact zones," defined by Mary Louise Pratt as "those social spaces where cultures meet, clash and grapple with each other, often in contexts of highly asymmetrical relations of power" (34). In the case of E306, those social spaces were American courtrooms. But in many argument courses, no particular social spaces (or events) can be "grappled" with since often none are clearly defined, creating confusion for students as to where they can enter a conversation. (126)

Schutt's solution to this problem is to group readings around the topic of the death penalty, which subsequently leads to discussions about the ways that courts dole out justice in our society. Students' writing exercises range from critical analysis of court documents with commentary on the success of the legal arguments, to writing about the perceptual impact of fictionalized accounts of death penalty issues in motion pictures on public opinion, and finally, critical analysis and essays addressing the impact of journalists on pubic opinions (129-30).

To be sure, there is no one way to incorporate liberatory rhetoric into the argument classroom. Although it is not without its inconsistencies, a program designed to prepare students for critical engagement with the world around them will expand their view of the possibilities for rhetorical inquiry. Once they begin to question authority, the realm of rhetorical invention will expand exponentially. Since much of the locus of discussion is on everyday artifacts, it will not be difficult to find discussion pieces or engage students in dialogue that asks them to critically question the assumptions that they hold.

Works Cited

Berlin, James. *Rhetoric, Poetics, and Cultures: Refiguring College English Studies.* West Lafayette, IN: Parlor, 2003.

Berthoff, Ann. "The Intelligent Eye and the Thinking Hand." *The Writer's Mind: Writing as a Mode of Thinking.* Ed. Janice N. Hays, Phyllis A. Roth, Jon R. Ramsey, and Robert D. Foulke. Urbana: NCTE, 1983. 191-96.

Bizzell, Patricia. "Paulo Freire and What Education Can Do." *JAC* 17.3 (1997): 319-322.

Ellsworth, Elizabeth. "Why Doesn't This Feel Empowering? Working through the Repressive Myths of Critical Pedagogy." *Harvard Educational Review* 59.3 (1989): 297-324.

Freire, Paulo. *Pedagogy of the Oppressed.* New York: Continuum, 2000.

Freire, Paulo, and Donaldo P. Macedo. "A Dialogue: Culture, Language, and Race." *Harvard Educational Review* 65.2 (1995): 377-402.

Lazere, Donald. "Back to Basics: A Force for Oppression or Liberation?" *College English* 54.1 (1992): 17-21.

Schutt, Robin Muksian. "Starkweather and Smith: Using 'Contact Zones' to Teach Argument." *Teaching English in the Two-Year College* 25.2 (1998): 126-131.

Shor, Ira. *Critical Teaching and Everyday Life.* Boston: South End, 1980.

—, ed. *Freire for the Classroom: A Sourcebook for Liberatory Teaching.* Portsmouth, NH: Boynton/Cook, 1987.

—. *When Students Have Power.* Chicago: U of Chicago P, 1996.
Shor, Ira, and Paulo Freire. *A Pedagogy for Liberation.* South Hadley, MA: Bergin & Garvey, 1987.

For Further Reading

Argument Textbooks

Alfano, Christine, and Alyssa O'Brien. *Envision: Persuasive Writing in a Visual World.* New York: Longman, 2005.
Charney, Davida M., Christine M. Neuwirth, David S. Kaufer, and Cheryl A. Geisler. *Having Your Say.* New York: Longman, 2006.
Clark, Irene L. *Writing About Diversity—An Argument Reader and Guide.* Boston: Thomson-Wadsworth, 2004.
Walsh, Sharon K., and Evelyn D. Asch. *Just War—A Wadsworth Casebook in Argument.* Boston: Thomson-Wadsworth, 2004.

The format of this book lends itself to use in a class that seeks deep exploration of cultural issues. The readings draw from political science, religion and ethical texts to weave a complex tapestry on the topic of violent confrontations being justified as "just wars," with an introductory section that asks the question, "is there such a thing as a just war"? The first part of the book offers foundational sections on rhetoric proceeded by a diverse body of articles with questions to consider following each selection. Many of the questions are aimed at pointing out contradictions between the points of view offered within the articles. There are other content topics within the Wadsworth Casebook in Argument series: immigration and civil disobedience.

Scholarly Works

Durst, Russell K. *Collision Course: Conflict, Negotiation, and Learning in College Composition.* Urbana: NCTE, 1999.

Much scholarship has been devoted to discussions of the classroom as a site of disagreement. Durst sees the field's lack of theoretical consideration of notions of conflict as a problem, so contemporary writing theory is examined within the context of "the ways first year writing students make sense of, engage, resist, and learn from the critical literacy approach practiced in the composition program" (10). The body of the text is comprised of data collected during a two-year qualitative study, focusing especially on two instructors and two students. Student resistance to writing instruction is also of importance within the book. The end call is for an ethic of "reflective instrumentalism" or respect for the exchange value of work from the student's perspective—teaching critical awareness in composition class while respecting the desire of students to receive more pragmatic instruction.

George, Ann. "Critical Pedagogy: Dreaming of Democracy." *A Guide to Composition Pedagogies*. Ed. Gary Tate, Amy Rupiper, and Kurt Schick. New York: Oxford UP, 2001. 92-112.

George's contribution to this anthology on pedagogy is historical in that it examines the roots of critical pedagogy; however, it does not stop there. She calls upon the work of Jonathan Kozol to support the notion that a critical pedagogy aimed at educating students to be citizens is sensible. Much of the chapter is in literature review form—identifying important texts and contextualizing the contributions of Freire, Shor, Giroux and others in the large body of work conducted on critical pedagogy. A vast array of pedagogical models are alluded to, which seems to be meant to underscore the importance of considering localized variables when implementing liberatory ideas into the classroom. George's work complicates the issue with a section on the means and ends of liberatory pedagogy (while many of the theorists agree on the ends, they part ways on the means) and asking questions such as "Who is to be Liberated from What?" Any attempt to map theoretical terrain will have holes, but George does a good job of not myopically focusing on the major figures and incorporating both old and new texts.

Kanpol, Barry. *Critical Pedagogy: An Introduction*. Westport, CN: Bergin & Garvey, 1994.

Kanpol is writing at a time when public education was beginning to lean heavily towards standardized testing and school choice, which he views as diversions away from the issues that are most in need of discussing, namely the lack of emphasis on civic engagement and bridging the gap between the quality of education that students receive in different parts of the country. Rather than critique the current institution, Kanpol instead outlines critical theory via a literature review of relevant topics related to critical theory, such as individualism and multiculturalism, and then focuses attention on issues that are readily apparent in classrooms across the country through examining three schools in case study form and allowing the localized problems to shine light on the larger systemic problems. The final chapter takes the form of an interview between a critical theorist and a student that is used as a vehicle to demonstrate the necessity of the dense theory that Kanpol is using to support his pedagogy. This text is particularly sensitive to the role that race, class and gender play in education. Many of the arguments expressed in this book have been articulated in other texts; however, the use of theoretical oppositions (deviance/resistance, multiculturalism/similarities within difference), although reductive, are effective for mapping out the terrain of traditional versus critical educational theory.

Lynch, Dennis, Diana George, and Marilyn Cooper. "Moments of Argument: Agonistic Inquiry and Confrontational Cooperation." *College Composition and Communication* 48.1 (1997): 61-85.

This article considers ways to get students to engage issues critically instead of separating them into two diametrically opposed positions and oversimplifying complex problems. The authors advocate a pedagogy that includes moments of conflict and agonistic positioning as well as moments of understanding and communication. They believe that by critically engaging complex issues, it is easier to show students where they jump to conclusions, don't thoroughly examine an issue and/or don't move beyond impractical logical arguments. Concrete examples of writing assignments and course goals are provided for two distinct argument classes. The topics covered in the article should be helpful in the areas of pedagogy, anticipating student misunderstanding, and basic theory of argument.

McLaren, Peter. *Life in Schools: An Introduction to Critical Pedagogy in the Foundations of Education.* New York: Longman, 1994.

McLaren sees critical theory as a method for understanding modern social problems. Through a narrative of his times as a teacher, he reveals his struggles to deliver to his students the empowering, justice-centered education that he feels should be the cornerstone of public education. What follows is a theoretical treatment of the "broken dreams, false promises" that McLaren claims traditional, uncritical educations leaves in its wake. Much like other texts on critical pedagogy, this book has an extensive section on the philosophical roots of liberatory models and the social construction of knowledge. The detailed explanation of terms such as "ideology" and "hegemony" is useful, as is the appendix that identifies "critical educators" and outlines their intellectual contributions.

Ronald, Kate, and Hephzibah Roskelly. "Untested Feasibility: Imagining the Pragmatic Possibility of Paulo Freire." *College English* 63.5 (2001): 612-32.

Ronald and Roskelly seek to align the work of Paulo Freire with North American pragmatic philosophy espoused by Cornell West, in an attempt to reconcile his ideas with the contemporary state of education in America because "for both philosophies, belief means a willingness to act and the assurance that reflection on action will lead to better, more hopeful acts" (614). A central theme is that Freire's work needs to be "imported" properly in the context that it will be used. The authors claim that many scholars read Freire as outsiders from a "voyeuristic standpoint," which undermines the importance of his message. University students may not be "oppressed" in the same ways or to the extent as Brazilian peasants; however, there are limited situations that dictate the possibilities for their lives. Thoughtful theorizing about the world can lead to changed assumptions about possibility. The North American pragmatic philosophical tradition also acknowledges the link between belief and action and the inherently communal nature of inquiry. There is not a tidy overlap of the two belief systems; the authors merely offer a new lens through which to read an old theory.

Steinberg, Shari J. "Liberation Theology and Liberatory Pedagogies: Renewing the Dialogue." *College English* 68.3 (2006): 271-90.

Whereas many articles approach liberatory pedagogy as a means of moving students to challenge the ideologies that they bring to the classroom, Steinberg's position is somewhat different. Citing the religious foundations of Paulo Freire's work and its ties to liberation theology, namely ending oppressive class structures through enacting the messages from the gospels, Steinberg makes a call to view the spiritual and the intellectual side by side if we are truly "to begin where students are." She sees this suggestion as particularly necessary to break liberatory pedagogy from the uncritical modernist binary that relegates religion to the private and politics to the public sphere. This means accepting students' religious convictions as a part of their identities and not as roadblocks to critical thinking. Steinberg sees community, solidarity, and reflection as key terms to both philosophical traditions. There are passages to elucidate the foundation of liberatory theology and other important concepts, as well as a passage describing students using liberatory rhetoric to supplement their understanding of how they fit into and continually shape their religious communities—a perspective that is all too often brushed off as uncritical.

Thelin, William H. "Understanding Problems in Critical Classrooms." *College Composition and Communication* 57.1 (2005): 114-41.

Thelin's central thesis is that the critical classroom framework is worthwhile even if there is "failure" in implementing the pedagogy. This is a reaction to scholarly work that focuses solely on the fact that in some cases, students don't respond to critical pedagogy to the extent that teachers would like them to and that even if they do respond, they may be parroting ideas that that they feel the teacher wants to hear. Thelin sees "failure" as a tool that can be used to strengthen critical pedagogy. Through an account of a "problematic class" of his own, Thelin outlines what he believes went wrong in that class and how the reflection on pedagogical miscues can inform critical pedagogy and move beyond traditional forms of assessment that aim to standardize experience, which are not calibrated to account for the fluidity of a liberatory model. While others view the continual flux of liberatory methods as a problem, Thelin accepts it as a necessary part of working with students who are dealing with the unpleasant moments that the questioning of the social, economic and institutional realities of their lives creates.

Welsh, Susan. "Resistance Theory and Illegitimate Reproduction." *College Composition and Communication* 52.4 (2001): 553-73.

Welsh examines the tension created when using "resistance theory" as a means of having students explore mainstream culture. The main critique is that "resistance theory" reduces the constraints upon emancipatory consciousness down to a product that can be analyzed, classified, and purified, and thus undermines the importance of contradiction. The teacher is the diagnoser of students' illness, especially of those students who hold fast to dogma. "Resistance theory commits teachers to hierarchical determinations of the distance that learners have traveled beyond the status quo and beyond the compromise of contradictory consciousness" (556). What this fails to consider is that an action that would be viewed as not resisting from a resistance theory standpoint may be an understanding of the situation and a willful embracing of part of the conventional narrative and rejection of other parts. Welsh is not suggesting that critical pedagogy is not worthwhile; rather, she sees the real value of it not in the isolation and subsequent expansion of beliefs, but in the struggle with contradictory discourses and circumstances as students reflect on the ideas that make up their worldview. Her rationale is that consciousness is far too complex to be represented as a "collapse into the status quo" or a movement towards liberation.

Feminism and Argument

A feminist approach to argumentation arose out of a need for alternative models to classical argument, and out of the need to focus less on agonistic and antagonistic models of argument that assume a "winner" and a "loser," or on models which assume that the use of available means of persuasion is to get one's way. Instead, feminist argument focuses on new strategies of approaching argument, from ethical alternatives that reposition actors outside of competitive action, to viewing argumentation in less antagonistic terms of mediation, negotiation, and cooperation.

In its earliest manifestations, alternatives to traditional Aristotelian argument took the form of compositionists appealing to the work of Carl Rogers, a psychotherapist whose works centered around client-therapist communication. Rogers's work was influential on the field of rhetoric and composition as early as 1970 with mention as an "alternative to traditional argument" (274) in Young, Becker, and Pikes's *Rhetoric: Discovery and Change,* in which Rogerian approaches were considered appropriate to "dyadic situations." Rogerian rhetoric was hotly contested in the late 1970s and throughout the decade of the 1980s with pieces such as Maxine Hairston's 1976 "Carl Rogers's Alternative to Traditional Rhetoric," Andrea Lunsford's 1979 "Aristotelian vs. Rogerian Argument: A Reassessment," Lisa Ede's 1984 "Is Rogerian Rhetoric Really Rogerian?," Nathaniel Teich's 1987 "Rogerian Problem Solving and the Rhetoric of Argumentation," and Phyllis Lassner's 1990 "Feminist Responses to Rogerian Argument."

Rogers's work, when adapted to composition and rhetoric, presented a theory of argument based on empathetic "listening and understanding," as well as on actors seeing the particular discussion from another's point of view, in order to "sense how it feels" to be in another's shoes in order to communicate effectively (Young et al. 285). This work was appealing to feminist ideologies emerging in composition studies, as Rogerian rhetoric offered "empathy instead of opposition, dialogue instead of argument" (Lassner 220). Yet Rogerian rhetoric has never been overtly feminist; as Catherine Lamb argues in her landmark work "Beyond Argument in Feminist Composition," Rogerian argument is critiqued as being "more feminine than feminist," as "It has always been women's work to understand others" (17). Theories of and approaches to feminist argument, then, occupy themselves with providing alternatives that are concerned with power and representation as well as empathy and care. As Lamb argues, seeing argument as processes of negotiation and mediation are viable alternatives to masculinist argument because the point of argumentation "is no longer to win but to arrive at a solution in a just way that is acceptable to both sides," just as the conception of power changes "from something that can be possessed and used on somebody to something that is available to both [parties] and at least has the potential to be used for the benefit of both" (18).

Cooperative approaches to argument involving negotiation and mediation are popular feminist standpoints on argument; however, they are not without feminist critics. Many scholars point out that they rely on a truncated view of classical argument (see, for example, Lunsford), or on an overly simplistic metaphor of "argument-as-war" (Fulkerson). As Susan Jarratt argues, often argument pedagogies that center on negotiation and mediation leave students, and particularly female students, "insufficiently prepared to negotiate the oppressive discourses of racism, sexism, and classism surfacing in the composition classroom," in contemporary American life, and in democratic processes (106). Similarly, Alexis Easley argues that the best strategy a writing teacher can use in approaching the differences between and conflict inherent in traditional argument and alternatives to traditional argument are to bring the conflict between the two to students as a contradiction that they must mediate and acknowledge through their writing. As Easley has it, students need to be given both the tools with which to argue as well as the knowledge to use these tools ethically, reflectively, and responsibly. Additionally, Fulkerson suggests that amending metaphors of argument to reflect less violence by an increasing focus on partnership works to view argument "as an interactive discourse form . . . built on a structure of claim plus support, and [reinforces the idea] that its purpose is to engage the interlocutors in a dialectical partnership with the hope of reaching some mutually enlightening understanding" (7). Nancy Fraser, in "Rethinking the Public Sphere," engages the concept of argument and dominant discourse by suggesting that in stratified societies, "specialized discursive arenas"(73)—in the form of subaltern counterpublics—are useful and necessary for those grappling with marginalized identities. Extensions of feminist theories of argument can also be found within modern rhetorical theory by scholars who incorporate the work of Kenneth Burke (see Foss and Griffin "Feminist"), standpoint hermeneutics (see Ryan and Natalle), and invitational rhetoric (see Foss and Griffin "Beyond").

Even as feminist theories of argument themselves are negotiated, practices emerge within the argument classroom that reflect major tenets of feminist thought and action. Fulkerson suggests having students write policy proposals, requiring students to

> investigate and write about some small local procedure or policy that they feel is not working adequately, and to address their argument not to an opponent to be beaten but as a memorandum to the person or committee with responsibility for the policy. I teach my students about the standard features and reasoning patterns of the genre, show them examples from previous students, suggest areas in which they might profitably look for topics, have them interview relevant parties (especially those who operate the present system), and go through our usual multi-draft writing process with peer review. We also discuss the

> relative persuasiveness to readers responsible for the policy of angry or aggressive attacks versus reasoned critiques with easily-adopted solutions. . . . When the papers seem strong enough, I ask the students to send them to the appropriate real audiences to see how much success they might have at doing some work in the world. (3-4)

Here, Fulkerson suggests that the policy proposal genre is one that addresses community injustices as well as approaches argument in partnership *with*—in order to come to mutually agreeable consensus about creating change through a democratic process.

Hildy Miller takes a different approach to feminist theories of argumentation in her Web-based course "Feminism and Expository Writing." Grounding the assignment within "feminist rhetorical issues," Miller articulates that

> Argumentation is one of the key ways we practice "procedural knowing"—that is, a kind of thinking that is systematic. Since argumentative skills are valued in this culture, it is important that we learn them. Yet many feminists and others object to traditional argumentation on various grounds. They say it is too often intolerant of opposing views and bent on converting or destroying opposition. (8)

In order to make students aware of this tension, Miller offers up an assignment in which she asks students to

> Team up with another person to "collaborate" on structuring an argument with each of you taking a different/opposing view of an issue of your choosing. Work together to develop ways of "arguing" that don't have traditional agonistic characteristics. How can we disagree in a way that is respectful, recognizes pluralistic perspectives, and still makes it[s] point? Is it possible while arguing to have a persona that is loving and connected? (8)

Thus Miller, much in the way Easley suggests, leaves it up to students themselves to articulate and negotiate the tensions inherent in feminist and traditional modes of argument.

Feminist practices and approaches to argument are conflicted; however, it stands to reason that these conflicts are what make these approaches viable and tenable. Appropriating feminist responses and approaches to argument in our classrooms not only may benefit students by giving them a variety of argumentative strategies that add to the rhetorical means available to them, but also encourages teacher-scholars to "break out of calcified, acritical approaches" (Palczewski 161) to argument and to teaching.

Works Cited

Easley, Alexis. "Toward a Feminist Theory of Teaching Argumentative Writing." *Feminist Teacher* 11.1 (1997): 30-38.

Ede, Lisa. "Is Rogerian Rhetoric Really Rogerian?" *Rhetoric Review* 3.1 (1984): 40-48.

Foss, Sonja K., and Cindy L. Griffin. "A Feminist Perspective on Rhetorical Theory: Toward A Clarification of Boundaries." *Western Journal of Communication* 56.3 (1992): 330-349.

—. "Beyond Persuasion: A Proposal for Invitational Rhetoric." *Communications Monographs* 62.3 (1995): 2-18.

Fraser, Nancy. "Rethinking the Public Sphere: A Contribution to the Critique of Actually Existing Democracy." *Habermas and the Public Sphere.* Ed. Craig Calhoun. Cambridge: MIT P, 1992. 56-80.

Fulkerson, Richard. "Transcending Our Conception of Argument in Light of Feminist Critiques." *Argumentation and Advocacy.* 32.4 (1996): 199-218.

Hairston, Maxine. "Carl Rogers's Alternative to Traditional Rhetoric." *College Composition and Communication* 27.4 (1976): 373-77.

Jarratt, Susan C. "Feminism and Composition: The Case for Conflict." *Contending with Words: Composition and Rhetoric in a Postmodern Age.* Ed. Patricia Harkin and John Schilb. New York: MLA, 1991. 105-23.

Lamb, Catherine E. "Beyond Argument in Feminist Composition." *College Composition and Communication* 42.1 (1991): 11-24.

Lassner, Phyllis. "Feminist Responses to Rogerian Argument." *Rhetoric Review* 8.2 (1990): 220-32.

Lunsford, Andrea A. "Aristotelian vs. Rogerian Argument: A Reassessment." *College Composition and Communication* 30.2 (1979): 146-51.

Miller, Hildy. "Feminist Expository Writing Assignment A: Feminist Expository Writing." 2003. *Teaching with Writing: Feminist Expository Writing.* University of Minnesota Center for Writing, 26 May 2005. 29 Oct. 2005. <http://writing.umn.edu/tww/policy/syllabi/art_feminist.html.>

Palczewski, Catherine Helen. "Argumentation and Feminism: An Introduction." Argumentation and Advocacy. 32.4 (1996): 161-170.
Ryan, Kathleen J., and Elizabeth J. Natalle. "Fusing Horizons: Standpoint Hermeneutics and Invitational Rhetoric." *Rhetoric Society Quarterly* 31.2 (2001) 69-90.
Teich, Nathaniel. "Rogerian Problem Solving and the Rhetoric of Argumentation." *JAC* 7 (1987): 52-61.
Young, Richard E., Alton L. Becker, and Kenneth L. Pike. *Rhetoric: Discovery and Change.* New York: Harcourt, Brace, and World, 1970.

For Further Reading

Argument Textbooks

Goshgarian, Gary, Kathleen Krueger, and Janett Barnett-Minc. *Dialogues: An Argument Rhetoric and Reader.* New York: Longman, 2003.
Infante, Dominic. *Arguing Constructively.* Prospect Heights, IL: Waveland, 1987.
Makau, Josina M., and Debian L. Marty. *Cooperative Argumentation: A Model for Deliberative Community.* Prospect Heights, IL: Waveland, 2001.

Makau and Marty stress the importance of deliberative communities as places from which to "develop tools for confronting disagreement peacefully, ethically, and effectively." In the first two beginning chapters, the authors explain concepts central to their theory of argument, such as critical thinking (getting into the "questioning habit"), and ethical and effective dialogue (developing empathy and compassion to increase dialogic skills and to establish nondefensive awareness of one's own "balanced partiality"). Rather than see argumentation as "winning something," the authors outline a method of interdependence, where decisions are made based on the "best or most justifiable decision in any situation." The authors contend that the purpose of deliberation is to help build and maintain democratic principles and help build "moral community" through the promotion of equity and reciprocity. Makau and Marty use a blend of classical rhetoric and an extended discussion of "context and the deliberative community" to frame their argumentative strategies, and conclude with sections on ethical advocacy and argument evaluation.

Scholarly Works

Emmel, Barbara, Paula Resch, and Deborah Tenney, eds. *Argument Revisited, Argument Redefined: Negotiating Meaning in the Composition Classroom.* Thousand Oaks, CA: Sage, 1996.

In this edited anthology, Emmel, Resch and Tenney negotiate the complexities of argument by revisiting scholarship about traditional and accepted theories of argument, and redefining the future of argument theory. The first half of the anthology is devoted to revisiting "named" and "traditional" theories of argument, such as theories of the enthymeme, classical and Aristotelian rhetoric, and theories of Stephen Toulmin and Carl Rogers. Part two, "Argument Revisited," offers essays which illustrate and analyze theories perceived to be a "threat" to traditional models of argument, such as those represented by feminism, narratology, and reflexive reading strategies. As the editors claim, what unifies this text is that both sections see argument as a "genre and as a process that can serve students well" (xi).

Faigley, Lester, and Julia M. Allen. "Discursive Strategies for Social Change: An Alternative Rhetoric of Argument." *Rhetoric Review* 14.1 (1995): 142-172.

The authors provide a repertoire of alternative argument strategies that have been used to enact discursive change by writers who, historically, did not or felt they did not have the power to engage in the dominant discourse; however, Allen and Faigley do not make claims "for the utility of any strategy." Strategies for social change that have been used are: creating new languages (such as "Laadan" for writer Suzette Haden Elgin); constructing new pronouns (such as "co" or "na"); using neologisms; reclaiming or redefining words (such as "spinster" or "dyke"); juxtaposing language and "creating struggle within and utterance" (as is demonstrated by Gloria Anzaldúa's Borderlands/*La Frontera*); using musical forms to structure written communication; utilizing "perspective by incongruity," which puts "one assumed truth into an incongruous situation to undermine its truthfulness;" playing with language and metaphor and "calling without naming" (referring to Gertrude Stein's prose); and using narratives as a way to make oneself heard politically. The authors assert that writing teachers need to rethink traditional assumptions about the validity and use of logical arguments' ability to shift social structure, given the wide range of forced alternatives that have arisen out of power struggles throughout history.

Gilbert, Michael A. *Coalescent Argumentation.* Mahwah, NJ: Erlbaum, 1997.

Gilbert presents an approach to argumentation that "could better serve everyday arguers." Part one, chapters one through four, addresses general aspects of argumentation theory. Chapter one offers a general view of the history of argumentation and different perspectives of different specialists in the field. Tackling ways of defining argument, chapter two offers six definitions of argument as well as a comparison between them. Chapter three addresses the relation between argumentation, critical reasoning, and informal logic. Discussing the influence of feminist theory on argumentation, chapter four touches on voices in the field such as Gilligan, Tannen, Warren and Nye. Part two, chapters five through ten, addresses different models of argumentation. The fifth chapter of Gilbert's text focuses on the relationships between arguments and their goals, delineating between *task goals,* which refer to the direct goals of the argument, and *face goals,* which concern relationships between the participants. In chapter six, Gilbert identifies and explicates the four modes that categorize arguments: logical, emotional, visceral, and kisceral. Chapter seven addresses the influence of different argument modalities on argumentation theory. Chapters eight and nine address coalescent argumentation, the theory of "joining together of two disparate claims through recognition and exploration of opposing positions" (102). The last chapter offers a summary of Gilbert's theory of argumentation as well as a call to "leave violent conflict behind us" (145).

Kroll, Barry M. "Broadening the Repertoire: Alternatives to the Argumentative Edge." *Composition Studies* 28.1 (2000): 11-27.

Kroll explores three alternatives to traditional thesis-driven argument: "conciliatory," "integrative," and "deliberative" approaches. The conciliatory approach is best represented by Rogerian argument, in which a writer introduces a problem that, rather than divide the writer and reader, insinuates they work together to solve a problem in a conciliatory way. The integrative approach, closely tied to mediation and negotiation in current publications, emphasizes participants' ability to combine values rather than "elevate one set of values over another." Deliberative approaches, according to Kroll, differ slightly from Aristotle's idea of deliberative rhetoric in that a deliberative argument will consider alternatives before arriving at a decision (similar to a delayed-thesis argument). Kroll stresses the need for students to broaden their argumentative repertoire by learning and practicing these alternatives.

Tannen, Deborah. *The Argument Culture: Moving from Debate to Dialogue.* New York: Random, 1998.

Tannen critiques contemporary American culture for the "warlike atmosphere" surrounding its approach to public dialogue. Claiming that Americans have grown accustomed to this "culture of critique" through popular press, politics, and litigation, Tannen argues that an approach beyond the adversarial is needed to diversify approaches to seeking and gaining knowledge. She espouses moving away from dualism, looking to other cultures' ways of negotiating conflict in order to move beyond dissensus and into dialogue.

Teich, Nathaniel, ed. *Rogerian Perspectives: Collaborative Rhetoric for Oral and Written Communication.* Norwood, NJ: Ablex, 1992.

This edited collection, broken up into three sections, includes two written works of Carl Rogers, as well as commentary and analysis on Rogerian rhetoric and communication. The first section, "Carl Rogers on Communication," includes a 1951 work by Rogers, "Communication: Its Blocking and Its Facilitation," as well as a 1984 piece co-written by Rogers and David Ryback, "One Alternative to Nuclear Planetary Suicide." The first section also includes a conversation with Carl Rogers, written by the editor. Part two, "New Views on Rogerian Theory and Practice," includes quite a few essays relevant to composition instruction, as well as referents to rhetoric and argument by writers such as Richard Coe and Richard E. Young. Essays most relevant to the teaching of argument are "Classical and Rogerian Persuasion: An Archeological/Ecological Explication," "Rogerian and Platonic Dialogue in—and Beyond—The Writing Classroom," and "Carl Rogers and the Teaching of Rhetoric and Composition." The last section of the book, "Empathy: The Heart of Collaborative Communication," is made up of contributions from the editor in which he negotiates competing definitions and implications of the concept of empathy.

Service Learning and Argument

Service learning within rhetoric composition has its roots in the "social turn" of the field, represented most clearly in Marilyn Cooper's 1986 piece "The Ecology of Writing," in which she alludes to writing pedagogy that is concerned with the writing process as well as that which reflects a "growing awareness that language and texts are not simply the means by which individuals discover and communicate information, but are essentially social activities, dependent on social structures and processes not only in their interpretive but also in their constructive phases" (366). The aims of service learning have been tied to the work of John Dewey, who asserted that education has an explicit democratic function, as well as to liberatory pedagogies, taking cues from the work of Paolo Freire as a way to create citizens who are critically conscious about institutions of power, and who work to change social inequities. Since the mid-1990s, scholars have been engaging service learning as a topic to be distinguished in the field with articles such as Bruce Herzberg's 1994 "Community Service and Critical Teaching," Ellen Cushman's 1997 Braddock-award winning essay "The Rhetorician as an Agent of Social Change," and Linda Adler-Kassner, Robert Crooks, and Ann Watters's 1997 edited anthology *Writing the Community: Concepts and Models for Service-Learning in Composition.* Recently, service learning has also been tied to the idea that effective writing takes *place;* that is, geographic locations beyond the classroom, in order to provide students with real, rather than unreal, rhetorical situations (see also Heilker, Mauk).

Specific to theories of argument, service learning emerges out of much older stock, from Quintilian's plea that a rhetor be a "good man speaking well"—that is, the assumption that one's ability to be persuasive in a given case is as much tied to the ethical character of a speaker and a speaker's civic duty to *do the right thing* as it is about the rhetorical matter at hand. Thus service learning pedagogy, put into the context of argument, is about producing a citizen-orator, someone "who could bring his discursive skills to bear when the community [s]he served faced a difficult political or judicial decision, or required a celebration of its uniqueness or cultural worth, or simply needed its morale boosted" (Crowley 318).

Yet such a pedagogy is not without its critics. Service learning has been critiqued as being "hyperpragmatic at the expense of sustained critical analysis" (Scott 301), of being too idealistic in its expectations of social change (Rozycki), and of paying too little attention to the power relationships at work between colleges/universities and communities, given the sudden popularity of funding initiatives based uncritically around service-learning agendas (Mahala and Swilky). As universities are increasingly compelled to advertise their community partnerships to gain funding, and as university mission statements increasingly include phrases which reaffirm their "commitment to public service" (William and Mary) or their "commitment to sustained, engaged service to local, regional, national, and international constituencies" (UCSC), many may find themselves under pressure to commit to service-learning initiatives. In addition, much has been argued—on both sides—about the authenticity of writing assignments and service learning's place in providing a located, authentic rhetorical situation from which to produce texts (see Deans, Petraglia).

However, despite the seeming heyday of service learning coming to an end, scholars have spent as much or more time defending service learning initiatives with scholarship that attests to the large-scale sustainability of such programs around the country (see Robinson; Cushman "Sustainable"). Service learning pedagogy arises out of a commitment to democratic action and service to community, usually includes some component of experiential learning outside the classroom walls, addresses a community need, and contains some type of structured reflection about the experiential component (Scott 303). Thus the best practices that surround service learning and argumentation are those that support the Quintilianic philosophy behind service learning, as well as contribute to a better understanding of experiential learning, community and geography, and critical reflection.

Engaging practices of service learning within the argument classroom may be as straightforward as assigning a proposal argument to address community injustices; it may also, as Jonathan Mauk suggests, be a way of getting students to think critically about citizenship and care:

> An investigation or explaining assignment begins with readings on political action. The students are prompted to find the names of city, district, state, and federal officials elected to serve their communities. Then they are prompted to write a brief essay [argument] or develop a pamphlet that explains how an average citizen can correspond with government officials. Students then deliver their texts to their neighbors. In a follow-up essay, students explore the significance of their work. They may draw on particular encounters and/or outside texts on civic action. (381)

Arguments that engage service learning activities can be slightly more complex, having students critique their experiences specific to experiential learning or ideas such as "civic literacy" that are central to Quintilian's model. Students might also negotiate argumentative writing within service-based classes by taking a stake in local political issues, as Cooper and Julier explain:

> Our students researched and collected information about the proposed amendment [to protect citizens from discrimination based on height, weight, family, student, sexual orientation, or handicap status] from the local press . . . [t]hey solicited position statements from various individuals and organizations. . . . Other students followed the debate as the City Council deferred discussion to the Human Relations Board. . . . Against that contextual backdrop, we asked our students to design and conduct a public opinion poll to help the Lansing Human Relations Board decide on whether or not to recommend the city council adoption of the ordinance . . . [resulting in a drafted memo] to the Human Relations Board advising it on what decision to make regarding the proposed ordinance. (86-88)

What is central to best practices of argument in service learning courses that observe a "democratic/rhetorical model of writing instruction" (91) is an emphasis on civic values in conflict resolution, as well as a commitment to getting students to engage in public discourse in hopes to "forge lasting affirmations of civic reciprocity and ethical obligation for our students" (92)—in short, to produce good men and women, speaking (and writing) well.

Works Cited

Adler-Kassner, Linda, Robert Crooks, and Ann Watters, eds. *Writing the Community: Concepts and Models for Service-Learning in Composition.* Washington, DC: AAHE, 1997.

Cooper, David D., and Laura Julier. "Democratic Conversations: Civic Literacy and Service-Learning in the American Grains." Adler-Kassner, Crooks, and Watters 79-94.

Cooper, Marilyn M. "The Ecology of Writing." *College English* 48.4 (1986): 364-75.

Crowley, Sharon. "A Plea for the Revival of Sophistry." *Rhetoric Review* 7.2 (1989): 318-34.

Cushman, Ellen. "The Rhetorician as an Agent of Social Change." *College Composition and Communication* 47.1 (1996): 7-28.

—. "Sustainable Service Learning Programs." *College Composition and Communication* 52.1 (2002): 40-65.

Deans, Thomas. *Writing Partnerships: Service-Learning in Composition.* Urbana: NCTE, 2000.

Dewey, John. *Democracy and Education.* London: Macmillan, 1916.

Heilker, Paul. "Rhetoric Made Real: Civic Discourse and Writing Beyond the Curriculum." Adler-Kassner, Crooks, and Watters 71-78.

Herzberg, Bruce. "Community Service and Critical Teaching." *College Composition and Communication* 45.3 (1994): 307-19.

Mahala, Daniel, and Jody Swilky. "Constructing Disciplinary Space: The Borders, Boundaries, and Zones of English." *JAC* 23.4 (2003): 766-97.

Mauk, Jonathan. "Location, Location, Location: The 'Real' (E)states of Being, Writing, and Thinking in Composition." *College English* 65.4 (2003): 368-388.

Petraglia, Joseph, ed. *Reconceiving Writing, Rethinking Writing Instruction.* Mahwah, NJ: Erlbaum, 1995.

Robinson, Gail. "Creating Sustainable Service Learning Programs: Lessons Learned from the Horizons Project, 1997-2000." *American Association of Community Colleges Project Brief,* 2000. 30 Oct. 2005. <http://www.aacc.nche.edu/Content/ContentGroups/Project_Briefs2/sustainability.pdf>

Rozycki, Edward G. "Romantics, Idealists, and True Service Learning." *Educational Horizons* 80.4 (2002): 159-161.

Scott, Blake J. "Service-Learning and Cultural Studies: Toward a Hybrid Pedagogy of Rhetorical Intervention." *Rhetorical Democracy: Discursive Practices of Civic Engagement.* Ed. Gerard A. Hauser and Amy Grim. Mahwah, NJ: Erlbaum, 2004. 301-07.

University of California, Santa Cruz (UCSC) "UCSC At A Crossroads: Advisory Report of the Millennium Committee." n.d. 14 May 2004. <http://www.ucsc.edu/planbudg/chanc/millcom/mcmtg-980624-final report.htm>.

William and Mary University Web. "Strategic Plan: Into the Fourth Century." n.d. 14 May 2004. <http://www.wm.edu/administration/provost/stplan/pubserv.php>.

For Further Reading

Argument Textbooks

Berndt, Michael, and Amy Muse. *Composing a Civic Life: A Rhetoric and Readings for Inquiry and Action.* New York: Longman, 2004.

Deans, Thomas. *Writing and Community Action: A Service-Learning Rhetoric with Readings.* New York: Longman, 2003.

Isaacs, Emily J., and Phoebe Jackson. *Public Works: Student Writing as Public Text.* Portsmouth, NH: Boynton/Cook, 2001.

Ross, Carolyn, and Ardel Thomas. *Writing for Real: A Handbook for Writing in Community Service.* New York: Longman, 2003.

Scholarly Works

Adler-Kassner, Linda, Robert Crooks, and Ann Watters, eds. *Writing the Community: Concepts and Models for Service-Learning in Composition.* Washington, DC: AAHE, 1997.

This edited anthology is part of a larger mission by the American Association for Higher Education to publish a series of works on service learning and individual academic disciplines. Covering both the theory and the practice of service learning within composition, the anthology offers essays from some of the field's most prominent scholars in service learning such as Bruce Herzberg, Tom Deans, and Nora Bacon. Each essay offers a theorized approach to a pedagogical practice that involves a facet of service learning, as well as a facet of composition. Topics covered are those such as basic writing, writing across the curriculum, civic discourse, and inquiry and logic.

Cushman, Ellen. "The Public Intellectual, Service Learning, and Activist Research." *College English* 61.3 (1999): 328-36.

Cushman argues for a wider consideration of the definition of "public intellectual," asserting that such a definition must move beyond professionals, policymakers, and administrators to include the local community at large. In order to do this, Cushman maintains that current public intellectuals as we know them should move their research, teaching, and service work into the locus of the community, particularly community members in "under-served neighborhoods" (329). Detailing her own experience with teaching a "Social Issues and Literacy" course, Cushman argues that creating service learning and outreach courses do unify teaching, research, and service—moving beyond a "liberal do-gooder stance" and toward critical, activist research while challenging the value systems in place in the academy.

Deans, Thomas. *Writing Partnerships: Service-Learning in Composition.* Urbana: NCTE, 2000.

Deans works to contextualize service-learning initiatives, situating English Studies within a framework of public service. This work offers three real-world examples of different kinds of service learning, broken into three major chapters. Chapter three uses the trope "writing *for* the community," and focuses specifically on writing as service, as students partner with outside agencies and perform writing related tasks. This is differentiated from "writing *about* the community," the topic of Chapter four, in which students do community service and then critically reflect on that service in writing (using Bruce Herzberg's synthesis course at Bentley College as a model). These two models are also different from "writing *with* the community," the focus of Chapter five, in which Deans explores the model of community partnerships with universities, as evidenced by the Community Literacy Center, a partnership of Carnegie Mellon University and the Community House of Pittsburgh. Deans concludes with a helpful chapter that provides assignments and heuristics for varied service-learning initiatives, as well as appendices that consist of course materials, student writing samples, descriptions of community writing courses, and service learning resources and contacts.

Eberly, Rosa A. "From *Writers, Audiences,* and *Communities* to *Publics:* Writing Classrooms as Protopublic Spaces." *Rhetoric Review* 18.1 (1999): 165-78.

Eberly uses her belief that pedagogy and criticism should have "public functions and reflect the social natures of reading and writing" to propose using "public" as an alternative vocabulary for the commonplace concepts of *readers, audience,* and *community.* She argues that the writing classroom should be thought of as a *protopublic space.* According to Eberly, this alteration will help students locate themselves in various overlapping publics, which will facilitate a keener sense of the situated concerns of rhetoric when addressing local issues. Her work is an attempt to address problems of teaching audience awareness in the writing classroom that have been expressed in previous scholarly work. She draws on the work of John Dewey, Richard Sennett, Jurgen Habermas, and Hannah Arendt to ground the idea that teachers can and should approach audience as "publics in process," which are continually morphing as people write, read, and speak about common interests.

Hauser, Gerard A., and Amy Grim. *Rhetorical Democracy: Discursive Practices of Civic Engagement.* Mahwah, NJ: Erlbaum, 2004.

This anthology brings together selected papers from the 2002 Conference of the Rhetoric Society of America. Divided into three sections: Plenary Papers, President's Panel: The Rhetoric of 9/11 and Its Aftermath, and Selected Papers, the anthology presents a wide range of perspectives regarding how teachers and students speak and write their way into the civic arena. Relevant to theories of argument, service learning, and best practices are Herbert W. Simons "The Temple Issues Forum: Innovations in Pedagogy for Civic Engagement," Rolf Norgaard's "Desire and Performance at the Classroom Door: Discursive Laminations of Academic and Civic Engagement," and J. Blake Scott's "Service-Learning and Cultural Studies: Toward a Hybrid Pedagogy of Rhetorical Intervention."

Herzberg, Bruce. "Service Learning and Public Discourse." *JAC* 20.2 (2000): 391-404.

Herzberg engages the question, "what is the theoretical justification for teaching public discourse writing in the composition classroom?," specifically focusing on service-learning courses. Four potential answers exist: that students are more engaged by current public issues, that the immediacy of public issues provides a better understanding for students of genre and audience, that such material provides backing for critical pedagogy, and that public discourse fits in with the historical ends of rhetoric. It is this fourth justification that Herzberg espouses, asserting that it is still within the realm of contemporary rhetoric teachers to emphasize a "traditional kind of public rhetoric" (399). Service learning courses, Herzberg argues, provide a space that bridges the gap between academic discourse and public discourse, and allows room for discussions about civic responsibility, citizenship, and public policy.

Jacoby, Barbara, and Associates. *Service-Learning in Higher Education: Concepts and Practices.* San Francisco: Jossey-Bass, 1996.

This edited collection represents a "how-to" resource for those considering pursuing service-learning agendas within places of higher education, as well as those who may already be involved with service learning and who have hopes to improve existing institutional structure and support for such programs. Part I, "Foundations and Principles of Service Learning," presents an overview of service learning in higher education, focusing on best practices and building and strengthening community-campus partnerships. Part II, "Designing a Spectrum of Service-Learning Experiences," contains five essays, each of which marks a range of experiential learning practices, from one-time and short term service-learning experiences to intensive multi-year experiences. Part III, "Organizational, Administrative, and Policy Issues," presents nuts-and-bolts topics for teachers and administrators interested in service learning, from essays on how to start a service-learning program to securing its future in the academy.

Writing Across the Curriculum (WAC) and Writing in the Disciplines (WID)

Writing across the Curriculum (WAC) is a pedagogical and curricular movement that holds as its central principle the idea that students retain knowledge better when they are asked to engage with content in writing. In the standard writing across the curriculum system, specific courses, in a variety of disciplines, are designated as writing intensive. Within these courses, students synthesize, analyze, and apply course content through writing. Although the two are often conflated, Writing in the Disciplines (WID) and WAC have separate foundational underpinnings. WID, "a research movement to understand what writing actually occurs in different disciplinary areas" (Bazerman et al. 10) followed WAC and filled a theoretical void missing in early WAC scholarship (Jones and Comprone 60). Whereas WAC is primarily concerned with fostering an atmosphere where writing is systematically encouraged, training teachers and getting students to write in content courses, WID aims to interrogate the theoretical differences inherent in disciplinary visions of the role writing and to examine in depth the types of writing that take place across disciplines (Bazerman 10). WAC and WID are relevant to best practices in argument in two different ways:

1. Those who teach in WAC Programs or do research in the area of WID have focused on theories of argument to be at the heart of their enterprise. Different modes of writing among disciplines come back typically to differences in modes of argument among disciplines.

2. The lessons, and in some cases the controversies, gleaned from the study of WAC and WID are often applicable to the realities of writing in writing courses.

As David Bartholomae points out in "Inventing the University,"

> Every time a student sits down to write for us, he has to invent the university for the occasion—invent the university, that is, or a branch of it, like history or anthropology or economics or English. The student has to learn to speak our language, to speak as we do, to try on the peculiar ways of knowing, selecting, evalu-

> ating, reporting, concluding, and arguing that define the discourse of our community. (589)

One of the earliest attempts to theorize argument formation across disciplines can be found in Stephen Toulmin's *The Uses of Argument.* Toulmin suggests first considering the distinction between field-invariant and field-dependent elements whenever one critiques an argument. Field invariance denotes the existence of conventions such as those mentioned by Bartholomae (37). These conventions remain relatively constant across disciplines. No matter the field, inquiry begins with a problem, considers constraints, and relies upon evidence to make a case. However, field-dependent elements are always in flux. They include, for example, the standards used to determine what subjects are worthy of study and which claims do and don't require support (37). Basically, the differences between how historians and biologists write are in the ways they go about making, supporting, and elucidating their arguments. Field-dependent elements can also fluctuate within a discipline. For example, in the field of English composition, there are scholars who hold divergent views on what constitutes data in research. Some privilege ethnographic, observational data and others prefer quantitative, empirical data. Differences in their views on what constitutes good writing can be traced back to their differences on what constitutes valid inquiry and sound argument.

Janet Emig, in her classic essay, "Writing as a Mode of Learning," was among the first to relate issues of WAC and WID to composition studies. She uses the theories of Vygotsky, James Britton and others to make the case that writing is a "unique" form of learning, in part because "writing can sponsor learning because it can match its pace" (12). The recursive nature of writing allows for one to process information and make sense of it in ways that speaking and thinking don't facilitate. Emig's essay legitimated early attempts at WAC.

Some of the controversies associated with WAC also have important implications for those reading argument in writing courses. David Russell's work on activity theory challenges the notion that writing is transferable across disciplines. Russell appropriates this theory from Vygotsky. Activity theory assumes the existence of "activity systems" similar to fields or discourse communities, that call upon specific contexts to make meaning (55). These activity systems have histories of interaction canonized in literature, and use tools (both physical—computers, calculators, and semiotic—speaking, writing) to articulate ideas and make meaning of the world. They change via discussions that take place within them and borrow and transform tools from other disciplines to meet their ends (56). From this perspective, there are few, if any, field-invariant elements and no part of writing is considered an autonomous skill.

To see the relevance of work done in WAC/WID to argument, consider work done in an economics course focused on helping students define constructs and terms. To hone sensitivity to these concepts, Dennis Palamini suggests using "rhetorical cases."

> The rhetorical case is a self-contained story problem that simulates a realistic communication situation. The case provides information about the experiential and education backgrounds of the writer and readers. More important, the case also specifies a particular writing situation (or forum) and thus the relationship of the writer to the readers, that is, their organizational roles with respect to each other and their respective purposes. The student then assumes the writing role described in the case and strives to explain persuasively how the economic analysis helps the readers to understand their business or other type of economic problem and make good decisions. (206)

To illustrate his method, Palamini gives the example of a staff union economist discussing cost-of-living information with a union team charged to negotiate a new contract. The author sees the value of "rhetorical cases" in the emphasis on consideration of audience in a localized context. Economists may know how to communicate with each other, but the nature of their job necessitates the ability to communicate abstract information in language that laypeople can understand and use. At the end of the article, Palamini outlines an extended rhetorical case.

Sharing the responsibility for writing instruction is an idea that has been slowly but steadily accepted in academic circles. Mass education systems all too often ignore the nature of writing and students suffer as a result of the uncritical, reductive models of writing that they encounter throughout the academy. Knowledge of specialized, disciplinary-specific rhetoric should be a staple of compulsory study in universities and colleges if students are to truly find and utilize the most effective means of persuasion. A more careful consideration of the role of writing in education can lead to more interest from educators in how best to learn and teach writing. Only by understanding how modes of writing and argument taught in non-composition courses differ from and resemble modes of writing and argument traditionally taught in composition courses can we make appropriate adjustments to our course and assignment designs.

Works Cited

Bartholomae, David. "Inventing the University." *Cross-Talk in Comp Theory: A Reader.* Ed. Victor Villanueva. Urbana: NCTE, 1997. 589-620.

Bazerman, Charles, Joseph Little, Lisa Bethel, Teri Chavkin, Danielle Fouquette and Janet Garufis, eds. *Reference Guide to Writing Across the Curriculum.* West Lafeyette, IN: Parlor and the WAC Clearinghouse, 2005.

Emig, Janet. "Writing as a Mode of Learning." *Cross-Talk in Comp Theory: A Reader.* Ed. Victor Villanueva. Urbana: NCTE, 1997. 7-16.

Garay, Mary Sue. "'Day of Absence': Preparing Students to Write Effective Instructions." *Business Communication Quarterly* 63.2 (2000): 73-78.

Jones, Robert, and Joseph J. Comprone. "Where Do We Go Next in Writing Across the Curriculum?" *College Composition and Communication* 44.1 (1993): 59-68.

Palmini, Dennis. "Using Rhetorical Cases to Teach Writing Skills and Enhance Economic Learning." *Journal of Economic Education* 27.3 (1996): 205-16.

Russell, David. "Activity Theory and Its Implications for Writing Instruction." *Reconceiving Writing, Rethinking Writing Instruction.* Ed. Joseph Petraglia. Mahwah, NJ: Erlbaum, 1995. 51-77.

Toulmin, Stephen. *The Uses of Argument.* New York: Cambridge UP, 1999.

Wilkes, John. "Science Writing: Who? What? How?" *The English Journal* 67.4 (1978): 56-60.

For Further Reading

Argument Textbooks

Hult, Christine A. *Researching and Writing Across the Curriculum.* 3rd ed. New York: Longman, 2006.

Mulvaney, Mary Kay A., and David A. Jolliffe. *Academic Writing: Genres, Samples, and Resources.* New York: Longman, 2005.

Schmidt, Diane E., ed. *Writing in Political Science.* 3rd ed. New York: Longman, 2005.

Tinberg, Howard. *Writing with Consequence: What Writing Does in the Disciplines.* New York: Longman, 2003.

Scholarly Works—General

Blair, Catherine Pastore. "Only One of the Voices: Dialogic Writing across the Curriculum." *College English* 50.4 (1988): 383-89.

Catherine Pastore Blair theorizes a "dialogic" Writing Across the Curriculum model for educators who are involved in interdisciplinary writing instruction. Her position is that WAC should not be housed in English departments because that would imply that English studies was master of the domain of writing, which undercuts the main premises of WAC. The dialogic model is grounded in Bakhtin's and Friere's social theories of knowledge—that meaning is created in context. If this is true, "the English department owns only its particular brand of writing that carries its particular cultural context . . . English department writing is no better than writing in anthropology. It is only better by its own local standards" (384). Whereas some scholars position English faculty as the oppressed and overworked, Blair reverses the order and positions English faculty as the oppressors, who reserve the right to final say in matters of writing (386). This model places all disciplines on level ground and relies upon an interdisciplinary committee to oversee the WAC program and mandates that members of all disciplines involved engage in dialogue about views of writing early and often.

Anthropology

Segal, Edwin S. "The Journal: Teaching Reflexive Methodology on an Introductory Level" *Anthropology and Education Quarterly* 21.2 (1990): 121-27.

Segal's work is focused on the interaction between field and field worker. He cultivates an "anthropological imagination," which can best be described as a feel for placing conclusions about situations in anthropological frames without relying upon stock patterns of response. Segal views the participant-observer relationship inherent in fieldwork as a dialectical process and views writing as a way to help students establish a systematic way of thinking about their own experiences so that they can account for the differences between the observer's and the participant's worlds when they are writing up their field observations. The value of journaling, according to Segal, is that students learn to connect the course content with their own experiences and to get them to reveal information about situations that they encounter and their responses to them. The article suggests using questions to guide journal discussions, such as "describe an event or incident occurring within the past two weeks in which you found your behavior constrained by our society's sex-gender system" or allowing students to respond to anthropological articles. Segal suggests that over time, if prompted, students will gradually question the social factors affecting situations and rely less upon their own personal reading. As a pedagogical tool, it is useful to help the teacher guide direction of the class and focus class time to areas that the journals call attention.

Business

Cox, Pamela L., Paul E. Bobrowski, and Larry Maher. "Teaching First-Year Business Students to Summarize: Abstract Writing Assignment." *Business Communication Quarterly* 66.4 (2003): 36-54.

Cox et al. pinpoint as a major concern for business writing the necessity to condense large quantities of information into relatively smaller chunks. They call upon studies that have demonstrated that although this skill is integral to the field, few people summarize well. The article discusses an assignment designed to have students create an abstract of a larger text through rhetorically selecting information that is going to be most pertinent to the task at hand. They believe that "The primary purpose of the writing-to-learn assignments is to have writers explain concepts or ideas to themselves, to ask questions, and to make connections" (37). This is important because, in business writing, the writer represents the employer, thus s/he must use language that is going to clearly articulate the needs of the employer. Attention to the needs of the audience is of the utmost importance when phrasing the messages to ensure that they are received in the manner that they were intended.

Griggs, Karen. "A Role Play for Revising Style and Applying Management Theories." *Business Communication Quarterly* 68.1 (2005): 60-65.

Griggs believes that role-playing is an effective teaching tool because it allows students to call upon their previous experiences in relatively low-risk situations. The rhetorical significance of role-play is that it places purpose and audience at the center of communicative interactions, with revision as the central focus of this particular activity. The assignment sequence offered in this article begins with a scenario. All of the students are asked to pretend that they work for a corporate communications manager who has written multiple drafts of a memo. The first draft berates the staff for making a mistake that led to the loss of a court case and the revision explains court rulings and asks the staff to be more careful in the future. Some students are asked to role- play the different versions of the memo, while the rest of the students are cast in the role of the staff. After the presentations are given, the staff is asked to match role-play characters with management styles. Griggs states that it is through the ensuing discussion of management style and the varying ways that the staff could perceive the draft that students see the value of considering audience and purpose when revising. If time permits, Griggs suggests that the impact of time on revision could also be discussed (additional variables may need to be considered if the document is revised over a long period of time). There is an appendix with drafts of the memo at the end of the article.

Kallendorf, Craig, and Carol Kallendorf. "The Figures of Speech, Ethos, and Aristotle: Notes Toward a Rhetoric of Business Communication." *Journal of Business Communication* 22.1 (1985): 35-50.

After noticing that business communication (advertising, internal and external company documents such as letters and annual reports, and oral presentations and speeches) were utilizing classical figures of speech such as anaphora, hyperbole, metonymy, simile, and metaphor, the authors assert that there is a firm connection between business communication and classical Aristotelian rhetoric. Kallendorf and Kallendorf assert that business writing is intrinsically persuasive, taking its "rightful place" beside deliberative, judicial, and epideictic rhetoric.

Kreth, Melinda L. "A Small-Scale Client Project for Business Writing Students." *Business Communication Quarterly* 68.1 (2005): 52-59.

Kreth's model offers a way to engage students in an activity that mimics interaction with an audience that has specific desires and needs that need to be met within the context of a specific interaction. The author suggests that client-based pedagogy of this kind is a better alternative than service learning because client-based pedagogy has as its central goal understanding and negotiating of "real world" problems, whereas service learning emphasizes social activism. This particular assignment calls for interactions with a client-serving company. Kreth's class met with a realtor and collaborated to break up into groups to create different versions of a "buying my first home" guidebook to help first time homebuyers prepare for the experience. During the process, they met with the realtor and other realtors at the firm and considered the needs of homebuyers and realtors when deciding which information was essential for the needs of both parties to be met with one document. Since the final products were not actually used by the realtor, the "real world" value of the exercise is token. A secondary benefit of the assignment is that the students in her class took ownership of the activity and were critical of the structural constraints of the process. The critical engagement with the conventions of the field could also be fodder for discussion.

Economics

Greenlaw, Steven A. "Using Writing to Enhance Student Learning in Undergraduate Economics." *International Review of Economics Education* 1.1 (2003): 61-70.

Greenlaw's purpose in this article is not pedagogical, but there are a few good writing prompts that could aid in getting students to see the complexity involved in defining principles of economics and defending the constructs that they create. For example, one question is, "One of the results of Hurricane Andrew several years ago was dramatic increases in the prices of most products in south Florida. This prompted complaints of 'price gouging' and demands for government protection of consumers and punishment of the price gougers. Write a one- to two-page essay using the theory of supply and demand to analyze the impact of Hurricane Andrew on goods prices in south Florida. Exactly why did prices increase? Show graphically and explain in detail. In your essay, be sure to consider the following points. Define 'price gouging' in your own words. Explain the extent to which the price increases in south Florida were examples of price gouging or not. Should government have prevented the price increases? Who would have benefited and who would have been harmed if the government had prevented those price increases?" Although writing is seen primarily as a way to prepare students for class discussion, the prompts could be used for a deeper theoretical discussion about how economists appeal to people, and how visual aids can used to tell stories and even ethics in economics.

Engineering

Thompson, Nancy S., and Elizabeth M. Alford. "Developing a Writing Program in Engineering: Teaching Writing to Teach Engineering Literacies." ERIC document. ED 409 584. n.d. 7 Feb. 2009 <http://eric.ed.gov:80/ERICDocs/data/ericdocs2sql/content_storage_01/0000019b/80/16/bd/f3.pdf >.

This document is the written version of a Conference on College Composition and Communication presentation on the authors' work in a WID writing center designated for engineers. While this is not a pedagogical piece per se, it does address the literacies that are field-dependent for engineering. They list "absence of personal voice" and valuing of information over author as particularly salient features of writing in the field of engineering. This is born out in the disciplinary reverence for the lab report, which Thompson and Alford label "the foundation of engineering literacy" (2). At the end of the article, there is a section on group learning theory in engineering as a way to better facilitate student acquisition of engineering literacies.

Political Science

Shellman, Stephen M. "Active Learning in Comparative Politics: A Mock German Election and Coalition-Formation Simulation." *Political Science and Politics* 34.4 (2001): 827-34.

Although this article does not have discussions of writing at the center, Shellman's mock German election includes components of writing that are particularly well-suited to address methods of inquiry in political science. For example, students are split up into parties corresponding to real German political parties and asked to write party position statements on various issues to develop a sense of how the parties articulate their positions on the issues through arguments. Later in the sequence, students, still acting as representatives of political parties, are asked to fill out "coalition agreement forms" with the other parties to move the government's agenda in their direction. This writing assignment asks students to perform cost/benefit analysis of proposals, consider the motives of the group, and to consider the implications of binding their cause with another group's cause to create movement on an issue. The author believes that, during the course of the assignment, students learn the importance of a number of discipline-specific concepts.

Computers and Writing

For most of the students in our composition courses, writing and computers seem a natural pairing: drafts are easily composed and revised in any of a number of word processing programs, and emails and chat messages are composed and sent out by the dozens on a daily basis. Electronically-produced composition dominates writing and composition studies. Of course, this hasn't always been the case. Some twenty-two odd years ago, when word processing was still commonly referred to as "text processing" (Palmquist 400) and the widespread availability of microcomputers was a new phenomenon, composition scholars were divided on exactly if and how computers would impact the field. 1983 saw the creation of *Computers and Composition,* a peer-reviewed scholarly journal devoted exclusively to the theory, practice, and praxis of computers and writing. It is within the pages of this journal that many of the most important arguments about computers and writing can be found, and where the most influential scholars in the field (Kate Kiefer, Cynthia Selfe, and Gail Hawisher have formed a triumvirate of leadership from the field's inception) continue to publish their writing. Any teacher interested in understanding the history and evolution of computers and writing should begin their studies with *Computers and Composition.*

Given the relative newness of this field and the polarized reactions of many teachers to technology (Perelman's "inertia" creating many neo-Luddites), several arguments about computers and writing can be found in the discipline's writings. One such early argument can be traced in the pages of *Computers and Composition* as teachers debated whether or not computer-based writing "had the potential to produce global improvement in the quality of student writing" (Moran 347). In "Planning and Implementing the Right Word Processing System," Brownell was adamant that "word processors do make it possible to write more in less time, and do make us better writers" (3). His claim was quickly contested by McAllister and Sommers and Collins, and later by Dowling and Collier and Werier. Interested teachers can use this argument to trace the polarity between technophiles who believe that computers will have a positive impact on student writing and those more cautious scholars (see Harris and Bangert-Drowns) who favor assessment and conclusive evidence before embracing computers in writing classes. This debate continues, with many scholars turning to students to provide their views on computer-mediated composition instruction (with researchers like Gos, LeCourt and Barnes, and Duffelmeyer leading the way).

Exactly how emerging computer technologies impact the study and teaching of argumentation is much debated. The continual advancement of hardware, software, and computer accessories each year adds new possibilities (and potential pitfalls) for teachers of argument. Gary Stephens was among the earliest scholars theorizing how computers might impact argumentation, claiming that computers would increase student argumentative skills. Of course in 1984 when Stephens was writing, computer technology meant word processing, but as the 20th century continues to shrink in the rear-view mirror, there are a variety of ways argument teachers might use computer technology in their classrooms. Several scholars have hypothesized ways arguments might be effectively constructed in hypertextual environments (see Marshall, Conklin and Begeman, Bolter, Landow, and Kolb). Locke Carter discusses argument in hypertext in great detail, drawing on Perelman's work extensively. Sean D. Williams uses Toulmin's views of argumentation and credits interaction as the key to Web-based persuasion. Kajder and Bull and Williams and Jacobs explore how Web logs (blogs) may function to provide students with audience awareness and a dialogic component crucial to constructing effective arguments. For those teachers of argument conducting class out of a computer-mediated classroom (CMC), McAlister, Ravenscroft and Scanlon and

Coffin and Hewings offer suggestions on how those spaces might be effectively used to support collaboration and argument construction. For those scholars seeking a more technical explanation of how computer technology might augment argumentation, the field of computer science has devoted space in its literature to this issue, noticeable recently in Andriessen, Baker, and Suthers, Reed and Norman, Kirschner, Buckingham and Carr, and McElholm.

For teachers of argument seeking more practical help in technological matters, many helpful academic websites exist. The reliability and citation of Internet sources remains a crucial issue, as students rely more and more heavily on websites to provide the grounds and backing for their arguments without first evaluating the ethos of the source(s) being used. Online rubrics at the Cornell University Library, the UC Berkeley Library, and the New Mexico State University Library offer a diverse sampling of evaluative questions and suggestions for further study related to evaluating online sources. Many other university websites provide additional teaching aides. The Purdue Online Writing Lab (OWL) was one of the first in the country and remains one of the most important, offering many heuristics and ideas for effective writing. Dartmouth College offers a comprehensive Internet site devoted to Web teaching, providing downloadable teaching resources, articles on teaching with technology, and case studies of teachers using the Internet in their teaching. Schoolcraft College's website offers similar materials, including worksheets, handouts, and teaching modules, including materials on teaching argumentation. Lingua MOO, an academic virtual community, offers teachers another space to visit to find additional teaching materials related to technology and argumentation.

The sources listed here serve as a good starting point for teachers who want to explore how computer technologies impact the writing and teaching of arguments. Teachers who desire additional scholarship on theoretical and practical applications of how argument might be taught with a variety of computer applications and/or in electronic spaces should follow the conversations taking place in the pages of *Computers and Composition,* the virtual pages of *Computers and Composition Online,* and in online academic sites like Lingua MOO, where classroom applications of cutting-edge technologies can often be found first.

Works Cited

Andriessen, Jerry, Michael Baker, and Dan Suthers. *Arguing to Learn: Confronting Cognitions in Computer-Supported Collaborative Learning Environments.* Boston: Kluwer Academic, 2003.

Bangert-Drowns, Robert L. "The Word Processor as an Instructional Tool: A Meta-Analysis of Word Processing in Writing Instruction." *Review of Educational Research* 63.1 (1993): 69-93.

Barker, Joe. *Evaluating Web Pages: Techniques to Apply & Questions to Ask.* University of California Berkeley, 22 Mar. 2005. 26 Jan. 2006. <http://www.lib.berkeley.edu/TeachingLib/Guides/Internet/*Evaluate.html*>.

Beck, Susan E. *The Good, The Bad, & The Ugly: Why It's a Good Idea to Evaluate Web Sources.* New Mexico State University, 6 Nov. 2005. 26 Jan. 2006. <http://lib.nmsu.edu/instruction/eval.html>.

Bolter, Jay David. "Topographic Writing: Hypertext and the Electronic Writing Space." *Hypermedia and Literary Studies.* Ed. Paul Delany and George P. Landow. Cambridge: MIT P, 1991. 105-18.

Brownell, Thomas. "Planning and Implementing the Right Word Processing System." *Computers and Composition* 2.2 (1984): 3-5.

Carter, Locke. "Argument in Hypertext: Writing Strategies and the Problem of Order in a Nonsequential World." *Computers and Composition* 20.1 (2003): 3-22.

Coffin, Caroline, and Ann Hewings. "Engaging Electronically: Using CMC to Develop Students' Argumentation Skills in Higher Education." *Language and Education* 19.1 (2005): 32-49.

Collier, Richard, and Clifford Werier. "When Computer Writers Compose by Hand." *Computers and Composition* 12.1 (1995): 47-59.

Conklin, Jeff, and Michael L. Begeman. "gIbis: A Hypertext Tool for Team Design Deliberation." *Proceedings of Hypertext '87.* Chapel Hill, NC: Association of Computing Machinery, 1987. 247-68.

Dartmouth College. *Web Teaching at Dartmouth College.* 8 Sept. 2003. 26 Jan. 2006. <http://www.dartmouth.edu/~webteach/>.

Dowling, Carolyn. "Word Processing and the Ongoing Difficulty of Writing." *Computers and Composition* 11.3 (1994): 227-35.

Duffelmeyer, Barbara Blakeley. "Critical Computer Literacy: Computers in First-Year Composition as Topic and Environment." *Computers and Composition* 18.3 (2001): 289-307.

Engle, Michael. *Evaluating Web Sites: Criteria and Tools.* Cornell University Library, 28 Oct. 2005. 26 Jan. 2006. <http://www.library.cornell.edu/olinuris/ref/research/webeval.html>.

Gos, Michael. "Computer Anxiety and Computer Experience: A New Look at an Old Relationship." *The Clearing House* 69.5 (1996): 271-76.

Harris, Jeanette. "Student Writers and Word Processing: A Preliminary Evaluation." *College Composition and Communication* 36.3 (1985): 323-30.

Haynes, Cynthia, and Jan Rune Holmevik. *High Wired: On the Design, Use, and Theory of Educational MOOs.* Ann Arbor: The University of Michigan Press, 1998.

Jordan-Henley, Jennifer, and Barry M. Maid. "Tutoring in Cyberspace: Student Impact and College/University Collaboration." *Computers and Composition* 12.2 (1995): 211-18.

Kajder, Sara and Glen Bull. "Scaffolding for Struggling Students: Reading and Writing with Blogs." *Learning and Leading with Technology* 31.2 (2003): 32-46.

Kiefer, Kate. "Computers and Teacher Education in the 1990s and Beyond." *Evolving Perspectives on Computers and Composition Studies: Questions for the 1990s.* Eds. Gail E. Hawisher and Cynthia L. Selfe. Urbana: NCTE. 113-31.

Kinkead, Joyce, and Jan Ugan. "A Report on the 1983 CCCC Special Session for Writing Lab Directors." *Writing Lab Newsletter* 7.10 (1983): 5-6.

Kirschner, Paul A., Simon J. Buckingham Shum, and Chad S. Carr, eds. *Visualizing Argumentation: Software Tools for Collaborative and Educational Sense-Making.* New York: Springer, 2003.

Klem, Elizabeth, and Charles Moran. "Computers and Instructional Strategies in the Teaching of Writing." *Evolving Perspectives on Computers and Composition Studies: Questions for the 1990s.* Eds. Gail E. Hawisher and Cynthia L. Selfe. Urbana: NCTE. 132-49.

Kolb, David. "Association and Argument: Hypertext in and Around the Writing Process." *New Review of Hypermedia and Multimedia* 11.1 (2005): 27-32.

Landow, George P. *Hypertext: The Convergence of Contemporary Critical Theory and Technology.* Baltimore, MD: Johns Hopkins UP, 1992.

LeCourt, Donna, and Luanne Barnes. "Writing Multiplicity: Hypertext and Feminist Textual Politics." *Computers and Composition* 16.1 (1999): 55-72.

Marshall, Catherine C. "Constraint-Based Hypertext for Argumentation." *Proceedings of Hypertext '87.* Chapel Hill, NC: Association of Computing Machinery, 1987. 253-68.

McAlister, Simon, Andrew Ravenscroft, and Eileen Scanlon. "Combining Interaction and Context Design to Support Collaborative Argumentation Using a Tool for Synchronous CMC." *Journal of Computer Assisted Learning* 20.3 (2004): 194-204.

McAllister, Carole H. "The Effects of Word Processing on the Quality of Writing: Fact or Illusion?" *Computers and Composition* 2.4 (1985): 36-44.

McElholm, Dermot. *Text and Argumentation in English for Science and Technology.* Berlin: Peter Lang, 2002.
Moran, Charles. "*Computers and Composition* 1983-2002: What We Have Hoped For." *Computers and Composition* 20.4 (2003): 343-58.
Palmquist, Mike. "A Brief History of Computer Support for Writing Centers and Writing-Across-the-Curriculum Programs. *Computers and Composition* 20.4 (2003): 395-413.
Purdue University. *The OWL at Purdue.* n.d. 26 Jan. 2006. <http://owl.english.purdue.edu/owl/>.
Reed, Chris, and Timothy J. Norman, eds. *Argumentation Machines: New Frontiers in Argument and Computation.* Boston: Kluwer Academic, 2004.
Selfe, Cynthia L., and Richard Selfe. "The Politics of the Interface: Power and Its Exercise in Electronic Contact Zones." *College Composition and Communication* 45.4 (1994): 480-504.
Sommers, Elizabeth, and James Collins. "Microcomputers and Writing." *Computers and Composition* 2.4 (1985): 27-35.
Stephens, Gary. "Computer Debating." *Computers and Composition* 1.4 (1984).
Williams, Jeremy B., and Joanne Jacobs. "Exploring the Use of Blogs as Learning Spaces in the Higher Education Sector." *Australasian Journal of Educational Technology* 20.2 (2004): 232-47.
Williams, Sean D. "Process-Product Ambiguity: Theorizing a Perspective on World Wide Web Argumentation." *JAC* 22.2 (2002): 377-98.

For Further Reading

Textbooks

Carbone, Nick. *Writing Online: A Student's Guide to the Internet and World Wide Web.* Boston: Houghton Mifflin, 2000.
Kolko, Beth E., Alison E. Regan, and Susan Romano. *Writing in an Electronic World: A Rhetoric with Readings.* New York: Longman, 2001.
Holmevik, Jan Rune, and Cynthia Haynes. *MOOniversity: A Student's Guide to Online Learning Environments.* New York: Allyn & Bacon, 2000.
Ulmer, Gregory. *Internet Invention: From Literacy to Electracy.* New York: Allyn & Bacon, 2003.

Ulmer's book provides a pedagogy of online learning and is meant as a supplement to texts that introduce students to the Web, html, and graphics design. Ulmer hopes to move students familiar with print culture (literacy) towards familiarity with electronic culture ("electracy") and the rhetorics that surround it. A self- proclaimed "workbook-reader-theory," the text comes with a partner website and is broken into sections that both extract electronic literacy out of conventional print materials, as well as provide explicit discussion about the theory and pedagogy behind assignment choices. Topics for discussion are broken into career, family, entertainment, and community discourses, "emblems of a wide scope," which is concerned with the creation, production, and consumption of images, and ends with a chapter that asks students to invest in world issues and create a website on public policy in "conclusion: culture wars or syncretism?"

Scholarly Works

Andriessen, Jerry, Micheal Baker, and Dan Suthers. *Arguing to Learn: Confronting Cognitions in Computer-Supported Collaborative Learning Environments.* Boston: Kluwer Academic, 2003.

Andreissen, Baker, and Suthers offer this edited collection as one that revolves around computer-mediated interaction and argumentation, and specifically, computer-supported collaborative learning (CSCL) environments. The collection offers an overview of these environments, as well as their role in collaborative inquiry, literacy projects, and scientific investigation. The collection includes essays such as "Argumentation as Negotiation in Electronic Collaborative Writing," "Elaborating New Arguments through a CSCL Script," and "CSCL, Argumentation, and Deweyan Inquiry: Argumentation *is* Learning." The collection offers instructional strategies for improving the quality of learning and of producing written arguments, as well as for avoiding the pitfalls often associated with computer-mediated and collaborative learning environments.

Coffin, Caroline, and Ann Hewings. "Engaging Electronically: Using CMC to Develop Students' Argumentation Skills in Higher Education." *Language and Education* 19.1 (2005): 32-49.

How might electronic conferencing provide students with opportunities to develop argumentation skills? The authors explore this question by collecting data from a post-graduate distance education TESOL course, examining the asynchronous conference posts of two different student groups over the course of the academic term. Using the concept of engagement ("the system of semantic options available to writers for negotiating and adjusting the arguability of propositions and proposals" [37]), the authors examine how often in their posts the participants either endorsed, distanced, or challenged the views of their classmates in this electronic space. Their findings suggest that even though electronic conferences can facilitate engagement with difference, students were still reluctant to challenge their peers (much in the same way they are in more traditional face-to-face classroom settings). Teaching argument in electronic spaces presents some of the same challenges as teaching it in non-virtual classrooms.

Ladikas, Miltos, and Doris Schroeder. "Argumentation Theory and GM Foods." *Poesis & Praxis: International Journal of Ethics of Science and Technology Assessment* 3.3 (2005): 216-25.

The authors apply Stephen Toulmin's model for argumentation to the European debate around genetically modified (GM) foods that took place in public writings in the late 1990s. Their goal was to see if Toulmin's model was useful in analyzing public debates. British newspaper articles on GM soya (the first GM product to enter Europe) were analyzed over a two year period, examining the warrants, backing, and rebuttal of the claims discovered. The authors concluded that the Toulmin model of argumentation was a very effective tool for analyzing public debates. This essay serves as a useful model for teachers who seek examples of how to apply argumentation to current news events.

Weger, Harry Jr., and Mark Aakhus. "Arguing in Internet Chat Rooms: Argumentative Adaptations to Chat Room Design and Some Consequences for Public Deliberation at a Distance." *Argumentation and Advocacy* 40.1 (2003): 23-38.

Does the format of the argumentation venue alter the form of the argument itself? The authors explore this question by examining the quality of chat room argumentation, collecting data from America Online (AOL) political chat rooms. Data was analyzed using the pragma-dialectical approach, which places emphasis on the functional utility of arguments in attempt to understand how Internet chat rooms "encourage or discourage critical discussion in the public sphere" (27).

Data analysis indicated that several features problematic for supporting critical discussion (lack of conversational coherence, under-developed arguments, and flaming) were typical in chat room spaces. The authors theorize that design elements of chat rooms (continuous scrolling transcripts, contribution limits, and unidentified participants) directly influence the form argumentation can take in these spaces. Rather than seeing chat rooms as a failed space for argumentation, the authors suggest seeing them as "an achievement of an alternative model of argumentative dialogue adapted to the format of the venue for public participation" (37).

Visual Rhetoric

In *A New Rhetoric,* Perelman and Olbrechts-Tyteca identify the importance of *presence* to argumentation. There, the authors describe presence as the combination of form and substance, psychologically influencing the audience through such techniques as omission, emphasis, choice, and selection. Even though these authors do not discuss much in the way of extra-verbal uses of the visual, it seems clear that this concept, which stresses putting something immediately in front of the audience, is particularly important in visual rhetoric, arguably the most dominant and pervasive types of appeals in our culture. The visual rhetoric of magazines (a glossy two-page spread in *Vanity Fair* for Lancome depicting a young female model lounging in a pink summer dress and inviting viewers to "Awaken to a new spring" line of cosmetics), television (a smiling and patient Alex Rodriguez helping children learn the basics of catching a baseball in a television promotional for Boys and Girls Clubs of America), and the Internet (at the Greenpeace International website, the wide-eyed face of a baby orangutan greeting visitors next to text that suggests "This fragile Earth deserves a voice. It needs solutions. It needs change. It needs action.") are among the almost 3000 messages that the average person encounters each day that are predominantly visual in their persuasive appeal.

However, we have been slow to fully embrace visual rhetoric studies in composition and rhetoric and argumentation. Carolyn Handa articulates this clearly:

> Composition and classical rhetoric as disciplines approach rhetoric and argument in strictly verbal terms

> . . . Within composition scholars by no means agree universally on the question of whether or not images can make arguments, especially as arguments are classically defined: linear sequences of claims, counter-claims, and evidence. Whether images can argue on their own or only in conjunction with words is an even more contentious subject. (305)

For those readers who have grown up in a culture dominated by imagistic rather than print-based media, the persuasive power of images, signs, and symbols seems a foregone conclusion. Why, then, has our discipline been so resistant to accepting visual rhetoric as a legitimate field of study?

Craig Stroupe helps situates this phenomenon by pointing out that rhetoric and composition programs are usually contained within English departments, and that it is English studies as a whole that has been staunch in its defense of verbal print culture and its "customary dismissal of popular, predominantly visual discourses" (609-10). Fear of technology (particularly computer technology) and disdain for popular "texts" contributed heavily to this early marginalization of visual rhetoric in the discipline. Visual rhetoric clearly complements many disciplines, but as other "new" fields of study have experienced, it also may threaten established academic disciplines, whose completeness, internal coherence, and boundaries may be called into question if visual rhetoric is recognized. Given these obstacles, the pace of visual studies' (re)emergence is more easily understood.

Rhetoric and composition's reticence to embrace visual rhetoric studies is ironic, given the importance of the visual throughout the history of the discipline since ancient times. Aristotle acknowledged the power of metaphor and visualization and Quintillian identified visualization as the surest means of arousing emotions. Plato placed great importance on light and vision in both the extra-sensory and the sensory worlds. Ernst Robert Curtius points out that in medieval times, epideictic rhetoric (with more emphasis placed on visual presentation) became much more important than deliberative rhetoric. Catherine Hobbs argues that Francis Bacon, by calling images *emblems,* accepted the premise that images are more memorable than words. She offers the following quote from Bacon as evidence: "It is easier to retain the image of a sportsman hunting the hare, of an apothecary ranging his boxes, an orator making a speech, a boy repeating verses, or a player acting his part, than the corresponding notions of invention, disposition, elocution, memory, [and] action" (60-61). The "new rhetoricians" of the Scottish Enlightenment (Smith, Blair, Lord Kames, and Campbell among others) were also influenced by Bacon's centering of imagery and imagination. The terms and concepts now recognized as integral to visual studies have a rich history in rhetoric. Gunther Kress and Theo Van Leeuwen and Hunter Gardner are among the scholars leading the academic conversation on the need to pay attention to visual rhetorics.

Many strong classroom applications of visual rhetoric exist. One of the earliest texts to demonstrate how to incorporate the study of visuals in the writing classroom was Stephen Bernhardt's "Seeing the Text." In this essay, Bernhardt argued that even verbal print texts are inherently visual in that they rely on spatial arrangements and decisions (font styles and sizes, locations of white spaces, paragraphing, etc.) that are rhetorical in nature. Bernhardt's essay includes copies of an environmental fact sheet produced by conservation-minded citizens and politicians pursuing wetlands protection legislation. Bernhardt's analysis of the construction of the fact sheet serves as a strong introduction to the notion that visual rhetoric need not include pictures, signs, or symbols, and provides a point of comparison for the many similar civic-minded fact sheets, advocacy pamphlets, and websites that exist.

In "Reading the Visual in College Writing Classes," Charles Hill shares some of his own techniques for introducing students to visual rhetoric. His examples are diverse, ranging from the rearrangement of the spaces between lines of text and the size of the text lines (similar to Bernhardt's essay) to the analysis of the rhetoric of famous photographs (United States Marines raising the flag over Iwo Jima) to the deconstruction of the cultural values hidden within a print-based advertisement for life insurance. Hill's analysis of each example helps clearly demonstrate the diversity of visual persuasive appeals and provides teachers and students with a strong pedagogical foundation from which to explore other examples of visual rhetoric in the sample categories provided.

For teachers who want to continue to explore the connections between visual rhetoric and culture, articles by Francis Frascina and Kenneth Zagacki offer complementary analyses of Norman Rockwell paintings. Frascina compares Rockwell's original World War

II-inspired paintings with the digitally altered versions of the paintings produced by *The New York Times* after 9/11 in an attempt to demonstrate the "collective cultural memory" powerful images can construct. Zagacki uses Rockwell's civil rights paintings to illustrate how visual works of art "may operate rhetorically to articulate public knowledge" and shape public perception. These two essays and the Rockwell paintings discussed in them offer excellent opportunities for teachers to introduce students to visual rhetoric concepts and methods through which they might analyze and deconstruct imagistic persuasive appeals.

Practical examples for other visual rhetoric genres exist as well. McCloud's *Understanding Comics: The Invisible Art* creatively uses comics themselves to analyze the rhetorical practices employed by comics. David Blakesley's analysis of the rhetorically reflexive verbal and visual components in *The Usual Suspects* provides a framework that can be applied to the study of visual rhetoric in cinema. Craig Smith's "Television News as Rhetoric" works well in conjunction with Joel Nydahl's "The Rhetoric of Television News" and John Hartley's *Uses of Television,* to provide representative examples of how television rhetoric can be studied and applied. Teachers who wish to combine the study of television and film might select Thomas Rosteck's 1989 article which analyzes the argumentative structure of Edward R. Murrow's "Report on Senator McCarthy" from the documentary series "See It Now" and George Clooney's 2005 film *Good Night, and Good Luck* which depicts the same pivotal situation in American history. Those interested in video game rhetoric and the ongoing argument about the impacts of violent video games might connect Lachlan, Smith, and Tamborini and the large amount of journalism covering the debate between Joseph Lieberman and game designers and players (Wikipedia.org has excellent coverage of this issue). These materials can be combined with the video games *Doom* and *Doom 3,* and *Doom: The Movie* to provide a practical example of how different visual rhetorics impact the same subject matter.

The next decade will see visual rhetoric studies gain increasing status in all relevant academic disciplines including rhetoric and composition; prescient teachers will begin to increase their literacy in visual rhetoric theory and pedagogy (drawing on the proliferation of cultural examples that surround them) in preparation for the increasing academic awareness of and appreciation for the persuasive power of the image and visually persuasive texts.

Works Cited

Bernhardt, Stephen A. "Seeing the Text." *College Composition and Communication* 37.1 (1986): 66-78.

Blakesley, David, ed. *The Terministic Screen: Rhetorical Perspectives on Film.* Carbondale: Southern Illinois UP, 2003.

Curtius, Ernst Robert. *European Literature and the Latin Middle Ages.* Princeton, NJ: Princeton/Bollingen, 1973.

Doom. Dir. Andrzej Bartkowiak. Perf. The Rock, Karl Urban, and Rosamund Pike. Universal, 2005.

Frascina, Francis. "The New York Times, Norman Rockwell and the New Patriotism." *Journal of Visual Culture* 2.1 (2003): 99-130.

Gardner, Howard. *Changing Minds: The Art and Science of Changing Our Own and Other People's Minds.* Boston: Harvard Business School, 2004.

Good Night, and Good Luck. Dir. George Clooney. Perf. David Strathairn, Robert Downey, Jr., Patricia Clarkson, and Ray Wise. Warner Independent Pictures, 2005.

Handa, Carolyn, ed. *Visual Rhetoric in a Digital World: A Critical Sourcebook.* New York: Bedford/St. Martin's, 2004.

Hartley, John. *Uses of Television.* London: Routledge, 1999.

Hill, Charles A. "Reading the Visual in College Writing Classes." *Intertexts: Reading Pedagogy in College Writing Classrooms.* Ed. Marguerite Helmers. Mahwah, NJ: LEA, 2003. 123-50.

Hobbs, Catherine L. "Learning from the Past: Verbal and Visual Literacy in Early Modern Rhetoric and Writing Pedagogy." *Language and Image in the Reading-Writing Classroom.* Ed. Kristie Fleckenstein, Linda T. Calendrillo and Demetrice A. Worley. Mahwah, NJ: LEA, 2002. 27-44.

id Software. *Doom.* id Software, 1993.

id Software. *Doom III.* Activision, 2004

Kress, Gunther, and Theo Van Leeuwen. *Reading Images: The Grammar of Visual Design.* New York: Routledge, 1996.

Lachlan, Ken, Stacy L. Smith, and Ron Tamborini. "Popular Video Games: Quantifying the Presentation of Violence and Its Context." *Journal of Broadcasting & Electronic Media* 41.1 (2003): 58-76.

McCloud, Scott. *Understanding Comics: The Invisible Art.* New York: HarperCollins, 1994.

Nydahl, Joel. "The Rhetoric of Television News." *Teaching English in the Two-Year College* 13.4 (1986): 290-97.

Rosteck, Thomas. "Irony, Argument, and Reportage in Television Documentary: "See It Now" versus Senator McCarthy." *Quarterly Journal of Speech* 75.3 (1989): 277-98.

Smith, Craig R. "Television News as Rhetoric." *Western Journal of Speech Communication* 41.3 (1977): 147-59.

Stroupe, Craig. "Visualizing English: Recognizing the Hybrid Literacy of Visual and Verbal Authorship on the Web." *College English* 62.5 (2000): 607-32.

Zagacki, Kenneth. "Visibility and Rhetoric: The Power of Visual Images in Norman Rockwell's Depictions of Civil Rights." *Quarterly Journal of Speech* 91.2 (2005): 175-200.

For Further Reading

Textbooks

Alfano, Christine and Alyssa O'Brien. *Envision: Persuasive Writing in a Visual World.* New York: Longman, 2005.

Faigley, Lester, Diana George, Anna Palchik, and Cynthia Selfe. *Picturing Texts.* New York: Norton, 2005.

McQuade, Donald and Christine McQuade. *Seeing and Writing.* Boston: Bedford/St. Martin's, 2000.

This textbook both asks and answers the question "what does seeing have to do with writing?" Designed to introduce students to elements of visual rhetoric, McQuade and McQuade divide each chapter into an opening set of images ("portfolio"), images juxtaposed with written text ("pair"), exercises, visual representations of history ("retrospect"), interviews, key concepts for writers ("visualizing composition"), a collection of visual and written readings ("looking closer"), and contextual historical and cultural images for difficult readings ("context"). The book makes explicit connections between visual and written texts and topics such as place, gender, difference, icons, and observing the everyday.

Ruszkiewicz, John, Daniel Anderson, and Christy Friend. *Beyond Words: Reading and Writing in a Visual Age.* New York: Longman, 2006.

Scholarly Works

Birdsell, David S., and Leo Groarke. "Toward a Theory of Visual Argument." *Argumentation & Advocacy* 33.1 (1996): 1-10.

Birdsell and Groarke assert that argumentation theorists are overly concerned with the verbal aspects of argument to the exclusion of the visual aspects of argument. This is problematic, they maintain, because of the changing nature of argument itself, particularly in new media such as television, the internet, advertising, and film. In creating a theory of visual argument, the authors assert that the unwarranted assumption that visual arguments are less precise than verbal arguments must be abandoned—they argue instead that both verbal and visual arguments may be vague and imprecise. The authors assert that a theory of visual argument will take into account the importance of context, arguing that just as verbal arguments themselves cannot stand in isolation, neither can visual arguments. The authors outline three types of context important to visual argument: immediate visual context, immediate verbal context, and visual culture. The last element in a theory of visual argument is the issue of representation and resemblance, to which the authors argue there is an argumentative component that is reflected in most visual texts.

Finnegan, Cara A. "The Naturalistic Enthymeme and Visual Argument: Photographic Representation in the Skull Controversy.'" *Argumentation and Advocacy* 37.3 (2001): 133-49.

Finnegan introduces the concept of the naturalistic enthymeme to the study of visual rhetoric: the assumptions we make about the argumentative potential of photographs, particularly nature photographs. She argues that because we perceive photographs as realistic, we assume them to be "true" or "real" until given a reason to doubt them. She uses the 1930s debate over the photographs taken by Arthur Rothstein for the Resettlement Administration depicting drought conditions in the Dakotas to support her claims. Through this article, the author hopes to demonstrate how visual cultural implications influence the perceived argumentative capacity of images.

Fox, Roy F., ed. *Images in Language, Media, and Mind.* Urbana: NCTE, 1994.

This anthology provides several demonstrations of how societal images are persuasive in nature. Operating under the assumption that "the most important kind of meaning is constructed from personal interactions with images" (xi), Fox has selected essays analyzing the visual persuasion of print advertising, news coverage of the Gulf War, television sportscasts, and the imagery of the Oliver North trial, among others. The range of subjects covered offer several starting points for exploring imagistic rhetoric and the terminology used by the authors (such as symbolspeak and hyperintertextuality) provide the beginnings of a vocabulary to aid in the discussion of visual arguments.

George, Diana. "From Analysis to Design: Visual Communication in the Teaching of Writing." *College Composition and Communication* 52.1 (2002): 11-39.

George argues that the current terms used to describe visual rhetoric in the field of composition studies limit the way such communication might be brought to bear in the writing classroom. Specific to George's argument is that visual literacy belongs in the writing classroom and is not simply a new strategy "for adding relevance or interest to a required course" (13). George charts the history of visual rhetoric in English studies, including discussion of some of the first visual assignments in textbooks. She asserts that incorporating visual elements in a writing course widen the possibilities for instruction, and will do so in growing ways as teachers incorporate technology into classrooms that allow students to both analyze and produce visual texts.

Slade, Christina. "Seeing Reasons: Visual Argumentation in Advertisements." *Argumentation* 17.2 (2003): 145-60.

Using advertisements to illustrate her point, Slade argues that visual media can function as argumentation. Arguing against Postman and Poster's claims that visual media function as irrational argumentation, Slade asserts that not only does the rational/irrational divide not hold up, but also that visual texts do function as reasoned discourse.

5 Glossary of Terms

Here in the glossary, we have tried to be as concise as possible in defining and describing terms. Our glossary of the terms is specific to our treatment of the teaching of argument in this text. This means that some terms specific to Kenneth Burke's *terministic screen* appear among traditional argument terms. By no means is this a definitive or exhaustive list, as most rhetorical terms are applicable to teaching argument. For more complete historical and theoretical definitions of key rhetorical terms, interested readers might consult one of the more comprehensive reference works, such as the *Encyclopedia of Rhetoric,* edited by Thomas Sloane, the *Encyclopedia of Rhetoric and Composition,* edited by Theresa Enos, or the *Sourcebook on Rhetoric* by James Jasinski.

Action vs. Motion—In *A Grammar of Motives,* Burke defines action as the "human body in conscious or purposive motion" (14). Action is something only human beings are capable of. A capacity to act, meanwhile, is a prerequisite for moral choices. A baseball, thus, is capable of motion but not action, as it "is neither moral nor immoral, it cannot act, it can only move, or be moved" (136). For Burke, action involves moving toward an ideal, creating novelty along the way. The transformations effected by action are all necessarily partial, by necessity, due to the paradox of substance. See also: **Magic**, the **Paradox of Substance**.

Agonistic/Eristical Argument—From the Greek *agon,* meaning contest or conflict, and *eris,* meaning strife; agonistic or eristical argument represents a model of argument stressing conflict and dispute, advancing one person's perspective at the expense of others. Agonistic/eristical argument has been challenged by feminist scholars, among others, as an adversarial, patriarchal model that promotes dissensus rather than consensus. Moreover, eristical argument has also been criticized for being unrealistic. Most contemporary models of argument are many-sided and reject the goal of defeating one's adversaries in favor of a more realistic goal such as increasing or decreasing participants' adherence to or identification with the arguer's position and/or loosening adherence or identification with alternative positions.

Analogy—See **Invention.**

Attitude—Burke used five terms to explain human motives: act, agent, agency, scene and purpose. Later on, he added attitude, a term describing the manner in which the act is carried out. It is a precursor to the act, what he calls an "incipient act." Rhetoric moves people to act or bends their attitude so as to incline them to act. It does not force people to act, it convinces them. Acts then become the representations of our attitudes.

Burkeian Pentad—Kenneth Burke believed that social communication was best analyzed and understood as drama, leading him to privilege a pentad of terms for rhetorical study: *act*, *scene*, *agent*, *agency*, and *purpose.* Outcomes for rhetorical actions are determined by the *ratios* (relationships) between these five elements. See also: **Rhetorical Situation.**

Casuistry— "The general and the particular directions of rhetoric overlap insofar as all unique cases will necessarily involve the application of the universal topics to the particular matter at hand, and insofar as even situations considered very broadly may possess uniqueness" (Burke, *Rhetoric* 72-73). For Burke, casuistries are philosophies, general principles extended to specific situations. While casuistry has negative connotations for many contemporary analysts, Burke sees it as unavoidable. However, "casuistic stretching" is often needed to persuade people that an original frame (like the United States Constitution, for example) is still viable, despite new variables in time and space. See also: **Identification**, the **Paradox of substance**.

Consubstantiality—See **Identification.**

Courtship—For Kenneth Burke, courtship is a form of persuasion that operates through identification in which one "entity" persuades the other. For courtship to exist, each entity must belong to a separate class, which leads to what Burke refers to as "estrangement." For individuals, this estrangement lies in the difference between sexes; in the social realm, the difference between the sexes finds its equivalent within the differences between social classes. Burke refers to communication between classes as "abstract" courtship. Within the realm of abstract courtship, members of higher social classes attempt to control less privileged classes through "doctrine" and "education." Thus, "[b]y the 'principle of courtship' in rhetoric we mean the use of suasive devices for the transcending of social estrangement" (Rhetoric 208). Within this relationship of social estrangement, parties are "mysterious" to one another and that mystery can be converted to power. A teacher, for example, might remain largely silent so as to add gravity to questions that s/he raises, thus appearing to "probe into the depths of things" in the eyes of the student (210).

Burke's courtship differs from Perelman and Olbrecht-Tyteca's notion of *adherence* in that it does not seek explicitly to use persuasion to increase the degree of agreement with the rhetor. An audience's degree of adherence to the rhetor's argument can vary greatly. By contrast, courtship focuses primarily on the unequal relationship between the persuader and those being persuaded, rather than employ means generally considered "persuasive." Through courtship, the "courtier" already commands a certain "captivation" of the audience. This "courted" audience thus yearns to transcend the gap of social estrangement to unite with the persuader, while the persuader "coyly" maintains that distance and thus captivation and power.

Deliberative Rhetoric—See **Species of Rhetoric.**

Dialectic—With his opening sentence in the Rhetoric, Aristotle defines Rhetoric as the counterpart to Dialectic. Both rhetoric and dialectic are faculties of furnishing arguments. Historically, dialectic is sometimes seen as rhetoric's counterpart; at times it has competed with rhetoric. Aristotle distinguishes demonstrative reasoning (causal) from dialectical reasoning (non-causal or contingent), defining the latter as "reasoning from opinions" that are generally accepted as probable truths. Dialectic reasoning can occur between interlocutors, or it can be an internal inquiry. The Socratic Method is the best known example of dialectic reasoning whereby one begins with a proposition then pushes it to its conclusion by questions and answers and by applying the law of contradiction. Dialectic reasoning is a test for truth, a meaning-making process. Propositions must be secured prior to argument; a proposition is dialectically secured when it passes the law of contradiction. The Hegelian model of dialectic involves thesis (a proposition), antithesis (the contradiction of the proposition), and synthesis (an incorporation of the first two elements).

Doxa—The Greek word for common or popular opinions, which is the root of English words like "orthodoxy" (straight opinion) and "paradox" (opinions alongside one another). Doxa are the opinions sometimes codified, that are generally accepted within a community. The notion of doxa places the locus of authority outside of the individual and in the community. The opinions of individual people are not solely theirs, but also that of many others, thus giving those opinions more importance. Placing opinions outside of the individual also opens the door for persuasion to take place.

Enthymeme—Sometimes called a "truncated syllogism," the enthymeme leaves out a premise, and then hopes its audience will tacitly supply it. The enthymeme, thus, is not to be judged by the conventions of formal validity, but rather by the laws of probability. The more widely accepted the premise, the more likely it is that an audience will grant assent to the enthymeme's argument. Aristotle labeled the enthymeme the "substance of rhetorical persuasion" (I.1). Since there is very little that can be known for certain, rhetors must rely on beliefs and assumptions of their audience.

Ethos—See **Pisteis.**

Example, Illustration, Model—Perelman and Olbrechts-Tyteca analyze how rhetors seek to establish a commonality with their audience through a resort to the particular, in the form of *example,* which makes generalization possible; *illustration,* which provides support for an established generalization; and *model,* which encourages imitation. These can be further defined as follows:

Example: A particular instance which provides a foundation for a rule and acts as the starting point of a generalization. An example must be, at least provisionally, a fact. Examples serve both to illustrate a generalization and to establish the truth of the generalization. According to Perelman, much of argument is designed to get audiences to recognize invalidating facts (i.e., those examples which contradict the generalizations or rules they also admit). For Aristotle, proofs come in the form of either enthymeme or example. An example is neither the relation of "part to whole, nor whole to part, nor one whole to another whole; instead, example is the relation of part to part, and of like to like." Examples might be historical (referencing past events) or invented (Aristotle identified the fable as one type of effective invented example).

Illustration: Illustration seeks to make an abstract rule or idea concrete through a particular case; it promotes understanding of the rule. Whereas examples must be beyond question, illustrations need not be. Illustrations can be detailed, but examples should be pruned to avoid distraction.

Model: Models are idealized illustrations of a general rule. Models are not simply to be understood; they are to be imitated.

Epideictic Rhetoric—See **Species of Rhetoric.**

Fallacies, Informal—Fallacies, in the most general sense, are defective arguments (Sloane prefers "deficient moves in argumentative discourse"). Arguments may be fallacious due to flaws in their structure and form. These are formal fallacies. Arguments that are invalid for any other reason besides the form of the argument are informal fallacies. Informal fallacies come in many forms. One example of an informal fallacy is a "spurious relationship": claiming two different groups that have no logical relationship are nevertheless connected. Wikipedia provides the following example: "an example of a spurious relationship can be illuminated examining a city's ice cream sales. These sales are highest when the city's rate of drownings is highest. To allege that ice cream sales cause drowning would be to imply a spurious relationship between the two. In reality, a heat wave may have caused both." For a more complete treatment of informal fallacies in arguments, see Fulkerson's *Teaching the Argument in Writing.*

Forensic Rhetoric—See **Species of Rhetoric.**

Heuristics—See **Invention.**

Identification—For Burke, the concept of identification is central to rhetoric and to argument. Burkeian identification relies on the concepts of merger and division. Person A experiences merger if s/he has common interests with Person B or if s/he is persuaded to believe that there are common interests: "in being identified with B, A is 'substantially one' with a person other than himself" (Rhetoric 21). In the process of acting together, individuals share common sensations, concepts, images, ideas, and attitudes. Burke's term for this is consubstantiality, a way of "acting together." To clarify, Burke speaks of consubstantiality in terms of parent/child relations. For example, a child is consubstantial with his/her parents in the sense that it is at once their offspring and an autonomous actor. Some modicum of separation (division) always exists, as each person is a "unique, individual locus of motives" (21). Through identification, rhetoric and argumentation are made possible as arguments use the principles of merger and division to bend attitudes and persuade. See also: **Paradox of Substance.**

Illustration—See **Example.**

Impartiality—The condition of being a member of a group that will be affected by the outcome of an argument without having one's decisions influenced by that fact, as "an impartial judge," whose rulings would apply to everyone, including the judge. Impartiality, therefore, involves balancing all points of view in an argument. This contrasts with *objectivity* as used by Perelman, where neutrality is maintained because the rhetor purports to be unaffected by the argument's outcome.

Inertia—Perelman's *The New Rhetoric* uses the term "inertia" to designate human resistance to change. Borrowing from physics, Perelman and Olbrechts-Tyteca describe the idea that an audience's attitudes, beliefs, and behaviors tend to stay on course through habit. Value is also placed on any attitudes, beliefs, and behaviors that conserve the status quo. Thus, inertia favors the norm; while it is not necessary to persuade toward that which is already accepted, any change will be questioned and will require justification—an audience's natural inertia places the burden of proof on the party who wishes to promote change.

Invention—From the Latin *invenire,* "to find," invention is the first of the five classical canons of rhetoric, followed by arrangement, style, memory, and delivery. Since Aristotle defines rhetoric as "the faculty of discovering the available means of persuasion," much of his *Rhetoric* focuses on invention. Invention concerns finding something to say; consequently, invention relates to *logos,* (i.e., *what* the rhetor says rather than *how*). *Heuristics* (from the Greek *heuriskein,* meaning "to find out, to discover,") are invention strategies by which the rhetor can investigate systematically, following a set of procedures. A rhetor might run through a series of questions or prompts as a means of exploring and investigating a problem or question. In the realm of argument, *stasis theory* functions primarily as a heuristic insofar as each type of claim raises different questions for those making and hearing the claim. In arguments, there are five main claim types: definition (is X a Y?), cause (does X cause Y?), evaluation (is X a good or bad Y?), proposal (should we do X?), and resemblance (is X like Y?). Resemblance arguments are the foremost contemporary versions of *analogies*, where the most general formulation is A is to B as C is to D. However, the formulation may have only three terms, as in B is to A as C is to B, or A is to B as A is to C. Perelman and Olbrechts-Tyteca quote Aristotle's analogy, "For as the eyes of bats are to the blaze of day, so is the reason in our soul to the things which are by nature most evident of all" to explain *theme* (reason in the soul, obviousness) and *phoros* (eyes of bats, blaze of day). In analogy, the theme and phoros must belong to different spheres; if they are in the same sphere, we have example or illustration. Analogy relies on transfers of value from phoros to theme and vice versa. Analogy is often viewed with distrust when used as a proof. Perelman views it as an unstable means of argument similar to informal fallacies. See also: **Stasis Theory.**

Kairos—Both kairos and chronos, roughly translated from the Greek, represent the concept of time. Aristotle used kairos in its classical sense as a critical moment in the unfolding of an argument when one has an opportunity to arouse one's audience.

More recently *kairos* has also been translated as a sense of appropriateness and timeliness. James Kinneavy uses the term to refer to the "situational context." In this second, fuller sense, *kairos* plays a role in the construction of the entire argument and every rhetorical choice.

Logos—See **Pisteis.**

Mediation—See **Negotiation.**

Model—See **Example.**

Mystification—A Burkeian term, mystification occurs when language is used to deceive rather than communicate between different classes. Mystification reduces the fertile potential of mystery by "bureaucratizing" hierarchy into a set scheme that privileges one group over another absolutely and by ginning up the mysterious differences between classes at the expense of their underlying identity. Such misdirected rhetoric is concerned primarily with coercion and control. Mystery and mystification are differentiated from *magic.* As a supernatural force, magic is based on a primitive conception of influence, but it has similarities to rhetoric in its persuasive ends. While magic mistakenly attempts to induce action in things (or to reduce human actors to objects to be moved), rhetoric (often through exhortatory speech) attempts to induce action in people. Burke notes that magic is also associated with novelty, in that it creates something out of nothing; every rhetorical act thus involves a hint of magic to the extent that it uses novelty in the inducement of action. See also: **Courtship**.

Negotiation—Negotiation is an agreement-oriented mode of reaching consensus through communicating, or "working out differences." The concept of negotiation has been accepted by many feminist scholars as an alternative to the agonistic model of argument and as a model for classroom interaction. Others, including some feminists, criticize negotiation insofar as it avoids conflict in situations where conflict is called for. The idea of critical negotiation has been raised as well by scholars such as Thomas West, who connects the concept of negotiation with postcolonial theory, identity formation, and hybridization. Mediation is a particular type of negotiation. In mediation, a disinterested party helps guide the course of an argument, rather than becoming involved in it, or making a judgment for either participant. In mediation the mediator has no power over any participant in the argument, as opposed to arbitration, in which the third party has power to decide the outcome of an argument. Mediation is increasingly used in legal dispute resolution.

Objectivity—Objectivity is the condition of having no interest in and being unaffected by the outcome of an argument. Most contemporary theories of argument reject objectivity as a realistic or even desirable stance for a rhetor or audience. Perelman, for example, acknowledges that outside of science, controversies are settled among interested parties. The best one can hope for is not objectivity but impartiality whereby people act in the name of what's best for all rather than what is best for them or their allies.

Offices (Teaching and Informing, Pleasing, Moving and Bending)—These three rhetorical purposes originated in Cicero's ideas of the three offices of the orator. Each office is said to have an appropriate style. More specifically, the first office, (to teach, inform, instruct), is thought to be a plain style. The second office, (pleasing), called for a more tempered style. The moving and bending aspect of oratory, meanwhile, requires a more grandiloquent style that is stirring enough to persuade an audience to action.

Paradox of Substance—"Literally, a person's or a thing's sub-stance would be something that stands beneath or supports the person or thing" (Burke, *Grammar* 22). Here, Burke traces the etymological roots of the word "substance" to help explain his concept of the paradox of substance, showing that the word itself implies the presence of externals. Burke's concept of substance contrasts markedly with Aristotle's. For Aristotle the substance of an entity would be entire unto itself. Burke inclines to Spinoza's view that no single entity could be understood as self identical but only by what it is not ("all determination is negation" [*Grammar* 25]). This concept is the heart of the Burkeian Paradox of Substance: in order to be able to understand what a given thing is, you must first place it "in terms of" something else. This is the fundamental logic underlying Burke's dramatism. For Burke, there is an "inevitable paradox of definition, an antinomy that must endow the concept of substance with unresolvable ambiguity" (*Grammar* 24): something's substance can only be known in terms of what it is substantially not. See also: **Identification** and the **Dialectic**.

Pathos—See **Pisteis.**

Pisteis—Aristotle identified two types of rhetorical proofs: (1) artistic (intrinsic) and (2) inartistic (extrinsic). Inartistic proofs come, not from a rhetor's own efforts, but from preexisting data that the speaker must discover and use: confessions, written contracts, and so forth. Artistic proofs must be furnished by methods of rhetoric through the rhetor's own efforts. **Pisteis** (coming from the Greek word referring to the means of persuasion available in an argument) are the three types of artistic proofs available to the rhetor: logos, ethos, and pathos.

The *ethos* (Greek for "character") of the speaker refers to the rhetor's credibility. In Aristotle's time, trust was created from the speech itself rather than from the type of man speaking. More recently, however, ethos often as not derives more from office or position. For instance, we trust those who are experts in their fields more than those who are generalists. *Pathos* (Greek for "suffering" or "experience") refers to the emotions of the audience when they are brought into a state that is favorable to increasing adherence to the argument itself. The rhetor can appeal effectively to pathos by knowing the beliefs and values of the audience and employing various rhetorical strategies accordingly. *Logos* (Greek for "word") refers to the rationality of the argument proper. The argument itself should be consistent, coherent, rational, well grounded, and plausible in its logical appeal.

Praxis—Praxis is an alternative to the bifurcated theory/practice pair in which practice is subordinate to theory. Praxis exists as theorized, informed, and situated practice. In composition it is what separates classroom "lore" (criticized as unreflective and ad-hoc, as well as over-theorized abstraction) from reflective teaching that is grounded in critical, pedagogically situated ways of knowing and learning.

Presence—Presence refers to the elements of selection, arrangement and/or omission of facts, judgments, or lines of reasoning that act directly on our sensibility. Those elements of an argument endowed with presence allow an audience to perceive what otherwise would be merely conceived. Lending presence to one's argument through use of metaphors, vivid examples, striking graphics, etc. greatly increases audience identification with one's argument.

Propaganda—Propaganda is a type of rhetorical persuasion aimed at a mass rather than individual audience. It is explicit, and is produced by an institution or group (like a government). Propaganda is also distinguished by its self-serving nature: it makes no attempt to find compromise between rhetor and audience. Relying heavily on the repetition of symbols and images in social media, propaganda often has negative connotations in Western society, as governments, organized religions, and corporate advertisers (among others) continue to produce propaganda at high levels. The arguments (often visual in nature) produced by propaganda provide vivid examples that foster productive discussion in argument classrooms.

Ratio—See **Burkeian Pentad.**

Rhetoric of Bureaucracy—Rhetoric of bureaucracy refers to a rhetoric of gesture, usually symbolic in nature. A modern US example of Rhetoric of bureaucracy is the toppling of the statue of Saddam Hussein after the invasion of US forces into Baghdad. This type of rhetorical gesture signified victory for the United States forces and the defeat of Iraq.

Rhetorical Situation—The rhetorical situation refers to the contextually situated call to persuade, whether it is oral or written. How best to determine how to persuasively impact a given target audience? What are the elements of a given rhetorical situation? There is no easy answer to this question, and scholars continue to offer competing theoretical and practical frameworks. One common framework used in writing instruction is the rhetorical triangle, with focuses on the interrelatedness of the message, the writer, and the audience. Other frameworks are even more specific, identifying five major components of the rhetorical situation: occasion, purpose, topic, audience, and writer. Kenneth Burke's Pentad also identified five essential elements: act, scene, agent, agency, and purpose. Notice that even as these different frameworks are comprised of different terminologies, the core elements are similar, providing variations on the rhetorical triangle. No matter which terminological framework is used, the key to understanding the rhetorical situation lies in recognizing the "ratio" of the terms: which elements are most important to the given situation

Rogerian Argument—This is a type of argument that attempts to explore and/or resolve issues by engaging in empathic listening. The fundamental principle is to regard communication from the standpoint of understanding another person. To participate in authentic communication requires one to see the ideas and attitudes of the other person so profoundly that one can sense how it feels to be that person. The goal is to bring about a change in perspective or to modify the other person's conception of reality so that mutually advantageous co-operation is possible. There are three strategies: (1) reassure the person s/he is understood, (2) discover the validity of the person's position and (3) find areas of similarity. Some problems with Rogerian argument are its practice of identification at the start of argumentation when argumentation presupposes identification as a possible result. There is also potential for its manipulative use. Used as a technique, identification may not be sincerely felt, creating a false empathy with others.

Rule of Justice—This term is at the heart of Perelman's theories of argumentation. The key to this formal rule is in giving "identical treatment to beings or situations of the same kind" (*New* 218). Observing the rule of justice is necessary to the construction of arguments for justice. Through this rule, precedents also acquire greater importance: past cases can influence future cases (provided the categories are essentially the same).

Sophistry—In popular parlance, *sophistry* refers to any specious argument intended to trick rather than legitimately persuade a listener. The term dates from the fifth century B.C. and the Sophists, a loose collection of pre-Platonic philosophers and teachers employed as instructors of rhetoric. In general, Sophists taught from practical experience rather than theory, and stressed real-world persuasive skills rather than the quest for a particular form of truth. That is, their tactics taught one how to "argue to win" regardless of one's position.

In Plato's *Dialogues,* the Sophists are used as convenient debate fodder and straw men for Socrates's questioning, their use of rhetoric exposed as selfish and amoral (see Plato's *Gorgias*). Against Plato's condemnation of rhetoric, the Sophists emerge as artful tricksters, using language to deceive rather than to find truth. Contemporary perspectives on rhetoric have rehabilitated many Sophistic concepts, including attention to the ambiguity of language and the contextual nature of truth and knowledge. Susan Jarratt's "rhetorical feminism," for example, links the political focus of contemporary feminism with Sophistic approaches to the real-world power of language use.

Species of Rhetoric—For Aristotle, there are three kinds of discourse, each with its own temporal emphasis. Firstly, *epideictic* (ceremonial) discourse has to do with praise or blame. An example of this type of discourse is eulogy. The speaker uses ceremonial speech to bolster important attitudes and beliefs in the present. Secondly, *deliberative* discourse is a call for some sort of action, typically legislative, that either exhorts to or dissuades from a particular course of action. Thirdly, *forensic* (judicial) discourse determines guilt, innocence, or causation based on an examination of past events.

Stasis Theory—From the Greek word *staseis* which means "to take a stand." In rhetorical theory, stasis theory can be used to find common ground on an issue or as an invention strategy that provides the rhetor with a series of questions that serve to discover the point of disagreement between two disputants. Since the 2nd C. CE, there has traditionally been a hierarchical order of the stasis questions; however, recently scholars have argued that the questions do not necessarily have to be asked in a specific order; depending on the rhetorical situation, some of the questions may not be applicable. The significance of finding the point of origin of a disagreement is invaluable if the goal of argument is to reach a resolution or at least a clearer understanding of the issue, as opposed to bickering, which is often the result of an argument where stasis has not been reached prior to engagement. The stases are divided into four questions:

1. Conjecture—is there an act to be considered?
2. Definition—how can the act be defined?
3. Quality—how serious is the act? What are the extenuating circumstances?
4. Procedure—what should we do? Is there anything about the act that calls for a non-standard ruling or lessened punishment?

Topoi (Topics)—Originally delineated by Aristotle, the *topics* are the available means of persuasion and are used during the invention phase of argumentation. Aristotle classified the topics under two headings: (1) those common to all subjects (commonplaces) and usable in all circumstances and (2) those from specialized fields, such as physics or politics. Perelman takes a different approach to topics. He applies his term *loci* only to premises of a general nature that can serve as the bases for values and hierarchies and that relate to choices we make. He classifies *loci* into: (1) loci of quantity (e.g., a greater number of goods is more desirable than a lesser number of goods), (2) quality (e.g., one truth is to be desired above one hundred errors or the unique is valued above the usual, the ordinary, or the vulgar), (3) order (e.g., that which is earlier is superior to that which is later, for instance the original is superior to copy), (4) the existing (e.g., that which is actual or real is superior to the possible, the contingent, or the impossible), (5) essence (e.g., the superiority of the value of individuals as embodying the essence, for instance a best of breed would exhibit the qualities of that breed better than its competitors), and (6) the person (e.g., the value of dignity, worth, or autonomy of the person).

Toulmin's Schema for Argumentation—Toulmin's schema and terminology for analyzing and creating arguments are often used in the teaching of argument. Central to Toulmin's model of the structure of arguments are several key terms. All arguments make a *claim* based on *data*. A *warrant* is a general proposition that establishes a connection between the claim and the data. Warrants often need *backing* (evidence helping prove the warrant). The claim may also need a *qualifier* (to prevent absolutist language) and conditions for *rebuttal* (exceptions to the rule formed by the claim) to maximize its persuasive potential. Toulmin's schema has proven to be applicable across academic disciplines and to popular arguments as well.

6 Annotated Bibliography

In compiling this bibliography we discovered anew what others before us have discovered—the paucity of published work on argumentation in journals and presses prominent in the field of rhetoric and composition. Richard Fulkerson's observation about the lack of scholarly debate about the teaching of argumentation was borne out by our own research. In response we broadened the scope of the bibliography slightly, including several book-length philosophical treatments of argument. We opted not to broaden the scope further on the grounds that it would likely make the bibliography less, not more, useful to our readers. Our primary focus is on works published within the past twenty years, with some important earlier works included. Any work that focused on the teaching of argument is listed here. A number of works referred to extensively in the body of this book—Toulmin, Perelman, and Burke—are left out on the grounds that one can derive a much fuller sense of their argument from reading the previous chapters. Few argument textbooks are included here. Those that are cited are included because of a unique focus. Our assumption is that readers may wish to consult these texts for ideas about teaching argument rather than adopting them wholesale for classroom use.

Allen, Julia M., and Lester Faigley. "Discursive Strategies for Social Change: An Alternative Rhetoric of Argument." *Rhetoric Review* 14.1 (1995): 142-72.

The authors provide a repertoire of alternative argument strategies that have been used to enact discursive change by writers who, historically, did not or felt they did not have the power to engage in the dominant discourse; however, Allen and Faigley do not make claims "for the utility of any strategy." Strategies for social change that have been used are: creating new languages (such as "Laadan" for writer Suzette Haden Elgin); constructing new pronouns (such as "co" or "na"); using neologisms; reclaiming or redefining words (such as "spinster" or "dyke"); juxtaposing language and "creating struggle within and utterance" (as is demonstrated by Gloria Anzaldua's Borderlands/*La Frontera*); using musical forms to structure written communication; utilizing "perspective by incongruity," which puts "one assumed truth into an incongruous situation to undermine its truthfulness;" playing with language and metaphor and "calling without naming" (referring to Gertrude Stein's prose); and using narratives as a way to make oneself heard politically. The authors assert that writing teachers need to rethink traditional assumptions about the validity and use of logical arguments and their ability to shift social structure, given the wide range of forced alternatives that have arisen out of power struggles throughout history.

Andrews, Richard. "Models of Argumentation in Educational Discourse." *Text* 25.1 (2005): 107-27.

This piece is a review of literature of the various models of argumentation formulated for educational settings during the past ten years. The first half of the article is used to delineate the various and competing definitions of argument and to ground the literature review in the process of developing arguments as opposed to the phenomenon of argument. Andrews positions logical constructions of argument at one extreme and rhetorical constructions at the other. As he examines the various models, suggestions are made as to their usefulness in the classroom. Andrews is concerned primarily with the pedagogical value of these models. The second half of the article focuses in on four models of argumentation: Toulmin, Mitchell and Riddle, Andrews, and Kaufer and Geisler. As theories such as the Toulmin model are outlined, Andrews pinpoints ways to "adapt" them for more suitable use in the classroom. He suggests that an analytic model, such as Toulmin, is better suited to test the strength of an early draft than to generate arguments, a charge that has often been leveled against Toulmin. According to Andrews, the generative value of these models for argument is a key to their usefulness in educational settings. At the end, there is brief section on visual argument and the value of argument in society.

Bay, Jennifer L. "The Limits of Argument: A Response to Sean Williams." *JAC* 22.3 (2002): 684-97.

In this response to Sean Williams's article, "Process-Product Ambiguity: Theorizing a Perspective on World Wide Web Argumentation," Bay applauds the attention that Williams draws to argument in cyberspace and his attempt at "retooling" Toulmin in order to "reconceptualize" argument on the Internet, but laments the lack of discussion of the "visual and performative aspects" of the Web and how these aspects affect argument and the writer's sense of agency. Whereas Williams views "links" in webtexts as persuasive devices because the "author" selectively places them, Bay challenges whether this is a WWW argument theory or just a traditional theory applied to the Web. In short, Bay suggests that Williams assumes that the Web is a "text-based structure." In fact, she implies that most pedagogical practices still rely on this classical model and value words over images. Bay calls for a rhetoric of the Web that accounts for its multimedia capabilities and attempts to open space for production and analysis of webtexts that are more than print arguments.

Berrill, Deborah P., ed. *Perspectives on Written Argument.* Cresskill, NJ: Hampton, 1996.

This collection of thirteen essays emphasizes the role of writing in everyday life and offers a variety of contemporary views on argumentation. The essays range from the theoretical (Andrew Wilkinson's "Argument as a Primary Act of Mind") to the practical (Anson and Beach's "The Nature of Argument in Peer Dialogue Journals") and it emphasizes a variety of non-traditional approaches drawn from non-Western and feminist models as well as traditional Western modes of argument. A number of the essays consider the relationship between argument and the learning process, focusing on use of peer dialogue journals as a learning tool and the use of New Rhetoric to respond to students' argumentative writing. Other essays consider alternatives to the argument-as-war model, which treats argument as a means of transformation rather than negotiation. The final four essays focus on alternate cultural styles in argument.

Biser, Eileen, Linda Rubel, and Rose Marie Toscano. "Be Careful What You Ask For: When Basic Writers Take the Rhetorical Stage." *Journal of Basic Writing* 21.1 (2002): 52-70.

The authors discuss the difficulties facing students as they begin to adopt rhetorical stances and public voices. Marginalized writers in particular face additional challenges beyond the conventional expectations of form, in that they often write from a perspective beyond the mainstream. The article examines a public email written by a deaf student at the Rochester Institute of Technology arguing for a faculty discussion of the role of interpreters in the classroom. Though the writer follows the conventions of argument—writing from a position of authority, using a collective voice for power, citing expert opinion—her argument had unintended consequences, generating a largely negative response from RIT's deaf population, many of whom viewed the letter as presumptuous. Essentially, the writer failed to consider the complex views of the deaf community she purported to represent. The authors note several implications for teachers of argument, including the responsibilities and obligations in employing the collective voice, the particular challenges of argument in an electronic format, and the need for students to address "taken-for-granted" ideas in reading such as tone and author bias.

Booth, Wayne C. *Modern Dogma and the Rhetoric of Assent.* Chicago: U of Chicago P, 1974.

Booth's book is a product of the author's disciplinary background and its historical origins. It is based primarily on his experiences as a university administrator during the tumultuous nineteen-sixties and seventies. The most striking aspect of the rancorous disagreements that characterized the times was, according to Booth, the tendency of opponents to speak past each other, a state of affairs in marked contrast to civil and efficacious debates among members of various professions and academic disciplines. The failure to listen charitably to other arguments or the corresponding tendency to lapse into a slack-minded "I'm ok, you're ok," denial of differences motivates Booth's argument. Hence his definition of rhetoric: "the art of discovering warrantable beliefs and improving those beliefs in shared discourse" (xiii). The major impediment to Booth's rhetorical ideal is the dogma of modernism, which according to Booth, splits facts off from value and renders values little more than expressions of feelings (motivism). Just as values are impoverished by their reduction to feelings, rational inquiry is reduced to instrumentalism calculation by being divorced from values. While the dogmas of modernism have been renounced in every field, they maintained their currency in the realm of public discourse. Booth's book is an ambitious, often entertaining effort to unseat these dominant dogmas.

Bruffee, Kenneth A. *Collaborative Learning: Higher Education, Interdependence, and the Authority of Knowledge*, 2nd ed. Baltimore: John's Hopkins UP, 1998.

This extensively revised edition presents Bruffee's argument regarding the necessity to redefine authority, teaching, and theories of knowledge construction in the university. He presents his approach, a model of collaborative learning based on a social constructionist theory of knowledge. The book is divided into two parts: the first defines the approach, explaining how and why it works. Included in this section is a model of collaborative learning (as distinguished from cooperative learning), an explanation of the role of writing in collaborative learning (and the role of collaborate learning in teaching writing), and a discussion of how colleges can institutionalize collaborative learning through peer tutors. The second part discusses university education from the perspective of the institution, explaining how in the past institutional concepts of knowledge have negatively affected not only education but also research. Writing plays a central role in collaborative learning because it relies upon interdependence—the ongoing conversations, verbal and print, that create and sustain knowledge within communities and academic disciplines. From this perspective, all writing is argumentative because it is a process of knowledge construction that is negotiated between people. It is simultaneously a communal act that requires a keen awareness of the "language games" that are acceptable in different communities and a tool that can be used to alter those communities.

Burns, Philip J. "Supporting Deliberative Democracy: Pedagogical Arts of the Contact Zone of the Electronic Public Sphere." *Rhetoric Review* 18.1 (1999): 128-46.

Philip Burns draws on his experience with the Electronic Democracy Project to theorize the role of technology in teaching "deliberation" (argument). He contends that "normal discourse," or literate practices, are increasingly linked to academic disciplines and should instead be taken from the public sphere. Because the Internet creates more space for public discourse, educators must shift focus away from the classroom and out towards the public sphere as a pedagogical site to engender a more civic understanding of argument. He is seeking a rhetoric that is less agonistic and more concerned with mediating asymmetrical interactions between individuals and groups. Burns draws from James Bohman to define "deliberation" as "dialogical interactions" that occur in a specific situation and that allow for the "give and take of reasons," the end result being cooperation among members of the forum despite acknowledged differences. Borrowing from Mary Louise Pratt's definition of the "contact zone" as a space in which inequalities of power always exist and are always challenged (yet not always significantly changed), Burns asserts that technology mediation (e-mail, listservs, and other Web-based sites of communication) provides such a contact zone in which exigency can occur naturally rather than being imposed without context through assigned readings.

Chambliss, Marilyn J. and Ruth Garner. "Do Adults Change their Minds After Reading Persuasive Texts?" *Written Communication* 13.3 (1996): 291-313.

Describing the nature and content of persuasive texts, Chambliss and Garner establish a frame through which an examination of audience, in this case, adults' reading tendencies, can be viewed. The Toulmin model (claims, warrants, evidence) is used to evaluate structure and an Aristotelian analysis (artistic proofs—ethos, logos, pathos) is used for content. The running example throughout is an editorial that ran after the first Gulf War about the Middle East remaining very much the same as it had prior to war. This article examines how arguments, although they are designed to earn the reader's warranted assent, can only work if the reader actually does agree in good faith to objectively read the argument. It is Chambliss and Garner's belief that more often than not, adult readers tend to adhere rigidly to prior opinions regardless of new information that may be in the written argument.

Carroll, Jeffrey. "Essence, Stasis, and Dialectic." *Rhetoric Review* 23.2 (2004): 156-70.

Carroll's essay is concerned with alerting students to the importance of "first steps" in creating arguments, which in this case is agreeing upon the definition of key concepts or contested terms to ensure that the argument is focused and fruitful. Another goal is to demonstrate to students the value of critically engaging with plurality of definition to find the definition that is most appropriate for the embedded situation instead of relying upon the dictionary as the arbiter of definitional correctness. In doing so, he draws upon invention techniques from Aristotle (commonplace of definition), Cicero (stasis theory) and Plato (dialectic) as possible methods to reach "winnowed" (movement away from universal) definitions that teachers could model for students. The author underscores the importance of considering the role of definition by drawing upon Chaim Perelman's assertion that definition is not about clarifying meaning of an idea, but rather shaping the issue so that it will produce the persuasive effects sought.

Corder, Jim W. "On Argument, What Some Call 'Self-Writing,' and Trying to See the Back Side of One's Own Eyeballs." *Rhetoric Review* 22.1 (2002): 31-39.

In this posthumously published essay, Corder claims that we overlook many arguments that do not look like arguments—the quick barbs, slaps, and insults that are shorthand arguments which represent a clash between ways of seeing the world. He notes that rhetoric textbooks fail to acknowledge that arguments pit worldviews against one another. His main contention is that our experiences embed in us "completed rhetorics" or "models of the world" and we live them in our interactions with others. This means that identities are at stake in argumentative exchange. Because of this, when people rely upon their deep and steadfast convictions, which they call "good reasons," "sense," and "judgment," argument is over when it begins since they are often unwilling to consider alternatives as viable options. Consequently, instead of focusing on proofs, he suggests we focus on narrative and description because arguers need less to declare than to show their thinking. Corder refers to this showing as "self-writing," or writing which honestly reveals our motivations, which shows ourselves in the world we live in. He admits that showing the rhetoric we are already in can be as hard as seeing the backs of our eyeballs, but we are always in a rhetoric, and so we must continually identify ourselves in our writing in order to acknowledge that rhetoric.

Crosswhite, James. *The Rhetoric of Reason: Writing and the Attractions of Argument.* Madison: U of Wisconsin P, 1996.

Crosswhite's argument sets out to find a way for composition between the opposing threats of postmodernism on the one hand and scientism on the other. He rejects post-modernists generally and deconstruction specifically on the grounds that they overlook matters critical to his "rhetoric of reason," particularly the latter's commitment to resolving practical problems and making choices. While choice-making implies a sense of agency, Crosswhite rejects the idea of the agent as essential self. Instead of the self using claims and counter-claims to *express* a fixed identity, Crosswhite sees the self as the *product* of the choices, the claims and counter-claims, it makes through argument. In response to the corrosive skepticism of deconstruction, Crosswhite's rhetoric of reason calls for the conversion of doubt to argument. The end of argument, meanwhile, is justice, the fair and equitable balancing of competing claims arising from differing "disclosures of the world." He in turn rejects scientism with its "transmission" model of education in favor of a commitment to producing "a kind of ideal human being, philosophical, practical, articulate and beneficent" (14). It's an ambitious and idealistic argument and constitutes an important theoretical defense of first year writing. The philosophic sources for Crosswhite's argument are many and varied, but include Heidegger, Dewey, Habermas, Levinas and Cavell.

de Velasco, Antonio Raul. "Rethinking Perelman's Universal Audience: Political Dimensions of a Controversial Concept." *Rhetoric Society Quarterly* 35.2 (2005): 47-64.

The major claim of this article is that Perelman's notion of the "universal audience" might best be utilized in political critique, as opposed to its common use as a standard for rationality in argumentation. de Velasco aims to redirect conversation to the "political dimensions" of the concept or the way that the universal addressee can be viewed as the partial and partisan advocate of claims about reality. By doing so, he is re-framing the primary critique of Perelman's work, namely, the idea that a constructed universal audience is not useful in establishing a standard for rhetorical discourse. de Velasco's contention is that "it is the potential for discourse to "transcend" differences, conflicts and inconsistencies in the social world that the concept of the "universal audience" so neatly captures" (50). This position posits that the differences of universal audience construction amongst groups will shine light on slippages in stability. The political dimension takes precedent in this model because it is through political critique that the struggle for rhetorical construction of the "universal audience takes place." Perelman's ideas are considered alongside those of political theorists Chantel Mouffe and Ernesto Laclau, as a means to discuss how "hegemonic forms of discourse" establish what is true in different rhetorical scenes.

Emmel, Barbara A. "Toward a Pedagogy of the Enthymeme: The Roles of Dialogue, Intention, and Function in Shaping Argument." *Rhetoric Review* 13.1 (1994): 132-48.

Emmel asserts that any argument pedagogy must involve an "enthymematic approach" because it enables students to become aware of the processes by which they produce well-reasoned arguments. However, she recognizes that the enthymeme itself is often an alienating concept to teachers and students of writing. She believes that "teaching enthymematically" is focused on meta-cognition about "how communication, both written and otherwise, achieves the shape of shared conclusions and shared knowledge." Instead of teaching the enthymeme as a "truncated syllogism," Emmel advocates an approach that invites students to see the connection of the intention and the function of the claims that they make. She demonstrates this through a student example showing how enthymemes may be used heuristically as a way to both discover and shape arguments and to see the relationship of related claims that can be connected. The author is interested in creating an atmosphere where classroom discussions provide the necessary feedback for students as they develop, revise, and draft ideas and as students begin to understand why some claims need to be supported and others attain warranted assent. The "real" audience of peers is meant to subvert the problem of addressing a constructed audience in the writing classroom. The author sees the enthymeme not as a form imposed on process, but rather a "form representative of how that process takes shape."

Fahnestock, Jeanne. "Teaching Argumentation in the Junior-Level Course." *Teaching Advanced Composition.* Ed. Katherine Adams and John Adams. Portsmouth, NH: Boynton, 1991. 179-93.

Fahnestock begins her discussion by questioning the assertion that there should be a clear distinction between informing and persuading. Her position is that all communicative acts are persuasive, and failure to acknowledge this is tantamount to "self-deception" because the process of argumentative construction that determines which information is selected and omitted remains unquestioned. According to the author, this leads to much writing that is uncritical and unfit to survive scrutiny of actual audiences. Fahnestock and many of the other contributors to this collection are theorizing ways around the problem of teaching audience awareness and the rhetorical situation in a more authentic way, within the writing classroom, to better prepare students for the writing that they will do outside of the classroom. Here, she offers a stases-based method of inquiry to supplement the more analytic models of argument theory, such as Toulmin, that don't emphasize the invention side of writing. She then proposes a methodology for introducing advanced composition writers to argument. Her most important contribution is to suggest that students adopt and expand one topic through the semester, at the end of which they are required to submit an actual proposal to a real audience. During the semester, students work through several stases, each one building upon the previous one, culminating in an authentic endeavor to offer suggestions for solving the problem that has been their focus project.

Ferris, Dana R. "Rhetorical Strategies in Student Persuasive Writing: Differences between Native and Non-Native English Speakers." *Research in the Teaching of English* 28.1 (1994): 45-65.

Ferris is interested in the variations of rhetorical structures across languages, and identifies elements of English persuasive writing that may be problematic for non-native speakers. Here, she offers an empirical comparative analysis between persuasive texts (considered synonymous with argument in this article) written by native English speakers (basic and advanced) and by non-native English speakers (basic and advanced), in first-year English, to pinpoint possible weaknesses. In her study, sixty persuasive texts were analyzed for thirty-three quantitative variables such as number of words and clauses, word length and clauses per sentence, topical structure percentage of parallel, sequential and extended parallel progressions, and topical depth. They were also analyzed for rhetorical variables; Toulmin scores were assigned for claims, data and warrant, openings and closings, rhetorical questions and counter-arguments. There were notable differences between native and non-native English speakers. The native English speakers wrote longer compositions, scored higher on the Toulmin analysis, cited counterarguments more, and had a lower subtopics-to-sentences ratio. Ferris suggests that differences in the texts produced by the non-native students derive largely from different sets of assumptions about rhetorical expectations. In addition, non-native speakers may have less exposure to formal persuasion and concepts such as Toulmin's claim, data, warrant, counterargument, and modeling. This study calls attention to the need to study cultural differences in argument within the argument classroom where non-native speakers are asked to construct arguments, which the author states should take the form of instruction of "formal schemata required in English academic writing."

Fisher, Walter R. *Human Communication as Narration: Toward a Philosophy of Reason, Value, and Action.* Columbia: U of South Carolina P, 1989.

For Fisher, narrative is a more fundamental aspect of human communication than argument or even rhetoric. Human beings are *Homo narrans* before they are citizens or partisans, and subsequently all discourse aims to tell a story of some sort. The kind of storytelling we would all recognize as such—anecdotes, novels, short stories, history—is that which "recounts" events. But even forms of discourse that appear not to tell stories attempt to "account" for the way things are and as such fall under Fisher's broad notion of story understood as "symbolic interpretations of aspects of the world occurring in time and shaped by history, culture and character" (xiii). Each individual story offers "good reason" for believing something. The two criteria by which we judge the efficacy of a story's reasons are coherence and fidelity, which combine to form what Fisher terms "narrative rationality." The tests for coherence or how well a story "hangs together," involve comparisons of a given story to stories one knows to be true, consistency of the story's argumentative points and, crucially, the reliability of the story's characters—are their actions consistent with their words/values? Fidelity, meanwhile, corresponds with more traditional measures of what constitutes good reasons as adumbrated by theorists, such as Toulmin and Perelman. Fisher's theory owes much to Alaisdair MacIntyre's *After Virtue* and its critique of the modern tendency to split fact off from value and the spiritual from the material. The concluding chapters of Fisher's book offer some excellent analyses of political, literary and philosophical arguments grounded in narrative.

Frank, David A. "Argumentation Studies in the Wake of the New Rhetoric." *Argumentation & Advocacy* 40.4 (2004): 267-83.

Frank examines the influence of The New Rhetoric Project (NRP), represented by the collective works of Perelmen and Olbrecht-Tyteca, on the field of twentieth century argumentation. In reviewing the work of the NRP, Frank's aim is to draw attention to the impact of this scholarship in cementing the "study of argument as a *humane art*" (267). The writer makes his claim in the face of two movements of argument that, in his terms, threaten the field: the fragmentation of argument into case studies, and argument theories of pragma-dialectics. Frank suggests that returning to the works of the NRP allows scholars to navigate "between fragmentation and enforced uniformity, and remains the most ethical and powerful framework available to scholars of argument" (268). Central to the NRP are recognizing the importance of internal dialogue and continually questioning received ideology. As well, Frank emphasizes that disagreement is not negative, as long as people resolve matters verbally; rather, it continually shines light on the diversity of beliefs. All of this is important because NRP proposes that "uniform agreement" is not the goal of argument. Argumentation is meant to cause action, but morality should trump even the call to action.

Fulkerson, Richard. *Teaching the Argument in Writing.* Urbana: NCTE, 1996.

Fulkerson offers a clear, no-nonsense guide to teaching argument in the context of the writing class. Fulkerson surveys the major approaches to teaching argument and analyzes and evaluates each one, leaving the reader with a clear sense of how he views the strengths and weaknesses of each approach. He is wary of using Toulmin in the classroom on the grounds that it is primarily an analytic tool far more helpful to readers of argument than it is to writers of argument. He is particularly supportive of the stasis approach to argument and devotes much of the middle of the book to its use in the classroom. He is also supportive of the use of informal fallacies in teaching argument and very critical of how most writing textbooks treat the subject. He then discusses in some depth eleven major fallacies (including some subtypes) that in his view are most commonly found in argument. While the authors of this text are extremely wary of using informal fallacies in writing classes, we highly recommend Fulkerson's treatment of the subject to anyone committed to the approach. By the same token, Fulkerson's discussion of formal logic, a subject we definitely discourage in the writing classroom, is clear, if less thorough than his discussion of informal fallacies. Fulkerson also offers a discussion of statistical argument and a useful tool of argument evaluation, STAR (a generalization backed by a Sufficient number of Typical, Accurate, and Relevant instances).

Gage, John T. "A General Theory of the Enthymeme for Advanced Composition." *Teaching Advanced Composition.* Ed. Katherine Adams and John Adams. Portsmouth, NH: Boynton, 1991. 161-78.

Gage emphasizes student writers as responsible members of a discourse community. To that end, he proposes that students compose and revise enthymemes as an invention strategy, taking into account the rhetorical situation that has been created through classroom discussions and readings. These enthymemes represent the intention of the essay. The benefit of using the enthymeme in this manner is that it includes the possibility of helping students understand that the composing process is made responsible because it melds the writer's aims with the audience's needs. Consequently, audience becomes a resource to be used rather than an obstacle to be overcome. In Gage's model the essence of rhetorical exchange is to construct knowledge out of what the writer contributes and what the audience already knows or acknowledges.

Garret, Mary, and Xiaosui Xiao. "The Rhetorical Situation Revisited." *Rhetoric Society Quarterly* 23.2 (1993): 30-40.

As the title indicates, this article explores the concept of the rhetorical situation as defined by Bitzer in 1968. Bitzer identified three main elements necessary for a piece of discourse to emerge: exigency, constraints, and audience. Unlike Bitzer (who stressed exigency as the catalyst of the rhetorical situation) or Vatz (who favored the speaker), Garret and Xiao suggest that it is the audience that is the pivotal element of the rhetorical situation. The authors also argue that a culture's discourse tradition plays a significant role in shaping speaker and audience perceptions of the elements of the rhetorical situation. Finally, the authors suggest that the rhetorical situation is much more interactive and organic than previous scholarship has indicated.

Garrison, Jim. *Dewey and Eros.* New York: Teachers College, 1997.

Garrison sets out to salvage the Platonic notion of *eros*—defined as the truly desirable—vs. "sheer satisfaction." by placing it in the context of Dewey's pragmatic understanding of the desirable outcome sought by practical wisdom. Garrison's discussion has several implications for argument instructors concerned with the philosophical foundations of what they do. It offers a specific vision of the thinking we want to encourage in students, and envisions teaching and learning as a continual form of growth. Ideally, education creates ethical, creative thinkers who consider alternative possibilities, in search of the best options to create a better world.

Garver, Eugene. *For the Sake of Argument: Practical Reasoning, Character, and the Ethics of Belief.* Chicago: U of Chicago P, 2004.

Philosopher Eugene Garver draws heavily on Aristotle's *Rhetoric* by way of expanding the definition of rationality so as to stress ethos (and pathos) as well as logos. Rather than justice, the end of argument for Garver is friendship. His model for argument, meanwhile, is not "bargaining between strangers," but rather "deliberation among friends" (5). Garver rejects the methodical, universalistic model of rationality, in favor of practical reason, the Greeks' *phronesis.* Such reasoning resists a prioris, ties rationality to character, and acknowledges the impact of context. In elaborating his theory of rationality, Garver analyzes a number of modern legal and political examples, including *Brown v. Board of Education* and the South African Truth and Reconciliation Commission. While he draws heavily on the work of Richard Rorty in outlining his theory of practical reason, Garver is careful to distinguish his position from Rorty's at several key junctures.

Godden, David M. "Arguing at Cross-Purposes: Discharging the Dialectical Obligations of the Coalescent Model of Argumentation." *Argumentation* 17.2 (2003): 219-43.

Godden discusses Michael Gilbert's concept of Coalescent Argumentation (CA) and its implications for argumentation theory. The author offers a theoretical overview of Coalescent Argumentation, describing its three tenets: that argument is multi-modal, that it is position-based, and that is it is goal oriented. Godden then discusses Gilbert's criticisms of the CA model, including that it posits the wrong subject of study (something other than argument); that its purpose is for dispute resolution rather than theorizing argument; that it requires the wholesale abandonment of other argument models such as the critical-logical model (or that it mischaracterizes those other models); and that it is not inclusive of perspectival approaches. After refuting these points, Godden concludes by asserting that CA has much to offer argument theory, as long as critical-logical models and CA models are not put into opposition with one another.

Grant-Davie, Keith. "Rhetorical Situations and Their Constituents." *Rhetoric Review* 15.2 (1997): 264-79.

Grant-Davie claims that teaching students to analyze the rhetorical situations from which rhetoric arises is one of the most important argumentative concepts. However, while Lloyd Bitzer's term *rhetorical situation* is commonly used in argument, Grant-Davie believes that there is confusion as to what this term means. Thus, he attempts to clarify the original definition and re-cast the concept to account for theoretical advances in rhetoric since Bitzer first published. Grant-Davie defines the rhetorical situation as the situation in which a speaker/writer uses rhetoric to effect a change in reality. Using Bitzer's division of exigence, audience, and constraints as a starting point, Grant-Davie argues for a more comprehensive analysis, that acknowledges the interconnectedness of *exigence, rhetors, audiences,* and *constraints,* each of which he claims could be plural, (i.e., multiple audiences and/or constraints). The possibility of plurality opens the door for discussion of identity and the dynamic roles of rhetor and audience, which moves discussion away from general questions like, "who is the audience?," and towards situational questions, such as, how does a discourse "define and create context for readers?"

Hardin, Joe Marshall. *Opening Spaces: Critical Pedagogy and Resistance Theory in Composition.* Albany, NY: State U of New York P, 2001.

Invoking postmodern social theories, Hardin argues for a critical pedagogy of resistance in composition studies, which he believes can empower composition students. While he recognizes the reality that students must learn to read and write within the standard conventions of cultural and academic discourses, he is most interested in teaching them skills of inquiry and resistance to ideological indoctrination. He positions himself as a scholar in favor of the writing classroom as a site of resistance; however, he believes that many critical pedagogy models need to be theorized more fully so that the critical inquiry is ethical, meaning that rhetoric and the production of argument, as opposed to the political messages that are analyzed, are central to the discussion. Much of the book is dedicated to addressing criticisms of critical models and offering suggestions for how to re-envision those models. He wants to encourage an ethics that is "driven by unrelenting and unending critique"—a self-reflexive critique and makes students feel ethically responsible for the choices that they make and empowers them through the composition class experience.

Heidlebaugh, Nora. *Judgment, Rhetoric, and the Problem of Incommensurability: Recalling Practical Wisdom.* Columbia: U of South Carolina P, 2001.

Nora Heidlebaugh focuses this work on the efficacy of values-laden debate. She notes the tendency to rely on the products of rhetoric (the actual arguments we observe) to pass judgment. However, because value systems differ, arguers tend to adhere to the values and beliefs that warrant their position. They assume that others should accept such values without question. The result is an impasse. Consequently, Heidlebaugh calls for more attention to the process of invention. She calls on parties to articulate their own argument in the context of opposing arguments and to begin to agree on "frames of reference" from which to discuss an issue. The author points to the rhetorical practices of the early Sophists and Greek poets as a model for overcoming the "problem of incommensurability" common in rhetorical practice and invention. Because the goal of an argument should be a productive outcome, this book's primary value is its potential to help one understand habits of argumentation that lead to impasse.

Johnson, Ralph H. *Manifest Rationality. A Pragmatic Theory of Argument.* Mahwah, NJ: LEA, 2000.

Johnson is primarily concerned with how to evaluate and criticize argument. He advances a rhetorical position on argument, namely that it is a socializing activity that relies upon a complex process of constructing, critiquing, and revising argumentative positions that is bound by community standards, habits, and customs that are subject to change. However, he quickly separates process from product (privileging product) and defines "rationality" as "the ability to engage in the giving and receiving of reasons." The goal of this book is to explain argumentation as the exercise of rationality and to reject traditional theories of argument based on formal and informal logic. Johnson's notion of rationality is pragmatic. The criteria for a rational argument include: acceptability, truth, relevance and sufficiency. In turn, Johnson offers four principles that underlie argument evaluation: the principles of vulnerability, parity, logical neutrality, and discrimination.

Joliff, William. "Text as Topos: Using the Toulmin Model of Argument in Introduction to Literature." *Teaching English in the Two-Year College* 25:2 (1998): 151-58.

Joliff's attempt to move his Introduction to Literature class to discussions beyond the "antiphonal" and "genteel" and into "a more authentic classroom" led him to adopt Toulmin's model of argument as a tool to "teach them how to fight" about literature and other ideas. Noting students' apparent unfamiliarity with the methods of academic argument and the lack of time in a literature class to teach informal logic, he advocates introducing students to Toulmin's use of claim, data, and warrant as a solution. In this model, students make a claim about a piece of literature, and support the claim with both data from the text and a discussion of warrants from their own experience. Interpretive claims work best, Joliff maintains, but factual and thematic claims also keep students engaged in connecting a piece of literature with their own lives. In addition, the retrogressive nature of the Toulmin model requires students to continually re-engage with the details of the text in their search for data to support the claims underlying the original claim.

Juthe, André. "Argument by Analogy." *Argumentation* 19.1 (2005): 1-27.

While relying upon the Western philosophical traditions' theories of argumentation, Juthe attempts to fill the void in theoretical discussion about argument by analogy, a commonly used comparative technique in everyday conversation, as well as academic discourse. As this is an often used rhetorical technique in argument, Juthe believes that it is in need of more academic consideration. Juthe characterizes the structure and function of arguments by analogy, and details the differences between arguments by analogy and typical inductive, deductive, or abductive arguments. The writer explicates different types of argument structures, separating argument by conclusive argument from argument by inclusive analogy. Finally, Juthe argues that arguments by analogy are not reducible to any other type of argument, and have distinct characteristics which put them in their own argument classification.

Kaplan, R.B. "Foreword: What in the World is Contrastive Rhetoric?" *Contrastive Rhetoric Revisited and Redefined.* Ed. Clayann Gilliam Panetta. Mahwah, NJ: LEA, 2001. vii-xx.

In the foreword to this insightful anthology, Kaplan articulates a set of questions that directly relate to the teaching of argument in an ESL environment. These five questions examine areas such as topic selection, authority roles in argument, genres, and arrangement of evidence. Kaplan looks at different cultural systems and their direct influence in the area of rhetorical patterns and style of speakers of other languages who are writing arguments.

Knapp, Mark L., and William J. Earnest. "Shall Ye Know the Truth? Student Odysseys in Truth-Seeking." *Communication Education* 49.4 (2000): 375-86.

In this article, Knapp and Earnest describe the results of the final assignment in their "Lying and Deception" course. The project called for students to interview faculty members concerning perceptions of "truth" in their respective fields; grappling with the responses would give students first-hand experience into how we know, a fundamental goal of education. The authors analyze responses to seven interview questions (including such prompts as "How should students seek the truth?" and "How do scholars and educators in your field determine what is true?"), detailing a clear trend towards equivocation, contradiction, and ambiguity. Often, interviewee responses exhibit a struggle between a single concept of truth (the "Truth") and multiple interpretations (truths) in their field, leading the researchers to wonder how students will react to this lack of certainty from their professors. In post-project reflective essays, however, many students displayed a subtle understanding of the complex, contextual nature of truth revealed through the exercise. Argument instructors will find this article applicable in several ways. Dealing explicitly with "truth-seeking," it maps the very rhetorical ground which we ask students to tread, and its practical example can serve as the model for similar critical awakenings in the writing classroom.

Kroll, Barry M. "Arguing about Public Issues: What Can We Learn from Practical Ethics?" *Rhetoric Review* 16.1 (1997): 105-19.

Stating that most arguments about controversial topics have an "ethical edge," Kroll warns argument teachers of the danger of students slipping into *applied ethics* that uses "theory-application," a top-down approach that has one first settling on moral principles and then applying them deductively to conflicts, a process that tends to oversimplify complex issues. Instead, Kroll argues that teachers should encourage students to use *casuist* and *pragmatic* approaches, both of which begin with particularities of an ethical controversy. He urges argument teachers to help students to see that inquiry is a part of argument and to recognize the complexity of issues rather than rushing towards a simple solution. He suggests using writing assignments such as the "issues brief" which asks students to present a fair-minded view of an issue, laying out fully and fairly the arguments on all sides of a dispute. This pedagogical model attempts to divert attention away from the intractable ethical differences at the center of a dispute and towards other contributing social factors that can be mediated across differences and possibly alter the circumstances that necessitated the original dispute. Kroll emphasizes making the goal of writing sustaining conversation and not necessarily resolving complex problems.

Lundsford, Karen J. "Contextualizing Toulmin's Model in the Writing Classroom: A Case Study." *Written Communication* 19.1 (2002): 109-74.

Lundsford writes this case study in a response to a call from Richard Fulkerson to conduct further research that examines the effectiveness of the Toulmin model in argument classes. Specifically, Toulmin's claim that an argument's participants inevitably inhabit a specific situation or context that must be taken into account when applying his model. A careful consideration of the "context" (sometimes used synonymously with "field" to problematic ends) will alert the reader to challenges that will probably arise because fields are governed by certain criteria that serve to limit rhetorical options. Lundsford is concerned with the ambiguity related to context, which she believes cannot be isolated to a particular moment because people within a group are always continually contextualizing. A detailed description of Toumin's model is provided with visual maps of the various terms and examples from Toulmin's *Uses of Argument,* as well as a literature review of responses to Toulmin. The case study follows the events of a class of ten high school students who took a non-credit college writing course. Toulmin's schema was slightly modified from its original form. The central question for Lundsford is, who situates context? The field (group)? The reader? Lundsford believes that although context is sometimes treated as universal, it needs to be co-constructed by the writer and the reader.

Lynch, Dennis, Diana George, and Marilyn Cooper. "Moments of Argument: Agonistic Inquiry and Confrontational Cooperation." *College Composition and Communication* 48.1 (1997): 61-85.

This article considers ways to get students to engage issues critically instead of separating them into two diametrically opposed positions and oversimplifying complex problems. The authors advocate a pedagogy that includes moments of conflict and agonistic positioning as well as moments of understanding and communication. This is an acknowledgement of the impact of agonistic public models of argument (i.e., talk radio and political news programs) on society in general and students in particular, and an attempt to theorize an argument for the writing classroom that is less competitive and more deliberative. The authors believe that opening a space where students can critically engage complex issues will make it is easier to show them where they jump to conclusions, don't thoroughly examine an issue and/or don't move beyond impractical logical arguments. They also offer a defense of cooperative models of argument against claims that confrontation is a more useful means of shining light on the interconnectedness of social forces. Concrete examples of writing assignments and course goals are provided for two distinct argument classes to illustrate the value of using confrontation and cooperation to teach argument.

Matalene, Carolyn. "Experience as Evidence: Teaching Students to Write Honestly and Knowledgeably about Public Issues." *Rhetoric Review* 10.2 (1992): 252-65.

Facing a new "argument track" for first-year composition, Matalene evaluates twenty-four students' responses to the new type of curriculum by reading their six-paper semester portfolios. Matalene notices the disjuncture of student voices between a public and private space, asserting through student writing samples that student voices seemed "disembodied." In order to resist this bifurcation of public and private voice, Matalene asserts that students should begin writing from personal experience and then move into personal writing about public issues, rather than the opposite. This is a break from the more conventional position that personal experience is not as valuable, as an end product, in college writing classes as information that has been adjudicated by a third party. Matalene believes that asking students to divorce themselves (the private) from issues (the public) contributes to their lack of power and agency in the classroom. While her position is skeptical of placing argumentation at the center of first-year writing, the focus on "shaping personal knowledge for public communication" effectively can be utilized in discussions of argument to negotiate the uncomfortable shift to an abstract, academic voice that she pinpoints as a problem.

McComiskey, Bruce. *Gorgias and the New Sophistic Rhetoric.* Carbondale: Southern Illinois UP, 2002.

McComiskey examines Gorgianic rhetoric from both a historic and contemporary point of view. Part One is devoted to an historical analysis of Gorgianic rhetoric by the examination of three of Gorgias's classical texts, "On Non-Existence," the "Encomium of Helen," and the "Defense of Palamedes". In Part Two, McComiskey views Gorgianic rhetoric through a contemporary lens, devoting time to appropriations of Gorgianic rhetoric by neosophistic scholars, the contributions such scholars have made to the field of rhetoric, and the impact of postmodernism on Gorginaic rhetoric. In his last chapter, the author discusses what implications Gorgianic rhetoric, specifically the concept of kairos, has on the concepts of multiculturalism and the idea of the "global village." McComiskey includes an appendix of selected bibliographic sources for further reading on sophistic rhetoric and philosophy.

McMillan, Jill J., and Katy J. Harriger. "College Students and Deliberation." *Communication Education* 51.3 (2002): 237-53.

The authors address the decline in political participation from young people by proposing that a focus on deliberation—defined as "group discussion of a political issue with the specific intent of finding a resolution"—in the college classroom can positively affect attitudes towards civic involvement. Anecdotal experiences with students reveal that deliberative skills (such as balancing speaking with listening and building consensus) are often challenged by conventional notions of defending one's point at all costs. That is, the traditional uses of rhetoric seem at odds with the goals of group deliberation, a dilemma the authors consider both research-rich and pedagogically useful. Argument instructors may find some application in this article—it highlights an age-old conflict about the purposes of rhetoric and dialectic within a contemporary classroom framework.

Meyers, Renee A., Dale E Brashers, and Jennifer Hanner. "Majority-Minority Influence: Identifying Argumentative Patterns and Predicting Argument-Outcome Links." *Journal of Communication* 50.4 (2000): 3-30.

This study investigates the communication activities of majority and minority factions in small group decision-making discussions. In particular, the study focuses on the impact of argument on the final group outcomes. Even though this study examines speech communication, the Conversational Argument research program that it uses for its framework is a conglomeration of the work of Toulmin (formal argument), Perelman and Obrechts-Tyteca (interactional patterns of group argument), and Jackson and Jacobs (features of argument convergence). The authors believe that by using this framework, they can "connect two bodies of literature—majority-minority influence and argument—which, to date, have remained separate, but when connected, provide a basis for identifying communication as a central explanatory and predictive mechanism" (10). The results of the study indicated that majorities (the opinion supported by the most members of the group) win more often than minorities, that there are differences in how the subgroups argue, and that consistency (defined in this study as "maintenance of one's position in interaction") in argumentation is an important predictor of subgroup success. These concepts may be helpful to teachers and students of written argumentation, particularly when considering audience.

Moxley, Joseph M. "Reinventing the Wheel or Teaching the Basics?: College Writers' Knowledge of Argumentation." *Composition Studies* 21.2 (1993): 3-15.

Struggling with whether or not argument is valuable to teach in the college classroom, Moxley begins by engaging in the question of teachers' purposes in the writing classroom: are teachers giving students "something they need but do not yet have," (a "Classical" notion of teaching) or are teachers giving students practice at abilities they already have a capacity for (a "Romantic" notion of teaching)? In order to answer these questions, Moxley evaluates three sample arguments based on Toulmin's argumentative model, and then has both experienced and inexperienced college writers rank and evaluate these samples. Moxley's findings about basic, first-year, and advanced composition students support both the Classical and Romantic hypothesis of what students know and need to know about arguments; he concludes by asserting that there is and should be a middle ground between these hypotheses.

Perkins, Sally J. "Toward a Rhetorical/Dramatic Theory of Instructional Communication." *Communication Education* 43.3 (1994): 222-35.

Using specific concepts developed by Bertolt Brecht, Perkins uses dramatic theory to examine how instructors communicate with students in classrooms. The author notes that classrooms, like the stage, are inherently rhetorical in that they provide space for symbolic action (a concept explored mostly by Kenneth Burke). Brecht's critique of theater indicts the dramatic genres of realism and naturalism, as they presume a universal depiction of human experience while serving as camouflage for transmitting dominant values and encouraging a passive audience role. In contrast, Brecht suggests that the stage should be explicitly addressed as a site of struggle through the tactical and ongoing use (and analysis) of alienation, historicization, and "gest." Perkins applies each of these ideas to classroom instruction, arguing that they help create a rhetorically rich learning environment and promote critical awareness in students. This article offers instructors of argument solid theory along with specific examples for using classroom roles and behavior as texts for analysis.

Poggi, Isabella. "The Goals of Persuasion." *Pragmatics & Cognition* 13.2 (2005): 297-336.

Poggi, a social scientist, attempts to examine the role of persuader and persuadee intentions and goals through a logical, categorical treatment of argumentative exchange. The model used positions both parties as always consciously or unconsciously working towards particular "goals" or "super goals." Like many other models, Poggi locates persuasion and thus argument at the center of social exchange. Social interaction is necessary because individuals don't have the power to reach their desired ends on their own. Discourse is deemed valuable to people if it is "a useful means to some goal" (300). Poggi attempts to theorize how Aristotle's appeals (ethos, logos, pathos) function in persuasive interactions. His contention is that people persuade others through "goal hooking" or persuading Party A that his/her goal will be met through siding with Party B via appeals to ethos, logos and pathos, which are always present in persuasive discourse and subject to enhancement to maximize persuasive potential. While the prescriptive binaries, such as the distinction between persuasion and convincing, utilized in this article may not be all that rhetorical, the author's overall point that argument is best envisioned as a non-coercive exchange between vested parties with free will is worthwhile.

Provis, Chris. "Negotiation, Persuasion and Argument." *Argumentation* 18.1 (2004): 95-112.

Provis complicates notions of negotiation and argument, exploring both the accepted definitions of the two concepts, as well as the blurring between the two terms that often happens in argument scholarship. After examining argument cases that use both terms of argument (conflicting opinion or belief) and negotiation (conflicting goals or interest), Provis concludes that there are no distinct rules, principles, or norms which always apply to differentiate argument from negotiation. Instead, Provis asserts, we should look closely at the context and purpose of the interaction before trying to categorize it as negotiation or argument.

Rice, Jim. "The 1963 Hip-Hop Machine: Hip-Hop Pedagogy as Composition." *College Composition and Communication* 54.3 (2003): 453-71.

This essay proposes an alternative invention strategy to Toulmin and Aristotle for research-based argumentative writing. In particular it focuses on an examination of how hip-hop music constructs discourse through its complex method of laying sampled hooks on top of each other and how such rhetoric functions within an argument class. The call is for students to draw upon whatever contrasting voices are at their disposal and strategically sample to find out where they stand on an issue. For the purposes of this article, the year 1963 is used to locate disparate voices, but specific spaces of public discourse, contemporary issues, and physical space could also work. No specific pedagogy is discussed, only hypothetical ways that students could engage issues; however, its grounding in cultural studies could prove helpful in the argument classroom.

Roberts-Miller, Patricia. *Deliberate Conflict: Argument, Political Theory, and Composition Classes.* Carbondale: Southern Illinois UP, 2004.

Roberts-Miller calls on writing teachers to be more aware of the relationship between their pedagogy and their political theory. By political theory she does not have in mind a specific political ideology, liberal or conservative, so much as a "model of argument." There are, she suggests, six models of argument in democracy and while any of the six (with one possible exception) might serve as the basis for an effective argument-based writing class, one in particular, the deliberative model, is most attractive. The six models include the following: (1) The liberal model of the public sphere which she calls utopian insofar as it exists only as an ideal, or an Enlightenment leftover that sees argument as a search for universal best interests; (2) the technocratic model which is less a full-blown model than a recurrent impulse that occurs within the context of one of the other models, calling on people to let experts decide what's best for them; (3) the interest-based model which is almost purely subjectivist and hence incoherent, leaving one with no means by which to arbitrate competing claims; (4) the agonistic model which is more conflictual but more coherent than the interest-based model insofar as it is not necessarily subjectivist; (5) the communitarian model that rejects the liberal ideals of the autonomous individual and the "trashistorical foundations for democratic practices" (Roberts-Miller 5); (6) the deliberative model which is distinguished primarily for being broader than the other models, embracing narrative, the particulars a given situation, and emotion as part of rationality. The deliberative model emerges as the preferred model while the interest-based model is rejected as unusable in the classroom. The metric underlying Roberts-Miller's judgment owes a good deal to Wayne Booth's *Modern Dogma and the Rhetoric of Assent*, in particular his critique of the motivistic (subjectivist) and the scientismus (calculative rationality) approaches to argument.

Schiappa, Edward, ed. *Warranting Assent: Case Studies in Argument Evaluation.* Albany: State U of New York P, 1995.

Lamenting a dearth of applied evaluation argument, Schiappa compiles a collection of essays devoted to filling the void. In defining argument evaluation Schiappa stresses the narrower metric of cogency over more diffuse concerns with context values. One of the liveliest chapters in Schiappa's book deals with abortion arguments and some of the perennial tropes that await those bold enough to tackle them.

Schroeder, Christopher. "Knowledge and Power, Logic and Rhetoric, and Other Reflections in the Toulminian Mirror: A Critical Consideration of Stephen Toulmin's Contributions to Composition." *JAC* 17.1 (1997): 95-107.

In recent years, argumentative writing has become a central tenet of first-year writing. However, Schroeder suggests that the theories used to support argument pedagogy, namely the work of Stephen Toulmin, need to be questioned more, especially since he believes underprepared instructors are relying too heavily on Toulmin's work (as relayed in textbooks), although he believes Toulimin has been an asset to argumentative writing theory. Among the many problems that Schroeder seems to have is that Toulmin's work is too logic based—a mere iteration on traditional logocentric methods of inquiry. Schroeder seems to be assuming that Toulmin will be taught in a vacuum devoid of other rhetorical theory or somehow positioned as superior and not a related issue to audience awareness and other rhetorical theories. At its best Schroeder believes that Toulmin is helpful in the classroom because it asks students to analyze arguments. At its worst, he views it as relativistic.

Segal, Judith. "Patient Compliance, the Rhetoric of Rhetoric, and the Rhetoric of Persuasion." *Rhetoric Society Quarterly* 23.3-4 (1993): 90-102.

Segal uses the topic of medical compliance to identify scientific rhetoric as fertile ground for further inquiry and to reach several conclusions about rhetorical theory and persuasive theory. She draws on the Burkeian concept of identification and Perelman's notion of adherence to support her claim that persuasion occurs most often when bonds are formed between parties, which is lacking in the Western medical tradition's reliance on the asymmetrical patient/doctor dyad. Among her main points is that rhetorical theory and persuasion theory can and should inform each other, as each has traditionally explored separate spheres with little overlap. She also argues that rhetorical theory has too often ignored discommunity or situations where asymmetrical power relations are used as leverage to warrant assent and that rhetorical theory needs to be applied to disciplines in the social sciences to deconstruct the ways that they formulate arguments.

Shand, John. *Arguing Well.* New York: Routledge, 2000.

Shand, a philosopher, sets out to write a logic book that will prepare newcomers to the field for "thinking." The importance of "sound logic" is espoused throughout. By sound logic, Shand means deductive soundness (true premises + valid arguments). In chapter two, Shand uses an art v. knack argument similar to Plato's Socrates, from the *Gorgias*, to make the distinction between logic and rhetoric. Logic is concerned with the form of argument (e.g., people being justified in holding certain opinions); rhetoric solely with persuasion (e.g., convincing people within a certain context). The theoretical foundation of this book is deductive reasoning and there is no mention of any other way to "argue well." There are also no pedagogical links made between this deductive structure and how it can be implemented in the classroom nor any mention of classical argument. (Shand's book stands in here for a host of similar textbooks on logic, formal and informal, produced by philosophers over the past three decades.)

Siegel, Harvey. *Rationality Redeemed? Further Dialogues on an Educational Ideal.* NewYork: Routledge, 1997.

Rationality Redeemed extends the argument Siegel made eight years earlier in *Educating Reason.* His argument is that rationality and critical thinking "constitute a fundamental educational ideal." For Siegel, critical thinking must involve the ability to evaluate reasons and to take stands on philosophical issues. It should be generalizable to all types of claims and be free from prejudice. In the second half of the book, Siegel considers his model in the context of contemporary philosophy and responds to critics of *Educating Reason* who challenged his modernist theory of knowledge construction and use of metanarratives.

Slade, Christina. "Seeing Reasons: Visual Argumentation in Advertisements." *Argumentation* 17.2 (2003): 145-60.

Slade argues against the claim that visual arguments function irrationally, and the equation made by many argument theorists between rationality and "linear, written, unemotional prose" (145). Using examples of advertisements to demonstrate her points, Slade outlines three tenets for a theory of visual argumentation, claiming that images may function as speech acts, that they should be interpreted in terms of specific semiotics, and that they contain their own argument structure.

Spigelman, Candace. "Argument and Evidence in the Case of the Personal." *College English* 64.1 (2001): 63-87.

The author argues that personal narrative, properly conceived, can achieve the ends of academic writing. She traces the personal to early theories of argumentation, situating its first dismissal in Plato, and its resurrection in Aristotle, who makes a case for personal narrative in epideictic, forensic, and deliberative argument. A comparison is made to generalizations drawn from the details of a narrative to "the missing middle term" of the enthymeme. Historically, the narrative has had a prominent role in persuasion, but was displaced, in the Enlightenment, by scientific objectivity. The current-traditional five-paragraph essay was the embodiment of this paradigm. In an age when even science acknowledges the limits of objectivity, personal writing narratives are seen by Spigelman as a means to segue into academic material. While personal narrative remains more difficult to evaluate than expository prose, Spigelman demonstrates that reasonable grounds for evaluation do exist.

Trail, George Y. "Teaching Argument and the Rhetoric of Orwell's 'Politics and the English Language.'" *College English* 57.5 (1995): 570-83.

Trail analyzes Orwell's influential essay in its historical context both to explain its appeal and to underscore the importance of historical context to audience response. According to Trail, too much of Orwell's appeal is attributed to the values he espouses and the strategies he employs. Trail's argument also calls attention to the political nature of all writing and not just overtly "political writing."

Van Eemeren, Frans H., and Peter Houtlosser, eds. *Dialectic and Rhetoric: The Warp and Woof of Argumentation Analysis.* Dordrect, Netherlands: Kluwer Academic, 2002.

This collection of essays emerged from colloquia on dialectic and rhetoric held at the University of Amsterdam in 1999, New York University in 2000, and Northwestern University in 2001. The purpose of the volume is to clarify the characteristics of dialectic and rhetoric, particularly as they pertain to argumentative discourse and argument analysis. Essays analyze the similarities and differences between dialectic and rhetoric, covering topics such as Aristotelian approaches to rhetoric and dialectic; legal, forensic, and constitutional practices and processes of dialectic and rhetoric; and the relationship or "delicate balance" between the two traditions.

Van Eemeren, Frans H., Rob Grootendorst, and A. Fransisca Snoeck Henkemans. *Argumentation: Analysis, Evaluation, Presentation.* Mahwah, NJ: LEA, 2002.

Based on pragma-dialectical approaches to argumentation, the authors provide an introduction to analyzing, evaluating, and presenting argument. In part one, Analysis, the authors discuss differences of opinion, the ideal model of critical discussion, standpoints and premises, and the structure of argument. Part two, Evaluation, covers how to determine the soundness of an argument, providing a comprehensive look at fallacies. The last section, Presentation, covers specifics on written and oral argument based on the approaches laid out in sections one and two, detailing analysis and evaluation of written and oral texts for the purpose of revising argumentative discourse.

Walker, Jeffrey. "The Body of Persuasion: A Theory of the Enthymeme." *College English* 56.1 (1994): 46-65.

A detailed study and survey of the enthymeme, this essay admits to a dual vision: (1) to establish that everyone enthymemes and (2) to demonstrate that the art of "enthymeming" requires exacting, demanding, disciplined study. The history details early Greek conceptions, explaining the relationship of the enthymeme to the syllogism and finding the same distinction Aristotle makes between rhetoric and dialectic: "antistrophos," a systematic difference combined with a similarity. Aristotle says enthymeme is essence. His contribution is "dialogic rationality." Isocrates's earlier conception combines style, kairos, ethos and pathos with a mastery of other rhetorical skills. Anaximenes's approach is more technical, eristic and somewhat mechanical.

Walker claims that the ancient concepts of the enthymeme have a direct influence on contemporary practice, which goes unnoticed because few modern writers are trained in the concept. Because of this gap in their rhetorical theory, they do not realize that they are employing enthymemes in their arguments. The irony is that the enthymeme remains vital even when not understood: it remains a device connecting an idea with a rationale, relying on the audience's ability to make that connection, which is precisely why enthymemes deserve more attention.

West, Thomas. "Beyond Dissensus: Exploring the Heuristic Value of Conflict." *Rhetoric Review* 15.1 (1996): 142-55.

West claims that, as microcosms of a multicultural society, composition classrooms can use tensions and conflicts already present among students as a heuristic for them to examine their own beliefs. While teachers often view the classroom as a community, reducing differences to a pluralism where "everyone is entitled to his or her own opinion," West suggests seeing it as a community of dissensus which acknowledges issues of race, gender, culture, class differences, privilege, disenfranchisement, and unequal access to the dominant culture. He argues that ignoring tensions between student/student, student/teacher, and reading/believing has a silencing effect. Instead, students should use issues as prompts to explore what and how they believe. Through reflection on their reading, writing, and beliefs, students can position themselves in relation to the range of competing discourses—academic, familial, work, religious. This is an attempt to cast conflict as a necessary part of advancing conversations, a principle that is central to the task of argument.

Westbrook, B. Evelyn. "Debating Both Sides: What Nineteenth-Century College Literary Societies Can Teach Us about Critical Pedagogies." *Rhetoric Review* 21.4 (2002): 339-56.

Westbrook treats nineteenth-century college literary societies as analogous to today's critical pedagogies. The literary societies were extracurricular, student-run societies in which public issues of the day were debated in a pro-con format, then put to a popular vote. Like latter-day critical pedagogies, the societies challenged students to consider non-dominant perspectives, reexamine their individual positions, and critique the status quo. Based on a case study of one literary society, she recommends having students debate both sides of all issues so as to allow them to try out ideas as they are figuring out where they stand on issues of the day.

Williams, Sean. "Process-Product Ambiguity: Theorizing a Perspective of the Word Wide Web of Argumentation." *JAC* 22.2 (2002): 377-98.

A central theme in theorizing Web-based forms of writing is the play between user's choice and author's structure. Williams agrees that the play inherent in Web-based writing is important; however, he believes that other theorists (Bolter, Landow, Joyce) have paid too much attention to the autonomy of the reader in constructing the message. His position is that Stephen Toulmin's theory of "process-product ambiguity," or the tension between the various messages that can be gleaned from a Web-text that an author creates, is in need of more theorizing because even in Web-based writing, the author has control over the possibilities that can come from navigating the various links within the document. The reader-writer dyad is relying upon a "shared rationality"; "given this formulation, interactivity becomes not only a matter of effective hypermedia design, but, in fact, a basis of persuasion" (381). This view assumes that the reader will be more persuaded by the work of an author who allows more room for the feeling of co-construction of ideas. Persuasiveness is judged by the openness of the context of relationships. A response by Jennifer Bay (see above) calls to question the limitation of Williams's ideas to written words.

Yeh, Stuart S. "Empowering Education: Teaching Argumentative Writing to Cultural Minority Middle-School Students." *Research in the Teaching of English* 33.1 (1998): 49-83.

This article is an empirical study using quasi-experimental and case-study research methods. Two heuristics, (1) a pyramid heuristic based on Stephen Toulmin's model and (2) a bridge heuristic based on a modern version stasis theory of classical rhetoric, were evaluated to measure their effectiveness in helping 116 middle-school students in four seventh-grade courses in two different schools to write argumentative essays. The student responses suggested that cultural minority students (Hispanic American, African American, and Asian American) benefited from being taught how to use the heuristics in writing an argument. Students in the experimental group were able to adapt their skills and transfer the heuristic knowledge to a range of topics. Students in this group also demonstrated more knowledge of argument structure and strategies in comparison to the control group. The results support the hypothesis that knowledge of argumentative procedures would improve student ability to generate arguments with adequate content and arrangement. The heuristics test seemed to have improved traditionally-underprepared students' ability to write academic essays.

Works Cited

Aristotle. *On Rhetoric: A Theory of Civic Discourse.* Tr. George Kennedy. New York: Oxford, 1991.

Bakhtin, Mikhail M. *Speech Genres and Other Essays.* Ed. By Caryl Emerson and Michael Holquist. Trans. Vern W. McGee. Austin: U of Texas P, 1986.

Bakthin, M.M. [V.N. Volosinov]. *Marxism and the Philosophy of Language.* 1929. Trans. Ladislav Matejka and I. R. Titunik. Cambridge: Harvard UP, 1886.

Belenky, Mary, et al. *Women's Ways of Knowing: The Development of Self, Voice, and Mind.* New York: Basic Books, 1986.

Berube, Michael. *The Employment of English: Theory, Jobs and the Future of Literary Studies.* New York: New York UP, 1998.

Bishops of the Episcopal Church. "On Waging Reconciliation." 26 Sept. 2001. 16 Jan. 2007 <http://www.msgr.ca/msgr-3/on_waging_reconciliation.htm>.

Bizzell, Patricia, and Bruce Herzberg, eds. *The Rhetorical Tradition: Readings from Classical Times to the Present.* 2nd ed. New York: Bedford/St Martin's, 2001.

Bitzer, Lloyd. "The Rhetorical Situation." *Philosophy and Rhetoric* 1.1 (1968): 1-14. Rpt. in *Rhetoric: Concepts, Definitions, Boundaries.* Ed. William Covino and David Jolliffe. New York: Allyn & Bacon, 1995. 300-10.

Blumenberg, Hans. "An Anthropological Approach to the Contemporary Significance of Rhetoric." *After Philosophy: End or Transformation?* Ed. Kenneth Baynes, James Bohman, and Thomas McCarthy. Cambridge: MIT P, 1987. 429-59.

Brown, Richard Harvey. *Society as Text.* Chicago: U of Chicago P, 1987.

Burke, Kenneth. *Attitudes Toward History.* 3rd ed. Berkeley: U of California P, 1984.

—. *Counter-Statement.* 2nd ed. Chicago: U of Chicago P, 1957.

—. *A Grammar of Motives.* Berkeley: U of California P, 1966.

—. *Permanence and Change: An Anatomy of Purpose.* 3rd ed. Berkeley: U of California P, 1984.

—. "Revolutionary Symbolism in America." *American Writers' Congress.* Ed. Henry Hart. New York: International, 1935. 87-94. Rpt. in *The Legacy of*

Kenneth Burke. Herbert W. Simons and Trevor Melia, Eds. Madison: U of Wisconsin P. 1989: 267-73.
—. *A Rhetoric of Motives.* Berkeley: U of California P, 1969.
—. *The Rhetoric of Religion: Studies in Logology.* Berkeley: U of California P, 1970.
Conley, Thomas M. *Rhetoric in the European Tradition.* Chicago: U of Chicago P, 1990.
Crosswhite, James. *The Rhetoric of Reason: Writing and the Attractions of Argument.* Madison: U of Wisconsin P, 1996.
Crusius, Timothy. *Kenneth Burke and the Conversation after Philosophy.* Carbondale: Southern Illinois UP, 1999.
Ellul, Jacques. *Propaganda: The Formation of Men's Attitudes.* 1965. New York: Vintage, 1973.
Eemeren, F. H. van, et al. *Fundamentals of Argumentation Theory: A Handbook of Historical Backgrounds and Contemporary Developments.* Mahwah, NJ: Erlbaum, 1996.
Feyerabend, Paul. *Against Method.* London: Verso, 1978.
Fish, Stanley. "Condemnation without Absolutes." *New York Times* 15 Oct. 2001: A22.
Freire, Paolo. *Education for Critical Consciousness.* Cambridge, Mass: Seabury, 1973.
Fulkerson, Richard. *Teaching the Argument in Writing.* Urbana: NCTE, 1996.
—. "Composition at the Turn of the Twenty-First Century." *College Composition and Communication* 56.4 (2005): 654-87.
Gage, John. *Argument Revisited, Argument Redefined: Negotiating Meaning in the Composition Classroom.* Ed. Barbara Emmel, Paula Resch, and Deborah Tenney. Thousand Oaks, CA: Sage, 1996. 1-15.
—. "Teaching the Enthymeme: Invention and Arrangement." *Rhetoric Review* 2.1 (1983): 38-50.
Geertz, Clifford. "Blurred Genres: and the Refiguration of Social Thought." *The American Scholar* 29.2 (1980): 165-79. Rpt. in: Geertz, Clifford. *Local Knowledge. Further Essays in Interpretive Anthropology.* New York: Basic, 1983.
Gilligan, Carol. *In a Different Voice.* Cambridge: Harvard UP, 1982.
Haswell, Richard. "Minimal Marking." *College English* 45.6 (1983): 600-04.
Heller, Joseph. *Catch 22.* New York. Simon and Schuster. 1961.
Hillocks, George. "What Works in Teaching: A Meta-Analysis of Experimental Treatment Studies." *American Journal of Education* 93.1 (1984): 133-69.
Jarratt, Susan. *Rereading the Sophists: Classical Rhetoric Refigured.* Carbondale: Southern Illinois UP, 1991.

Johnson, Samuel. *Johnson's Dictionary; a Modern Selection.* Ed. E. L. McAdam, Jr. and George Milne. New York: Pantheon, 1963.

Kennedy, George. *Classical Rhetoric and its Christian and Secular Tradition from Ancient to Modern Times.* 2nd ed. Chapel Hill: U of North Carolina P, 1999.

Lakoff, George. *Moral Politics: How Liberals and Conservatives Think.* 2nd ed. Chicago: U of Chicago P, 2002.

Leo, John. "Cultural Relativism Leaves Some Blind to Evil." *Arizona Republic* 15 October 2001: A18.

Miller, Carolyn. "Genre as Social Action." *Quarterly Journal of Speech* 70.2 (1984): 151-67.

Perelman, Chaim, and Mme L. Olbrechts-Tytecha. *The New Rhetoric: A Treatise on Argumentation.* Tr. John Wilkinson and Purcell Weaver. South Bend, IN: U of Notre Dame P, 1969.

Perelman, Chaim. *The Realm of Rhetoric* Tr. William Kluback. South Bend, IN: U of Notre Dame P, 1982.

—. "Theory of Practical Reasoning." Rpt. in Bizzell, Patricia, and Bruce Herzberg, eds. *The Rhetorical Tradition: Readings from Classical Times to the Present.* 2nd ed. New York: Bedford/St Martin's, 2001. 1384-409.

Rorty, Richard. *Achieving Our Country.* Cambridge: Harvard UP, 1997.

—. *Philosophy and the Mirror of Nature.* Princeton: Princeton UP, 1979.

Spellmeyer, Kurt. *Common Ground: Dialogue, Understanding and the Teaching of Composition.* Englewood Cliffs, NJ: Prentice Hall, 1993.

Spigelman, Candace. "Argument and Evidence in the Case of the Personal." *College English* 63.1 (2001): 63-87.

Taylor, Charles. *Sources of the Self: The Making of the Modern Identity.* Cambridge: Harvard UP, 1989.

Toulmin, Stephen. *The Uses of Argument.* Cambridge: Cambridge University P, 1958.

Young, Richard E., Alton L. Becker, and Kenneth L. Pike. *Rhetoric: Discovery and Change.* New York. Harcourt, 1970.

Index

About the Authors

John Ramage worked in higher education for over thirty years at Montana State University and Arizona State University. He taught undergraduate literature and composition courses at all levels, and graduate courses in rhetorical theory and argumentation. He was also a writing program administrator for more than a decade, overseeing writing centers, composition programs, writing across the curriculum programs, and academic support programs. *Writing Arguments*, a textbook coauthored with John Bean and June Johnson, is now in its eighth edition.

Zachary Waggoner teaches courses in rhetoric, composition, videogame theory, and new teaching assistant education for the department of English at Arizona State University. He is the author of *My Avatar, My Self: Identity in Video Role-Playing Games* (McFarland Publishers, 2009) and several co-authored articles devoted to the teaching of writing, including "One Size Fits All?: Student Perspectives on Face-to-Face and Online Writing Pedagogies" with Lauren Yena (*Computers and Composition Online*) and "Sustainable Development: Thinking Globally and Acting Locally in the Writing Classroom" with Peter Goggin (*Composition Studies*).

Micheal Callaway is Residential Faculty at Mesa Community College in Mesa, Arizona. Currently, he is focusing on teaching and developing curriculum for developmental writing courses. He also teaches introductory writing courses. In addition to his teaching duties, he is also interested in assessment issues, especially the intersection of race and writing assessment.

Jennifer Clary-Lemon is Assistant Professor of Rhetoric at the University of Winnipeg. She is co-editor, with Peter Vandenberg and Sue Hum, of *Relations, Locations, Positions: Composition Theory for*

Writing Teachers (NCTE, 2006). Her research and teaching interests include examining the rhetorics of representation, as well as composition history and disciplinarity. Recent publications have appeared in *Composition Studies*, *American Review of Canadian Studies*, and (with Maureen Daly Goggin and Duane Roen) the *Handbook of Research on Writing*.